Introduction

The Jumbo Book of Preschool Activities was developed as a simple, organized way to present topics of interest to young children. The book contains a collection of weekly units, including objectives, discussion ideas, and five daily activities. Detailed directions for the pages within each unit are found on the teacher sheet at the beginning of each section (after the cover sheet).

The units in this book are sequenced according to a traditional school year. If followed as presented, they should lead the teacher through a curriculum that corresponds nicely to seasons, holidays, and related themes. However, the units can certainly be varied, as desired, without losing any of their impact.

Each unit comes with a cover sheet that can be attached to a large, folded piece of construction paper (12" x 18"/30 cm x 45 cm). Children can color the cover sheets. As the discussion and activity are completed each day, they can be placed into the folder. By the fifth day, the booklet can be stapled together and sent home. (If the material is used in a school setting, the rest of the weekly work can be put in the back of the booklet.)

Although most pages have a pattern for the children, use of the pattern is only a suggestion. Some teachers may prefer not to use patterns and to reinforce the daily ideas in another way.

The supplies needed for most of the activities are likely to be found in the classroom or home. The directions are simple to read and follow. An illustration on the teacher sheet will give an idea as to how the finished activity can look. Many work sheets also have written material on them; even though the children can not read all of it, parents can easily see the ideas presented. The teacher can also read the directions and other words aloud to the class, thereby helping pre-readers to make the connections between oral and written language that will be necessary as they learn to read themselves.

Following the units is a series of alphabet activities, one for each letter. These activities can be introduced in a variety of ways. Patterns, directions, and a list of necessary supplies for these activities can be found in the back of the book.

The weekly booklets put together from *The Jumbo Book of Preschool Activities* will provide parents with a record of the ideas covered during the week. Teachers will also have a way to organize thoughts and materials (stories, music, and visuals can be added for reinforcement). Finally, the children will have an organized way to take home their weekly work, and they will enjoy making a new book each week.

Look at Me

Look at Me

Objectives:

Each child will learn . . .

- how he or she is different.
- about his or her hands.
- activities people like to do.
- how he or she is like others.
- about his or her face.
- about his or her feet.

Discussions:

As a group, the class can discuss the . . .

- kinds of clothing they wear.
- colors of their eyes.
- placement of features on their faces.
- number of fingers on their hands.
- shapes of their feet.
- uses for their feet.
- different activities people enjoy doing.
- names of the children in the group.
- sizes of the children in the group.
- colors of their hair.
- shapes of their hands.
- importance of hands.
- number of toes on their feet.
- reasons for shoes and socks.

Activities:

Each child is given an appropriate child pattern (page 6). After discussing hair, features, and clothing, each child colors the figure to look like him or herself. If desired, affix the colored pattern to another sheet of paper and allow the child to color a background setting. Be sure to provide a variety of crayons for the many skin, hair, and eye tones that can be found among any group of children.

When each child is given a head pattern (page 7), discuss hair and the placement of features so that the children can use crayons to make their faces. Have the child write or dictate his or her name. (Note: The teacher can write each child's name, allowing the child to trace the name in crayon.)

Each child is given the poem sheet (page 8). After explaining to the children how they can make a hand a pattern by spreading it at the bottom of the sheet, have them use crayons to trace around their hands and add fingernails, rings, knuckles, and so forth.

Give each child a shoe and sock pattern (page 9) to color. Add yarn through the hole to make a shoelace. Fold the shoe over the sock. If desired, the sock section can be glued to a sheet of construction paper so that the child can easily fold the shoe back and forth.

Each child is given a copy of What I Like to Do (page 10). The child can dictate or write a word or phrase to complete the sentence. Then instruct the child to draw a corresponding picture.

Child Pattern

Color the pattern to look like you.

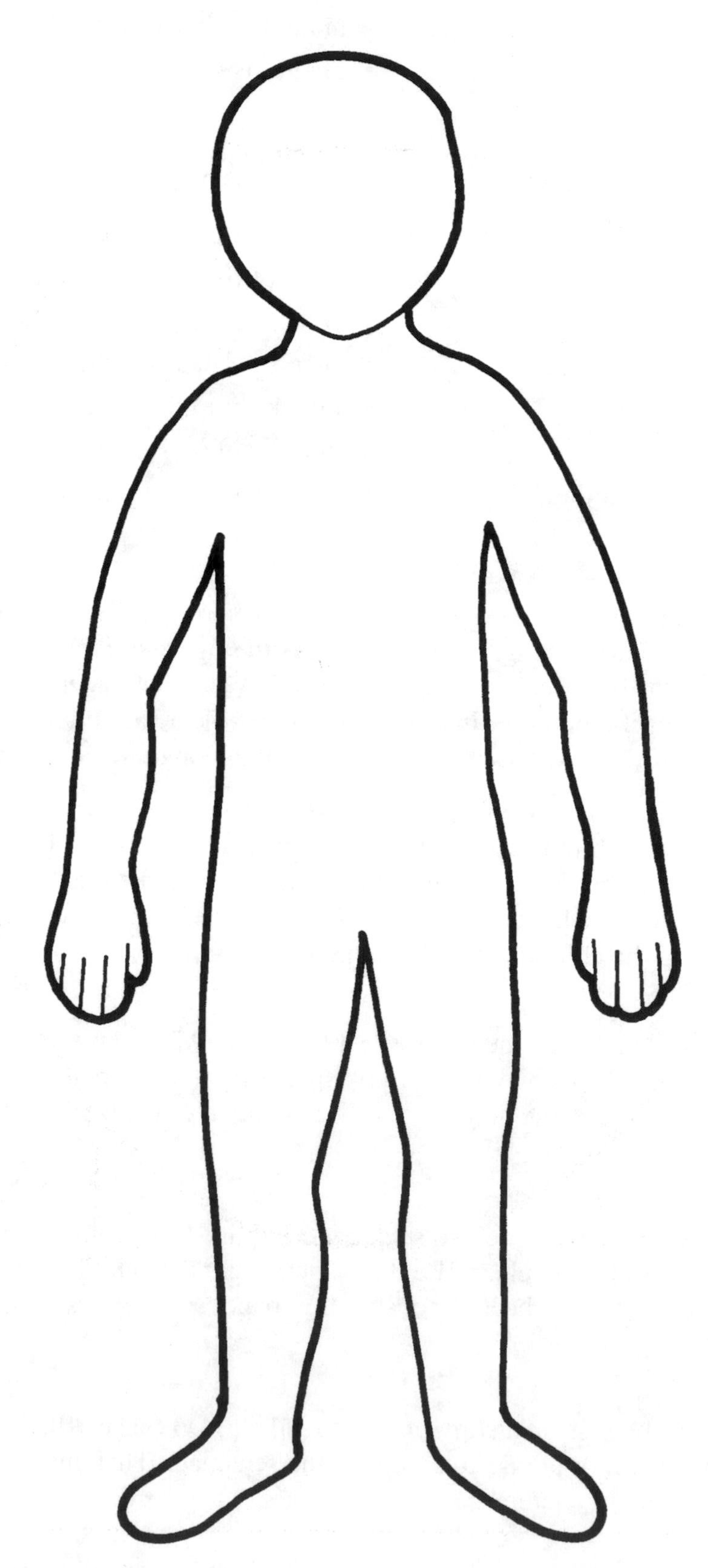

Here I Am

Color your face and hair to make the pattern look like you.

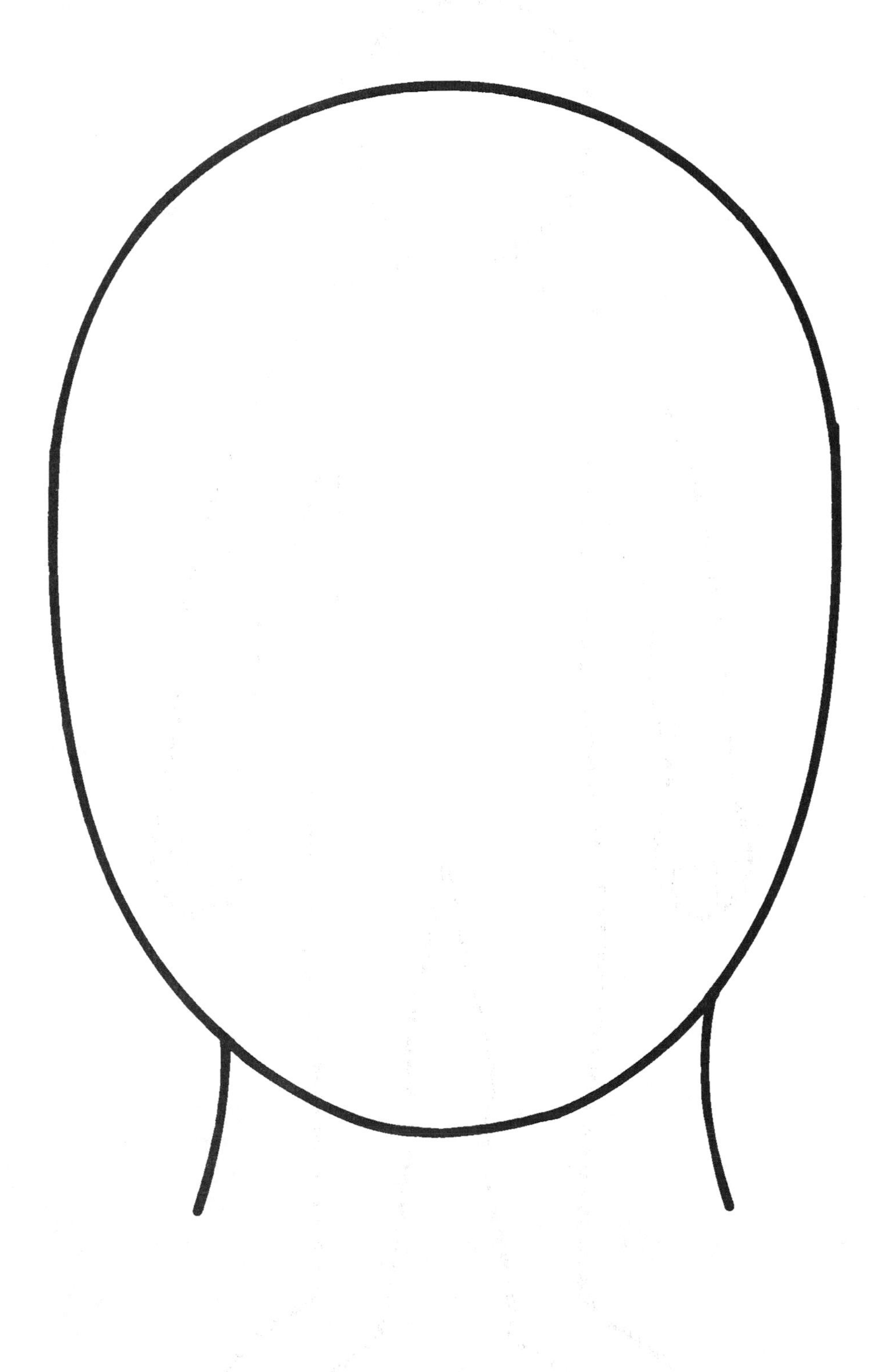

My name is ____

My Hand

Read the poem. Trace your hand below it. Color your hand and add details.

Look at my hand.
What do you see?
It is a special helper,
As useful as can be.

Editor
Dona Herweck Rice

Editorial Manager
Ina Massler Levin, M.A.

Editor in Chief
Sharon Coan, M.S. Ed.

Illustrator
Barb Lorseyedi

Cover Artist
Sue Fullam

Art Coordinator
Cheri Macoubrie Wilson

Creative Director
Elayne Roberts

Imaging
Ralph Olmedo, Jr.

Product Manager
Phil Garcia

Publishers
Rachelle Cracchiolo, M.S. Ed.
Mary Dupuy Smith, M.S. Ed.

JUMBO BOOK of Preschool Activities

Author
Shirley Jones

Teacher Created Materials, Inc.
6421 Industry Way
Westminster, CA 92683
www.teachercreated.com

Reprinted, 2001
ISBN 0-7439-3648-5
Made in U.S.A.

Table of Contents

Shoe and Sock Pattern

Color both sides of the shoe and sock. Cut them out on the dotted line. Add a shoelace through the hole. Fold the shoe on top of the sock.

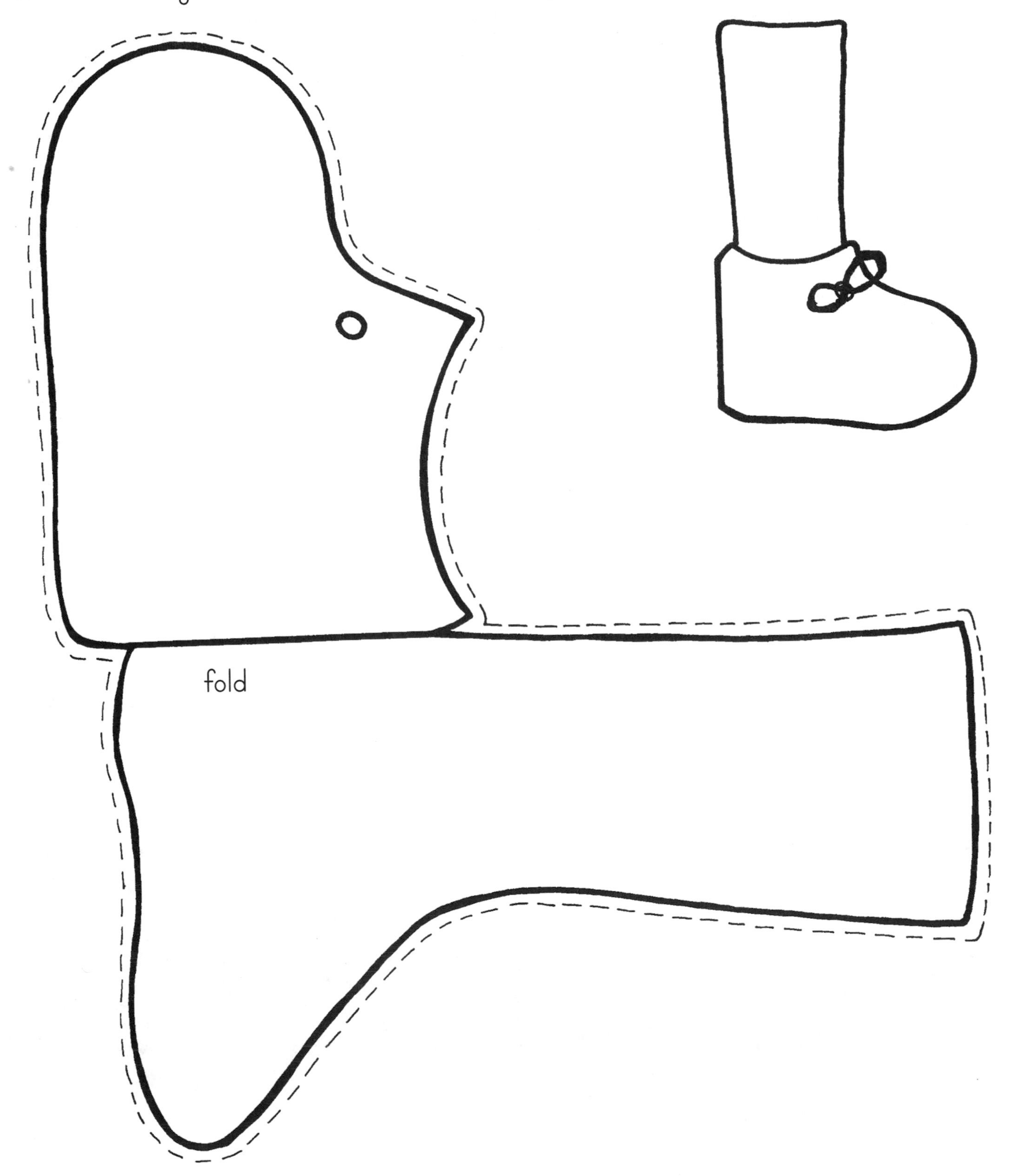

What I Like to Do

Finish the sentence below. Color a picture to show what you like to do.

I like to ____.

My School

My school is nice
As you can see.
There are many fun things
Just waiting for me.

My School

Objectives:

Each child will learn . . .

- how the outside of a school looks.
- about the activities done in different rooms of a school.
- about people who work at a school.
- how school helps us.

Discussions:

As a group, the class can discuss the . . .

- outside of the school building (doors, windows, construction materials, etc.).
- size of the building or buildings.
- school grounds.
- rooms in the school.
- uses for various rooms.
- people who work in the school.
- cafeteria arrangement.
- reasons meals are served at schools.
- things to do at the media center.
- reasons we have schools.
- things we can learn at school.
- ways we can make a good school.

Activities:

Give each child a folded paper. (See page 13.) After taking a walk outside to see the school building, instruct each child to draw the windows, doors, etc., of the school on the outside of the folded paper.

Using the paper from the previous activity, instruct each child to draw the people, equipment, windows, etc., of the school on the inside of the folded paper. Attach the school drawing to another sheet of paper. (Use staples at the top so the drawing on all sides can be seen.) Affix the three sentences from page 13 below the school drawing. Instruct the children to color the school surroundings on the paper around the building.

Provide each child with a copy of the cafeteria tray pattern (page 14). Have the children cut out the fork pattern (or the teacher can do this). Also cut a triangle from a piece of paper to represent a folded napkin. Discuss the foods that are good to eat for lunch. Instruct each child to draw a good meal and to add the fork and napkin at the side. If desired, everything can be pasted in place onto a large sheet of construction paper.

Give the book pages (page 15) to each child. Help the child to color the balls appropriately. The child or teacher can then fold the paper into a book. Staple the book to a sheet of paper and label it with the sentence at the bottom of the page.

Give a sheet of standard-size paper to each child. Instruct the child to fold the paper in many directions. The child can then open the folded paper and trace over the fold lines, coloring the created shapes in your school colors. Affix the colored sheet to a larger paper. Have the students write, "Our school colors are _______ and ________," filling in the blanks. Alternatively, provide the children with a copy of page 16, instructing them to color a pretty design by filling in the shapes with school colors and completing the sentence at the bottom.

My School Building

Fold a sheet of 18" x 6" (45 cm x 15 cm) construction paper as shown. Color the outside of your school building on the outside of the paper. Open the paper to color the inside of your school. Staple the school to the top of another sheet of paper. Glue the sentences on this page beneath your school building. Color grass and trees around your school.

My school has many doors.

My school has many rooms.

There are many things to do.

The Cafeteria

Color a healthful meal on the cafeteria tray. Color and cut out the fork, too.

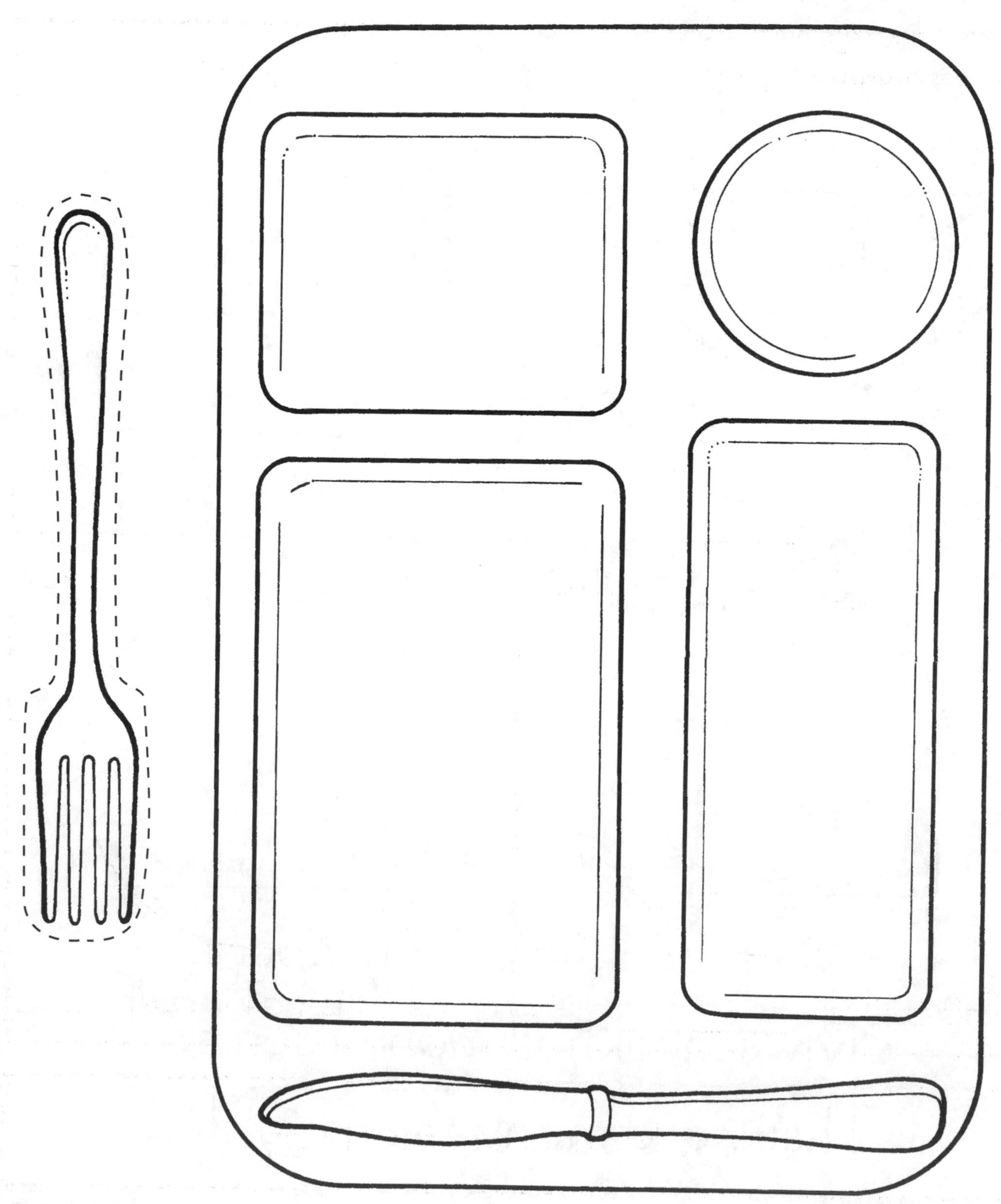

The Library

Color the pages of the book, writing a color on page 4. Cut the book along the dotted lines. Fold the book. Staple it to another paper. Glue the sentence strip below the book.

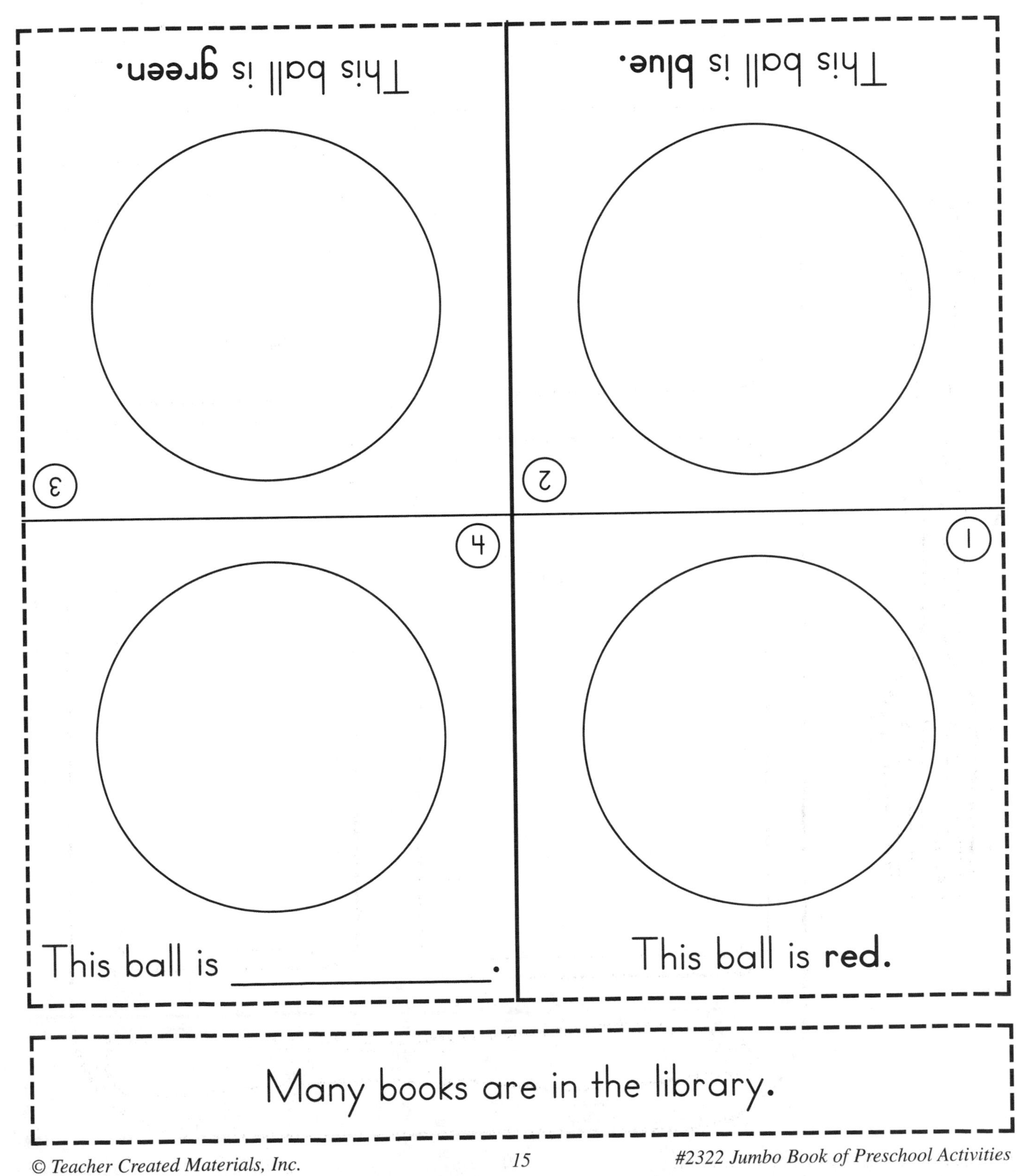

School Colors

Color each shape in one of your school colors to make a colorful design.

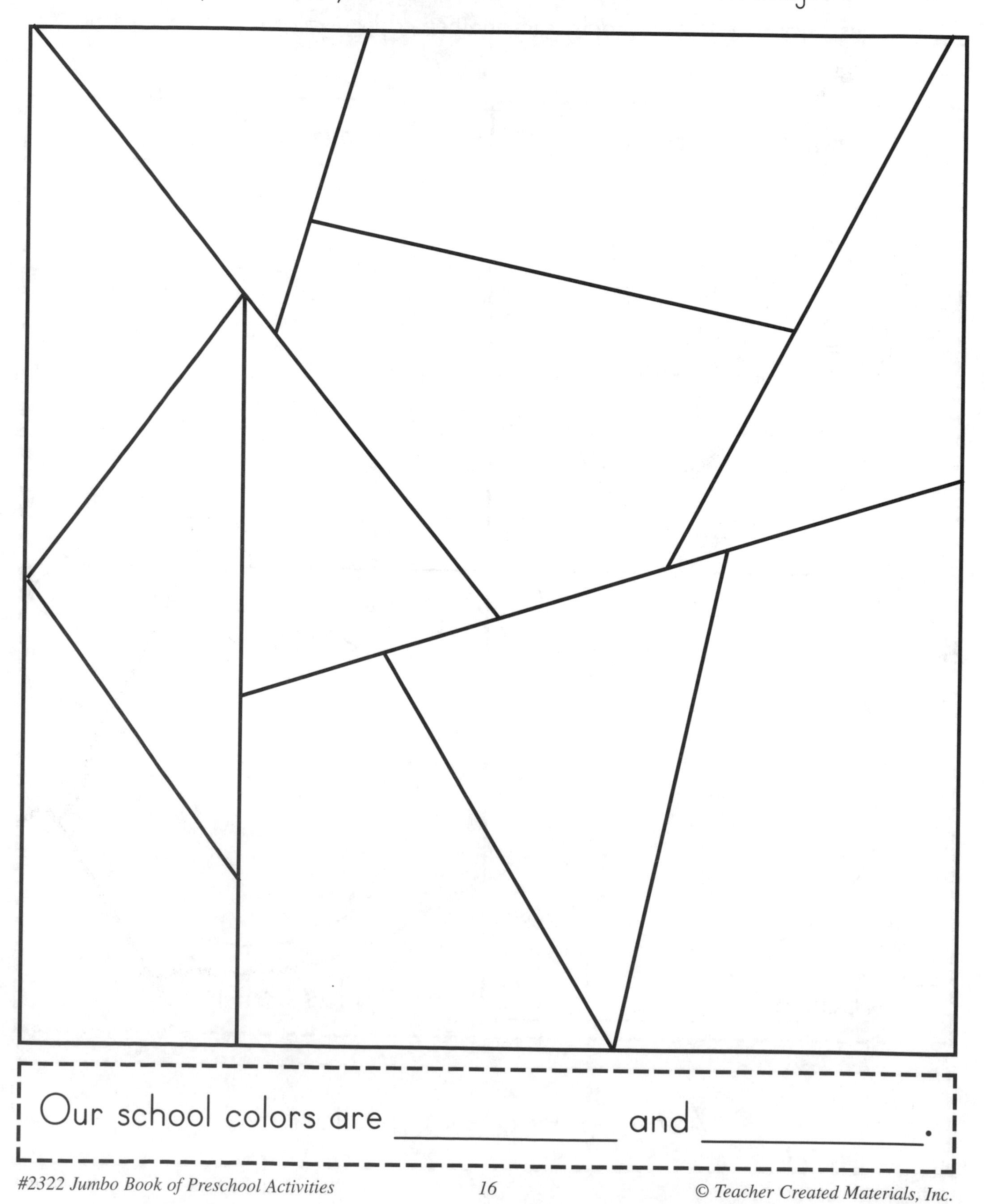

Our school colors are ____________ and ____________.

Friends

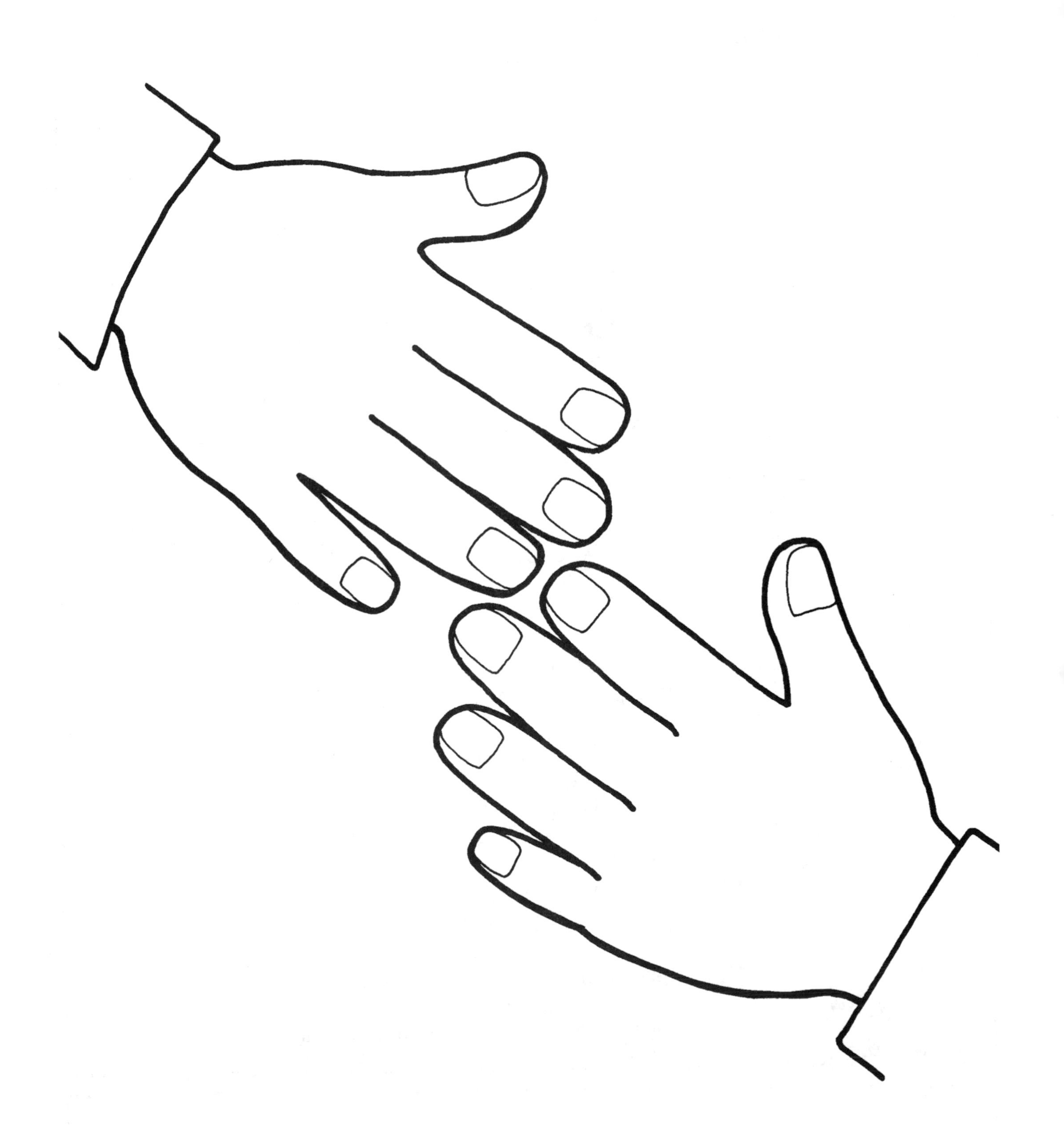

Friends

Objectives:

Each child will learn . . .

- the meaning of and need for friendship.
- ways to make and keep friends.
- about feelings when we lose friends.
- how friends can help.

Discussions:

As a group, the class can discuss the . . .

- meaning of a friend.
- reasons for having friends.
- ways we make friends.
- ways we keep friends.
- ways that fussing can lose friends.
- times and ways that friends can help.

Activities:

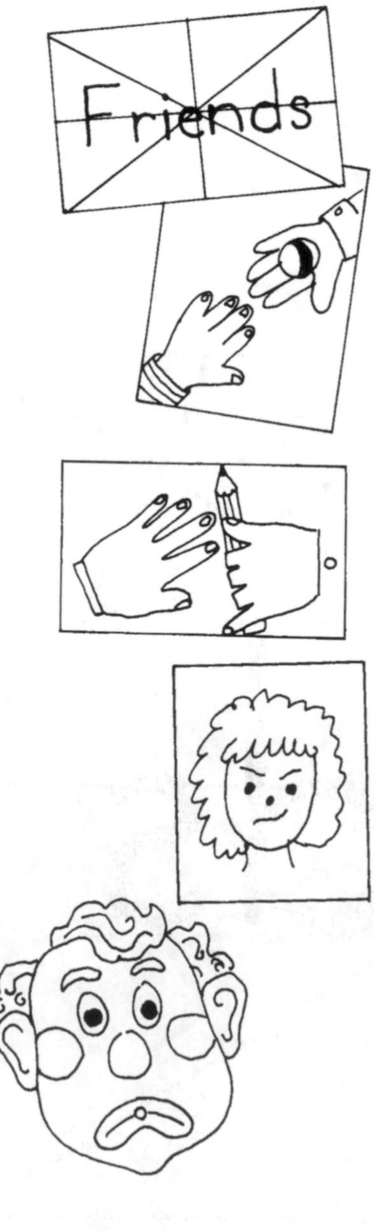

Give each child a copy of the activity sheet (page 19). After talking about the poem and the word "friend," instruct the children to color the rectangle, using only two colors. The two colors can represent the child and a special friend.

Have the children make suggestions about what they can share with a friend. Then ask the children to choose one of the suggested things and draw it on the work sheet (page 20).

Instruct the students to color the hand and pencil patterns (page 21). Help them to cut out the top hand and pencil as well as the dotted slot. Wrap the fingers of the cut hand around the pencil and tape the pencil in place. Affix the wrist of the hand through the slot with a brass fastener. The hand can then wiggle up and down as though handing the pencil to a friend.

Ask the children to color the figure on page 22.

After coloring the clown face and mouth patterns (page 23), the children can attach the mouth at the dot, using a brass fastener. The mouth can turn up or down to make a smile or frown.

True-Blue Friends

Read the poem. Choose two colors and color the shapes in the rectangle.

True-blue
Me and you,
Friends forever,
Through and through.

Sharing

What can friends share? Draw something that one friend could share with another. Color the picture.

Friends share.

Helping Hands

Color the hands and pencil. Cut out the top hand and pencil. Fold the fingers around the pencil and tape the pencil in place. Cut the slot. Put the wrist in the slot and fix it in place with a paper fastener.

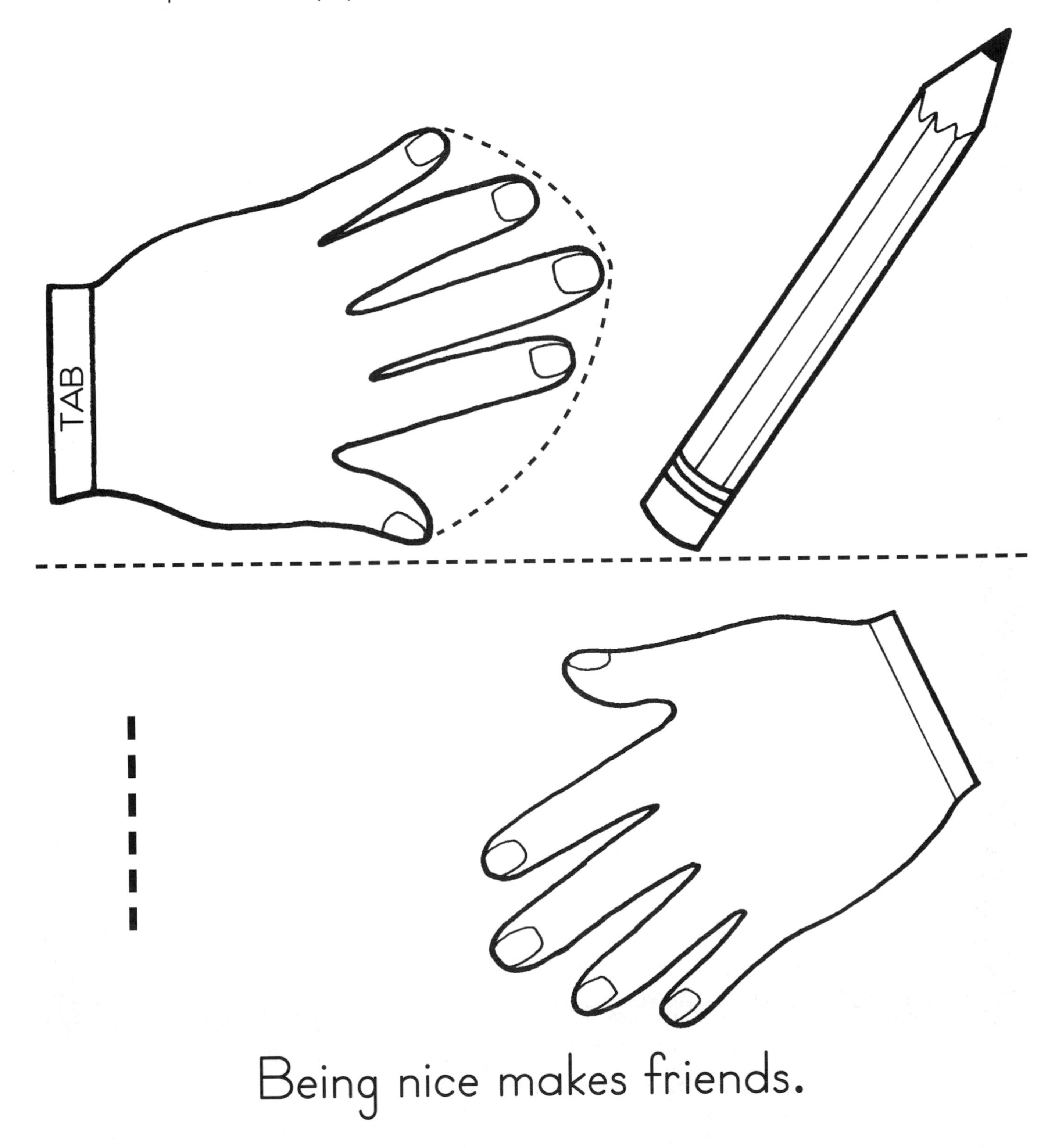

Being nice makes friends.

Don't Fuss!

Draw and color a head with a fussy face.

Fussing loses friends.

Happy and Sad

Color the face and mouth patterns. Cut out the mouth. Attach the mouth to the clown with a paper fastener. Make the clown happy or sad.

Friends can help when you are happy or sad.

Our Flag

I pledge allegiance to the flag
of the United States of
America,
and to the republic for which it
stands,
one nation, under God,
indivisible,
with liberty and justice for all.

Our Flag

Objectives:

Each child will learn . . .

- the size of our flag.
- the colors of our flag.
- what the stars and stripes represent.
- why we have a flag.
- what the pledge means.
- where we can see the flag.

Discussions:

As a group, the class can discuss . . .

- where we live (city, state, country).
- flags that represent different countries.
- how our flag looks.
- the colors used and why they were chosen.
- the number of stars and stripes.
- why our flag is displayed.
- how the flag is displayed.
- places we see the flag.
- the Pledge of Allegiance.
- what the pledge means.
- America.
- the national anthem and other songs.

Activities:

Give each child a map of the United States (page 26). Instruct the child to color the state where you live as well as other states according to the teacher's directions.

Each child is given a flag (page 27) and crayons. Instruct the child to color the stripes and field of blue. (Care should be taken to color the stripes correctly.)

Provide the children with page 28 and crayons. The children can draw themselves and cut out the figure (boy or girl). Fold the arm so the hand is over the heart. Glue the figure and a copy of the Pledge of Allegiance (page 24) to a sheet of construction paper. Glue the sentence from page 28 to the paper as well.

Give each child a copy of the star pattern (page 29) to cut out. Add drops of glue to the star and sprinkle silver glitter on the glue. Let dry. Glue the star and sentence strip to a sheet of blue construction paper.

The United States of America

Stars and Stripes

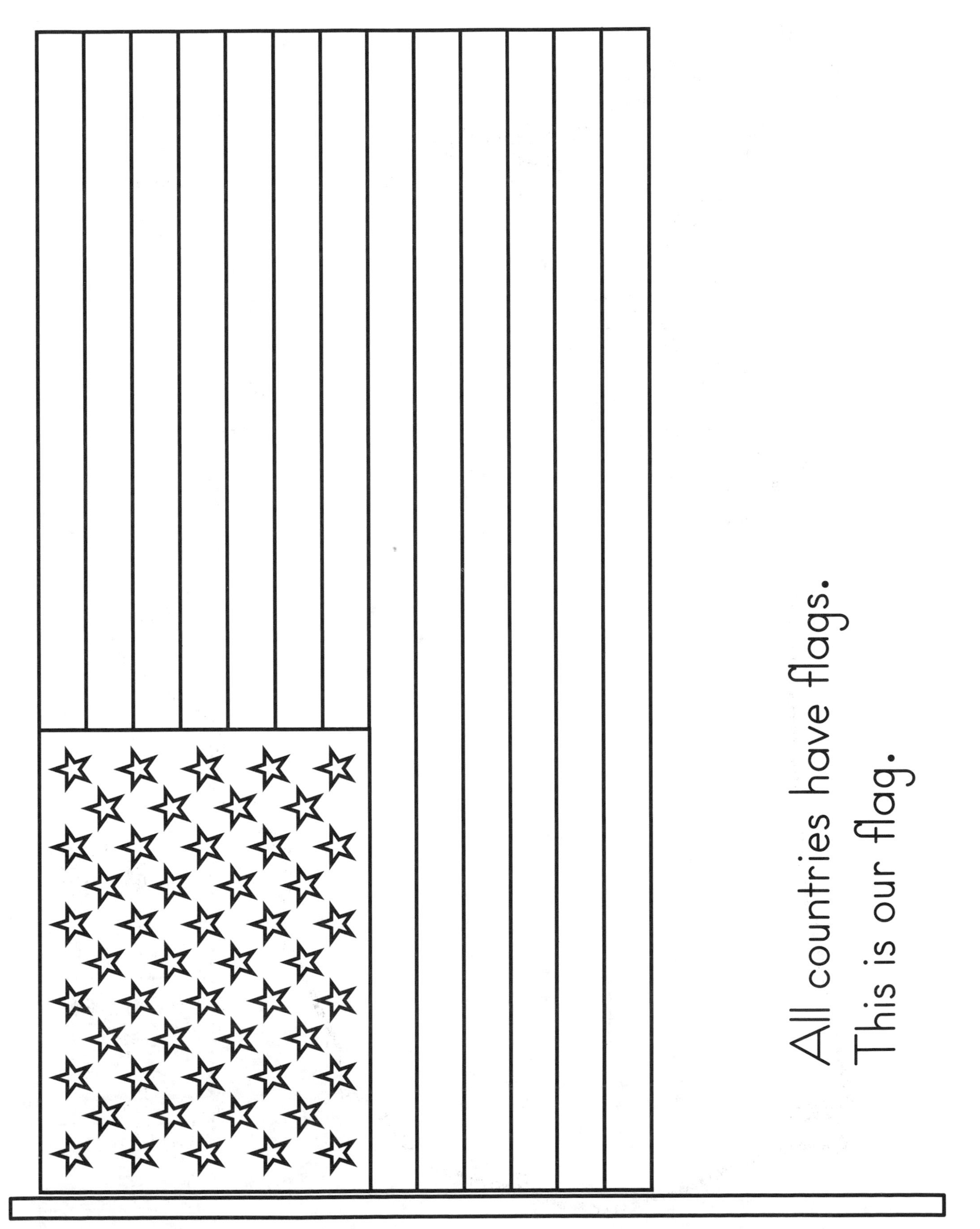

The Pledge of Allegiance

Color and then cut out the person. Fold the arm over the heart.

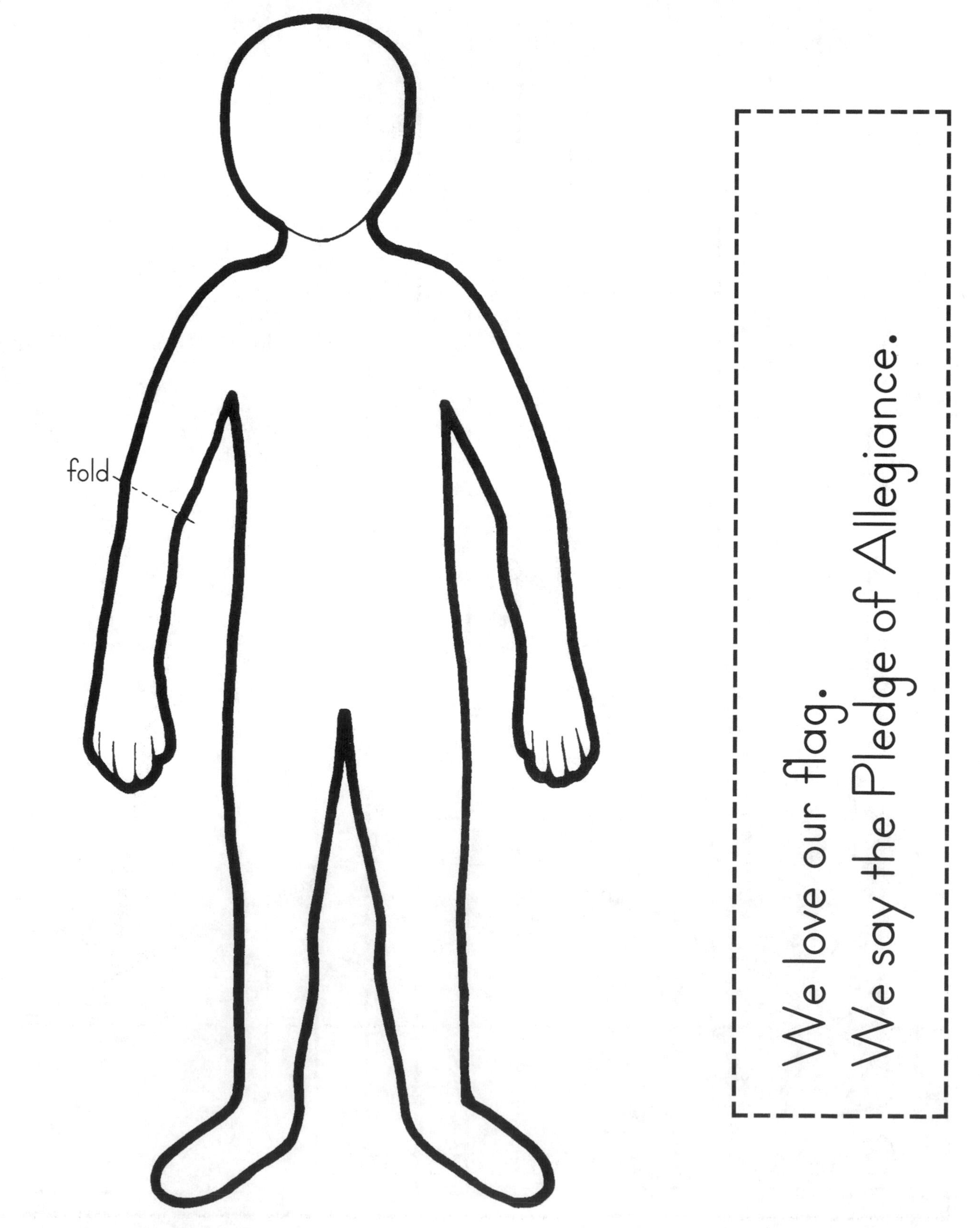

Star

Cut out the star. Cover it with glue and glitter.

Our flag has 50 stars.
One star is for each state.

Building a Good Me

Building a Good Me

Objectives:

Each child will learn . . .

- how actions reflect character.
- how others are affected by our actions.
- the benefits of positive actions.

Discussions:

As a group, the class can discuss . . .

- what actions tell about a person.
- how behavior can help or harm ourselves and others.
- respect for others.
- responsibility for actions.
- everyday honesty.
- helpfulness to others.
- fairness in work and play.
- character and how it is demonstrated in a person's behavior to others in everyday situations.

Activities:

Provide the children with a copy of page 32 and crayons. Instruct them to color additional books in the scene. If desired, have them trace the letters of the spoken words. Tell them that this page is about respect.

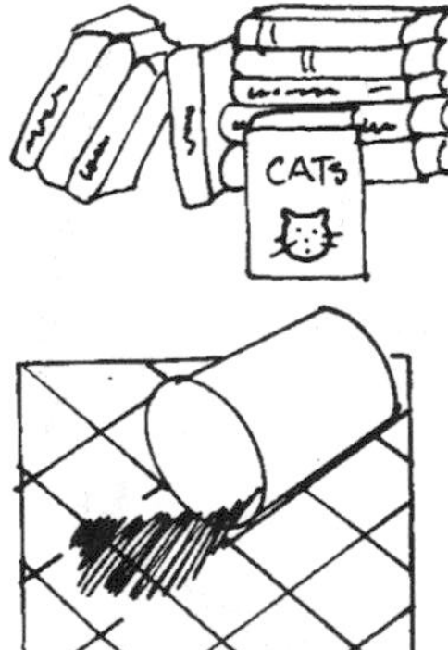

Instruct the children to color page 33. If desired, have them trace the letters of the spoken words. Add a splotch of white glue from the lip of the cup onto the tablecloth. When dry, let the children color it brown to make spilled chocolate milk or soda (or red for fruit punch, etc.). Tell the children that this page shows responsibility.

Ask the children to draw people working together to lift and carry the box (page 34). Colored tape like packing tape can be added to the box. If desired, have the children trace the letters of the spoken words. Tell them the page is about being a good friend and neighbor.

Children can draw and color the girl going over the finish line ahead of the other child (page 35). The rest of the picture can be colored as well, and the letters of the spoken words can be traced, if desired. For an added touch, glue ribbon to either side of the girl to show that she has broken through the finish line. Tell the children the page is about being fair in play and not cheating or whining.

After the picture is colored (page 36), sparkling cord or sequins can be glued to the cushion on the chair to make jewelry. If desired, allow the children to trace the letters of the spoken words. Tell them the page is about being honest.

Respect

Respect others' things.

Responsibility

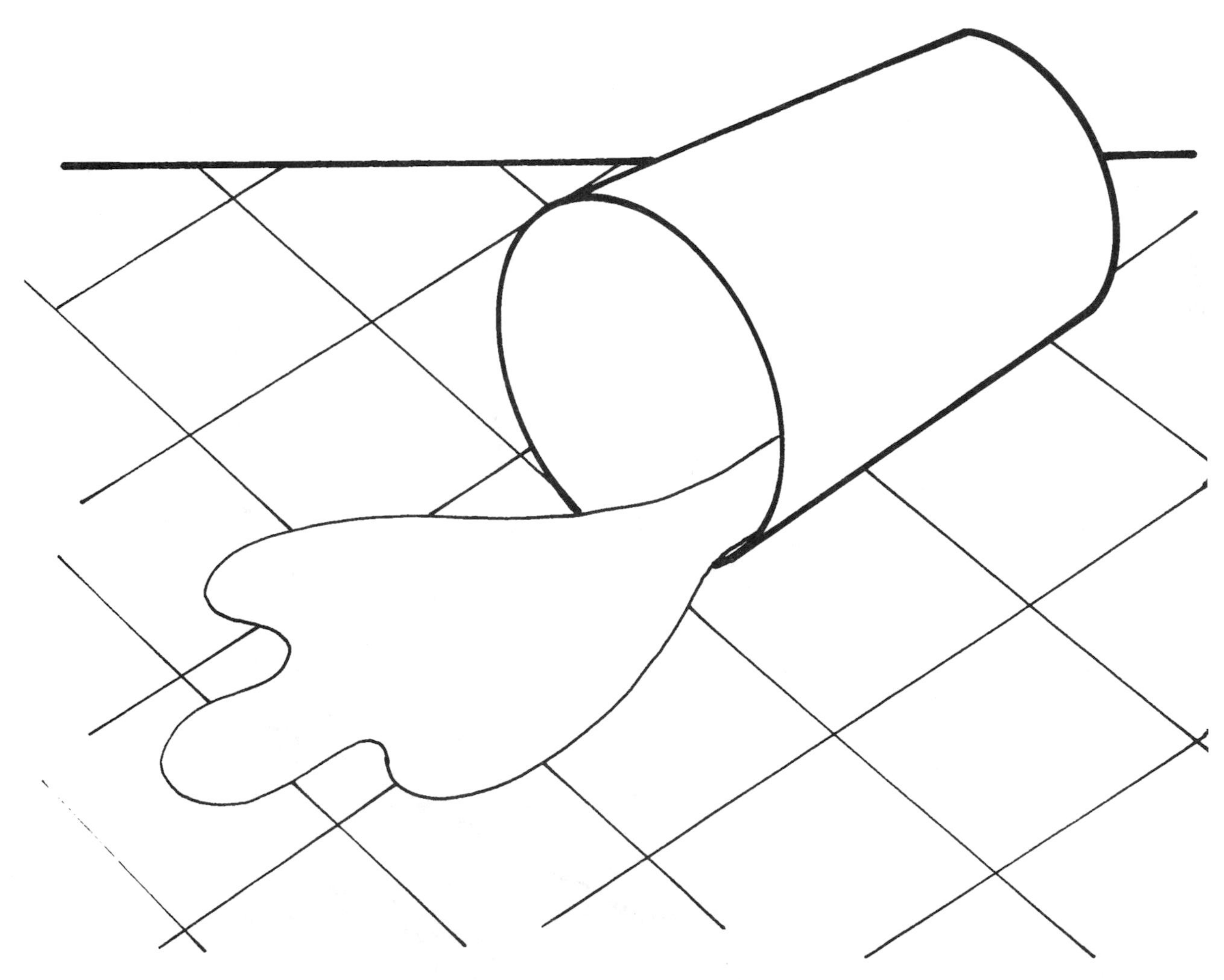

Admit mistakes.

Helping

Help others.

Fairness

Play fair.

Honesty

Tell the truth.

Safety

Safety

Objectives:

Each child will learn about safety . . .

- at home.
- near the street.
- at school.
- at play.

Discussion:

As a group, the class can discuss . . .

- taking care of toys.
- being careful on stairs.
- using caution with medicines.
- not playing with matches.
- not playing near traffic areas.
- proper behavior in cars and buses.
- road signs and lights and how they help us.
- using play equipment.
- taking turns.
- school safety.
- walking safely.
- the danger of pushing.
- stranger danger.

Activities:

Give each child a copy of the patterns on page 39, an 8" (20 cm) length of yarn, and crayons. Instruct the children to color the ball and kite. Glue the yarn to the kite to make a tail. Ask the children to color and fold the paper to make a cupboard. Let them arrange and glue the two toys inside the cupboard. Glue the cupboard to another sheet of paper. Glue the sentence strip to the bottom of the sheet.

Provide each child with a copy of the patterns on page 40, glue, and crayons. Let each child cut out and glue the car and wheels to the paper above the sentence. Have them color passengers and scenery, as desired. The passengers should be wearing seatbelts!

Provide each child with the patterns on page 41. Instruct them to color the circles as indicated and to glue the circles in sequence onto the rectangle (red on top, yellow in the middle, and green on the bottom). Help them to write "STOP," "WAIT," and "GO" on the corresponding circles. (Heavy black marker will work best.) Let them glue the signal to another piece of paper, attaching the poem beneath it. If desired, provide the patterns in colored paper, using brown for the signal box.

Give each child two figure patterns, one ball pattern, one strip pattern, and the background pattern (page 42). They will also need glue, a paper fastener, and crayons. The child can color the ball and figure patterns, paste the ball to the strip, color the background, and glue the people in place on the labeled sheet. The teacher can cut the dotted slot on the background and stick the paper strip though it, affixing the strip with a brass fastener at the circle. In this way, the ball can be tossed between the players.

Each child is given a door sheet with the sentence and one pattern (boy or girl) to color and glue in front of the door. The door and walls can also be colored.

Cleaning Up

Color and cut out the toys and cupboard. Add yarn to the kite for a tail. Glue the toys in the cupboard. Fold the doors to close them. Glue the cupboard and word strip to another paper.

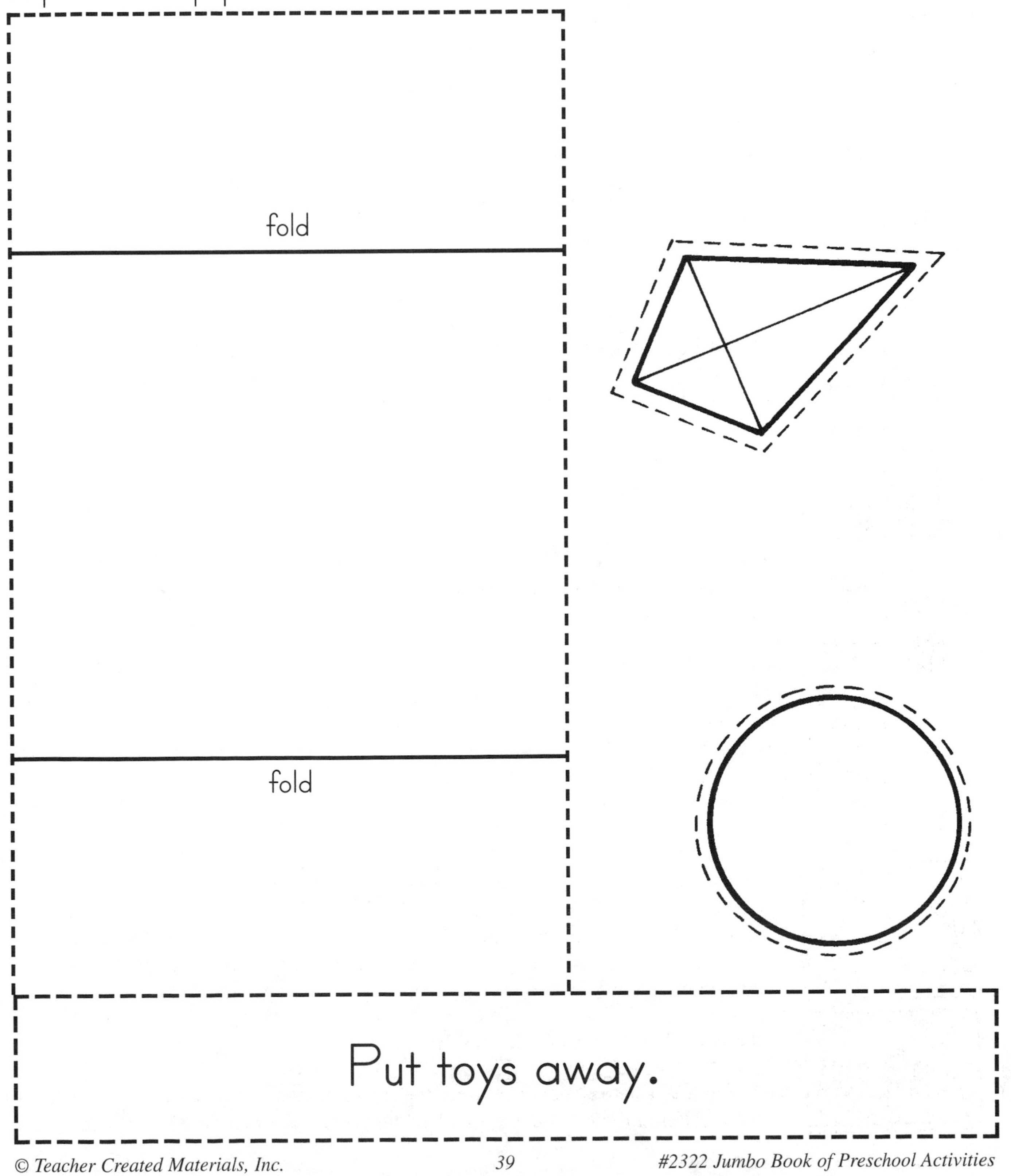

Have a Safe Trip!

Color the tires and car. Cut them out. Glue the car and tires to the sheet of paper. Draw passengers wearing seatbelts in the car, a road, and any other scenery you would like.

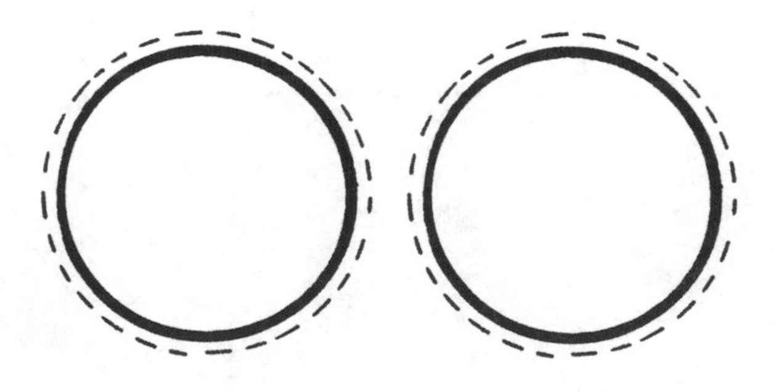

Fasten your seatbelts.

Traffic Light

Color the circles red, yellow, and green. Glue them in the right places on the traffic light box. Glue the signal and poem to another paper.

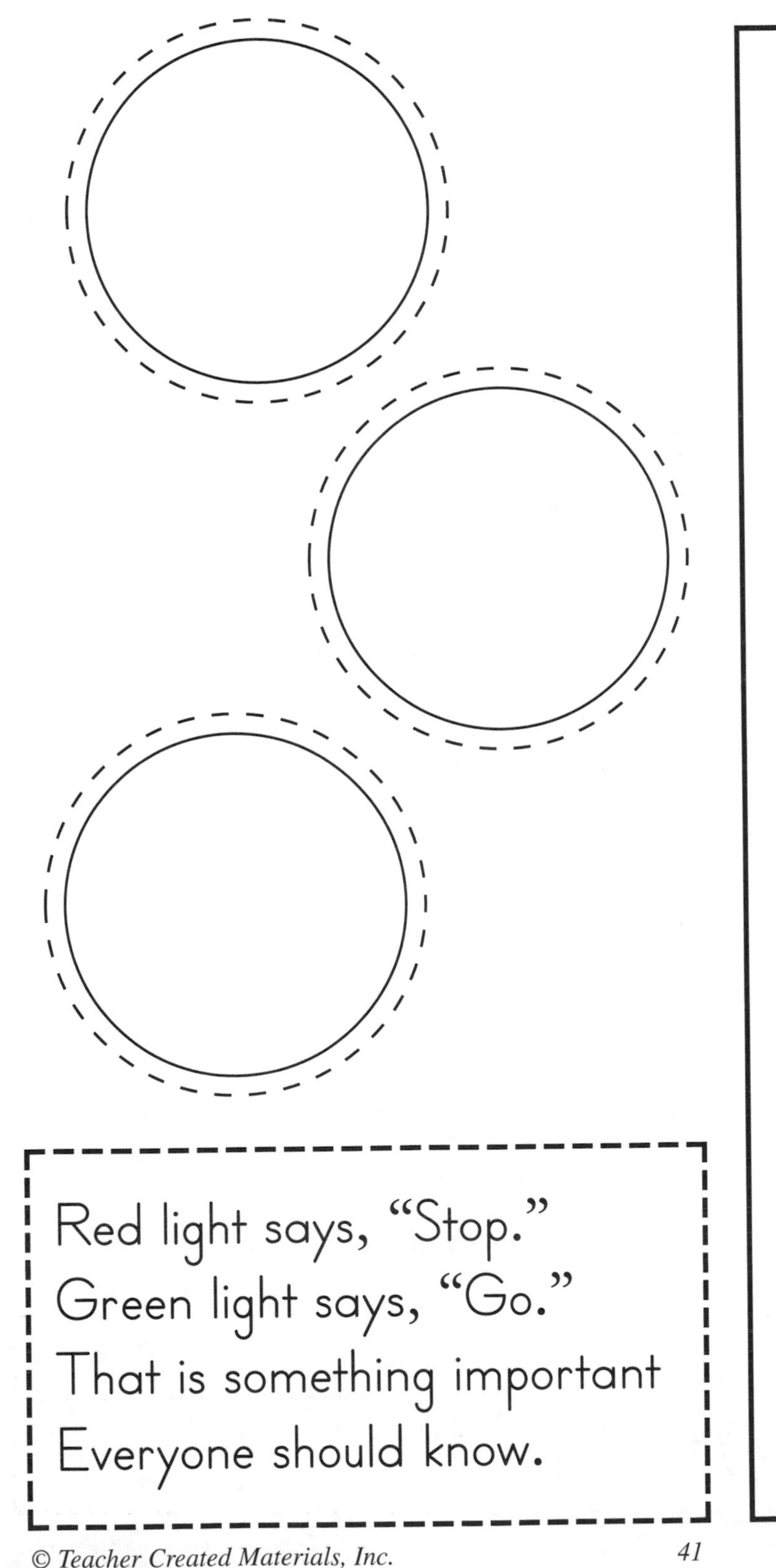

Red light says, "Stop."
Green light says, "Go."
That is something important
Everyone should know.

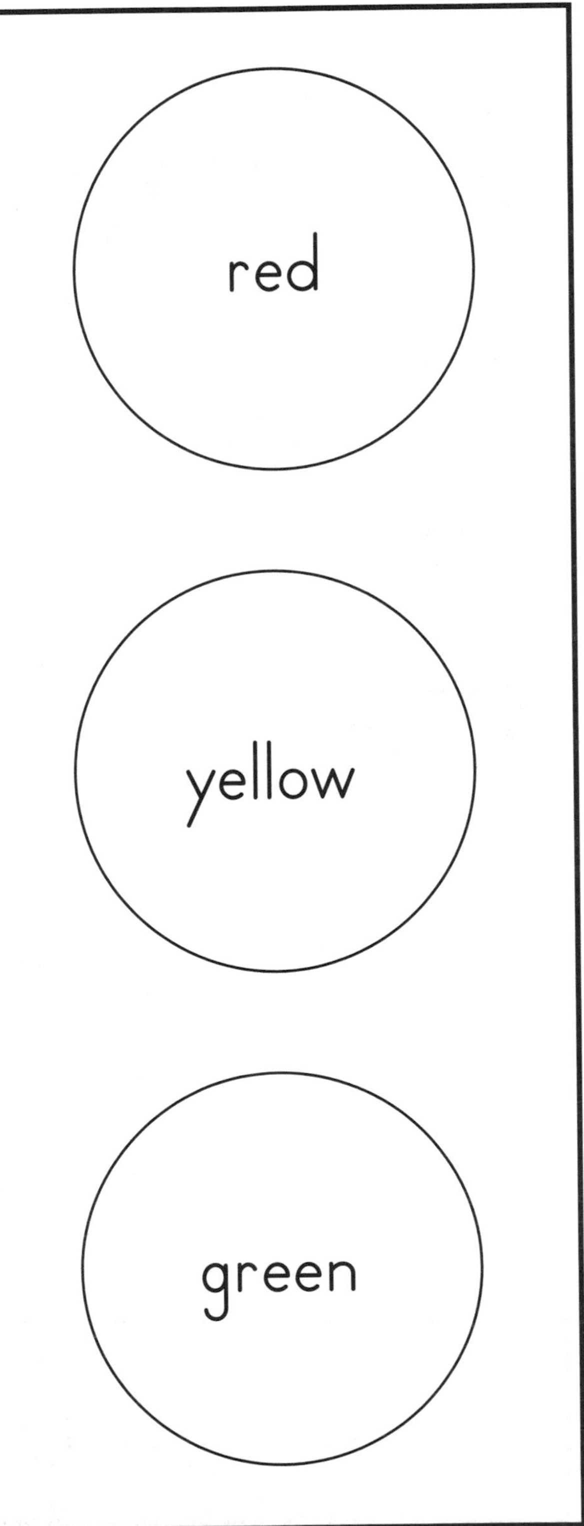

Let's Play

Color the ball and children. Glue the ball to the strip. Cut the dotted line to make a slot. Put the strip through the slot. Attach the strip to the background with a paper fastener. Move the ball back and forth.

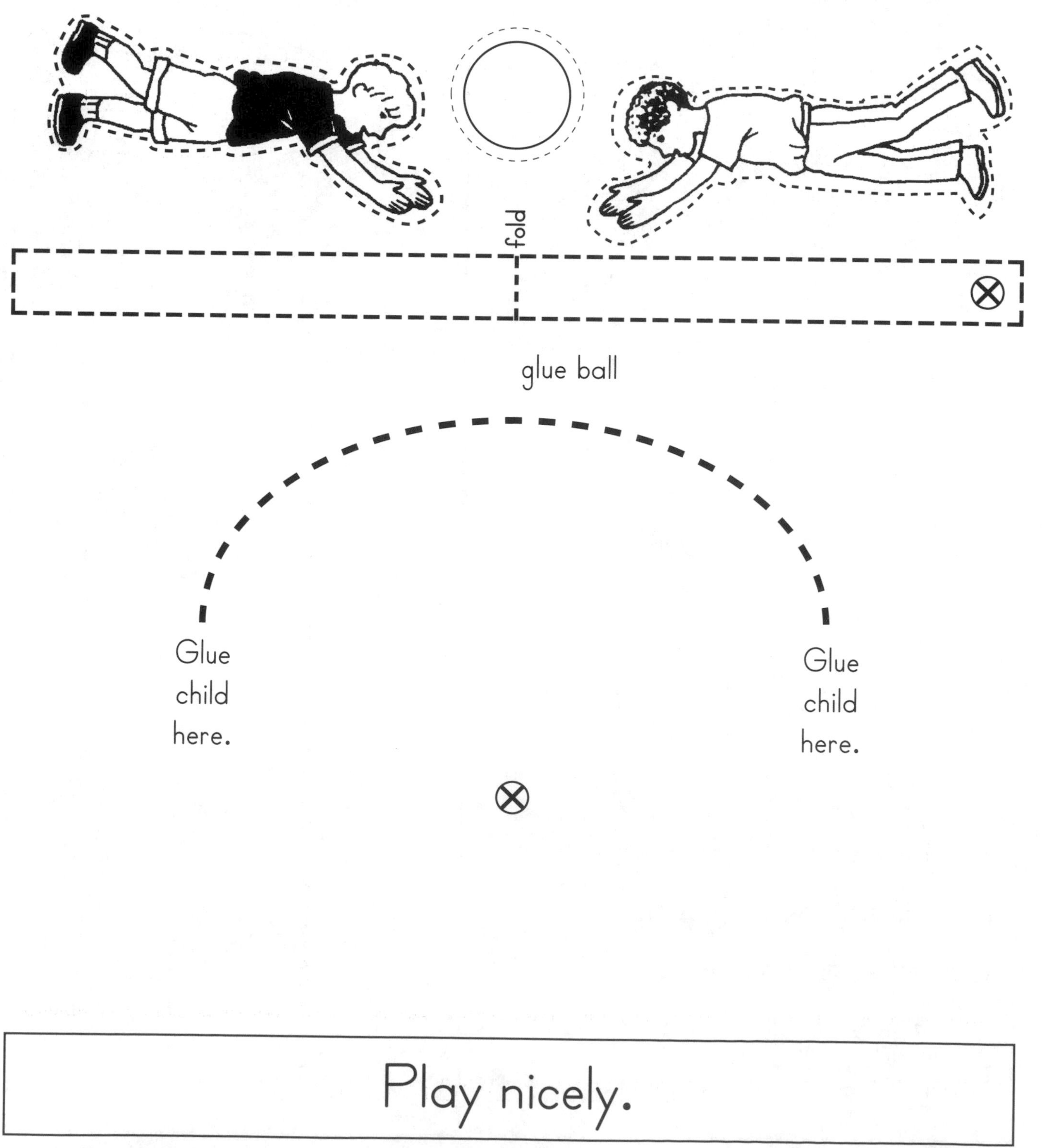

Play nicely.

Door Danger

Color one child. Color the door and the room. Glue the child in front of the door. Be sure never to play in front of doors!

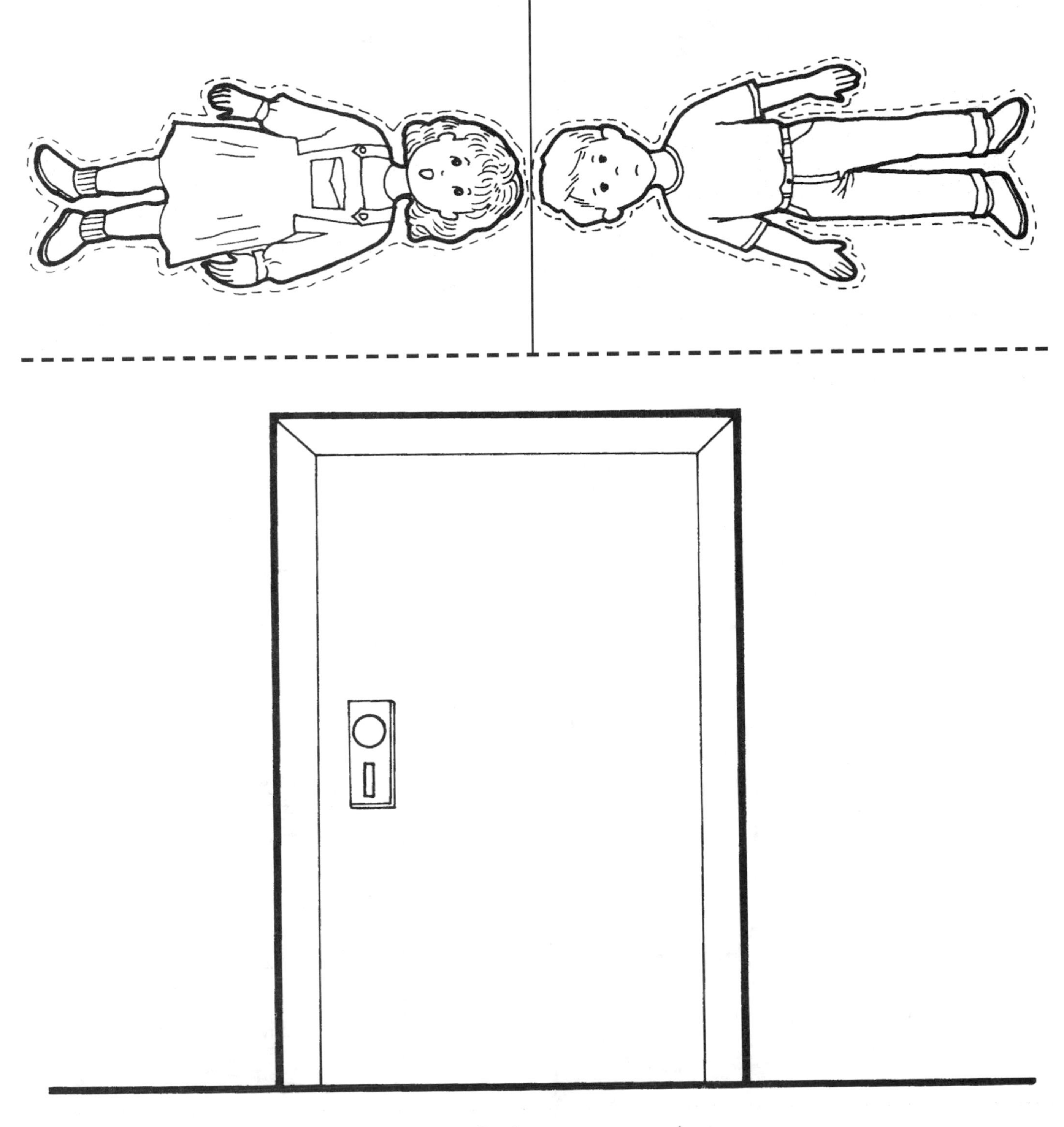

Be careful near doors.

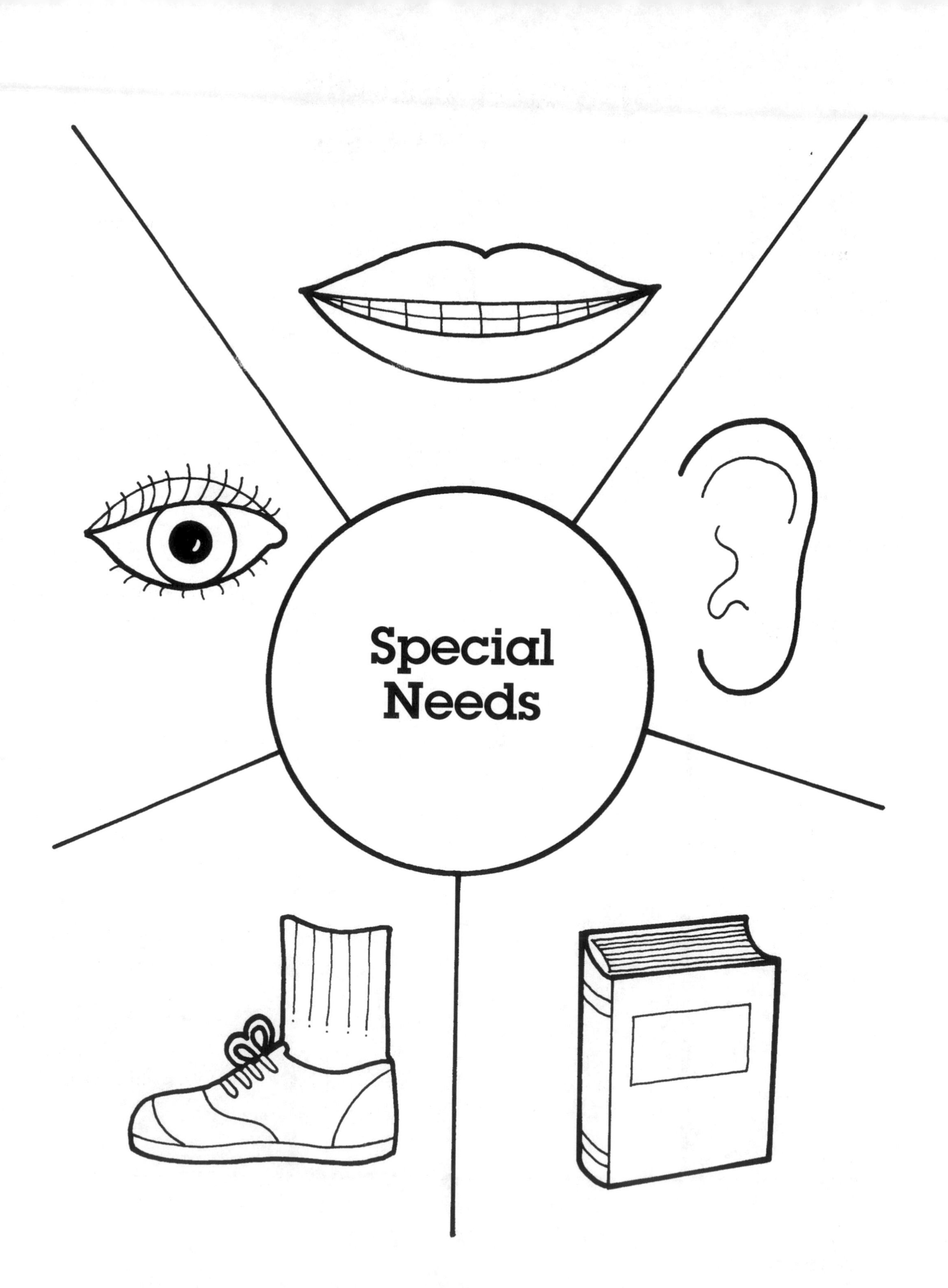
Special
Needs

Special Needs

Objectives:

Each child will learn . . .

- about special needs related to seeing, hearing, learning, moving, and speaking.
- how special problems come about.
- how we should act towards people with special needs.

Discussions:

As a group, the class can discuss . . .

- the importance of treating all people with kindness.
- disabilities that concern sight, hearing, physical movement, learning, and speech.
- how life for those with special challenges can be made easier.
- how everyone can help to make life better for those with special needs.

Activities:

Distribute page 46, crayons, and a chenille stick. Instruct the children to color the picture. Show them how to bend the chenille stick to make glasses. Glue the glasses in place.

Before working with the children, cut lined notebook paper to 3.5" x 2.5" (8.75 cm x 6.25 cm). Staple together one set of small paper (about four sheets, stapled along one long edge) per child. Let the children color the book cover (page 47). Cut a slit along the dotted line. Insert the stapled part of the lined paper through the slit and glue it in place to make a book. Instruct the children to draw a pencil, crayons, or other school supplies around the book.

Instruct the children to color the girl (page 48) and the chin. Cut out the chin and affix it to the face with paper fasteners to make the mouth move.

Instruct the children to color the face and ears (page 49). Cut out the ears and the slits at the sides of the head. Push the ear tabs through the slits and glue or tape them in place.

Color the body, arms, and legs (page 50), adding details to the face and clothes. Cut out the arms and legs. Attach them with paper fasteners to the body.

Sight

Color the picture. Add glasses to help the boy see.

A person may have trouble seeing.
Sometimes glasses help.

Learning

Color the book. Add other school supplies around the book. Glue pages into the book.

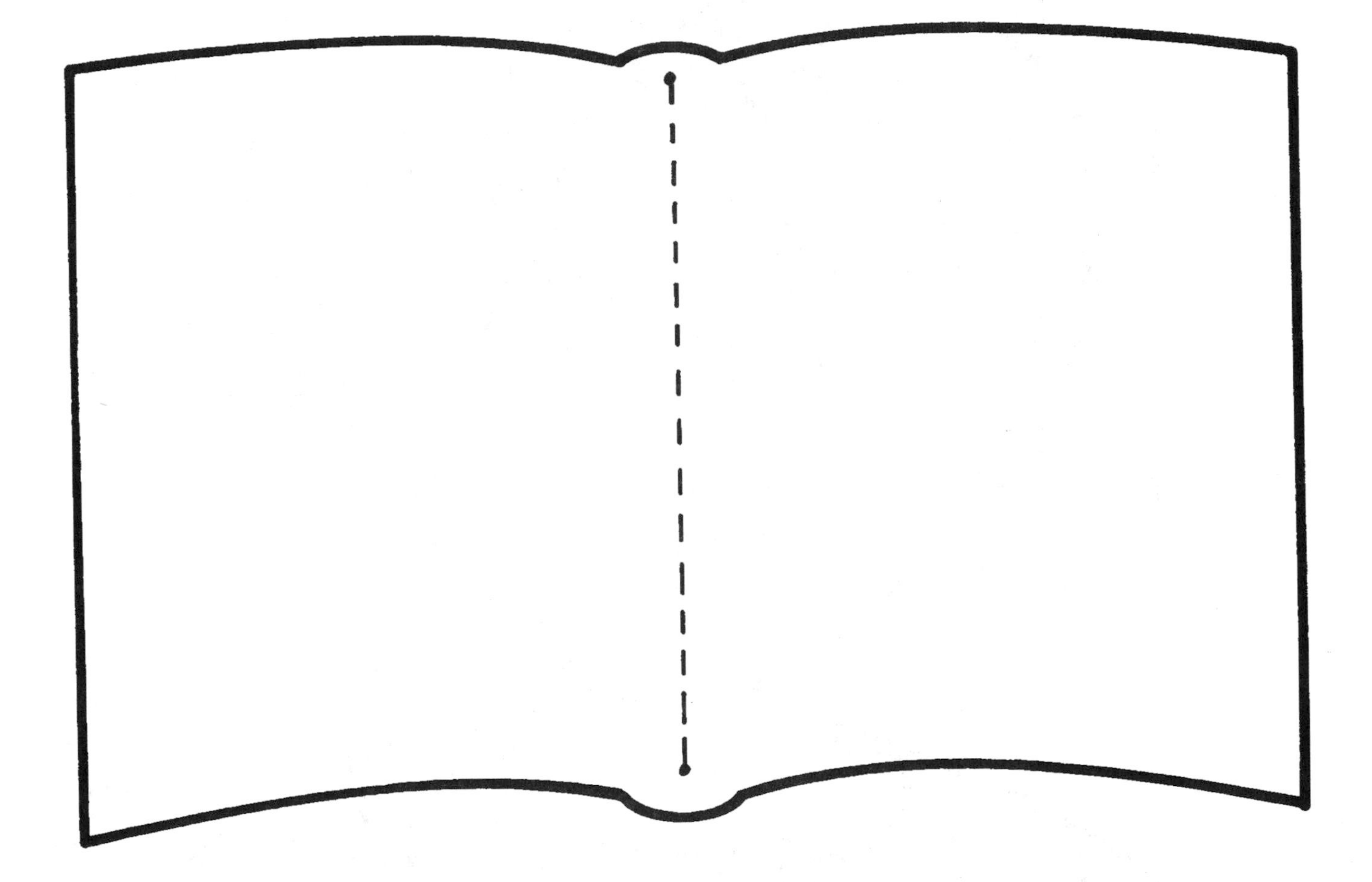

A person may have trouble learning.
Teachers and friends can help.

Speaking

Color the girl and the chin. Cut out the chin. Use paper fasteners to put the chin in place. Move the chin to help the girl speak.

A person may have trouble making some sounds. We use our mouths to speak.

Hearing

Color the boy and his ears. Cut out the ears and glue them in place to help the boy hear.

A person may have trouble hearing sounds. Sometimes hearing aids can help.

Movement

Color the girl and her arms and legs. Use paper fasteners to put the arms and legs in their right places. Move them around.

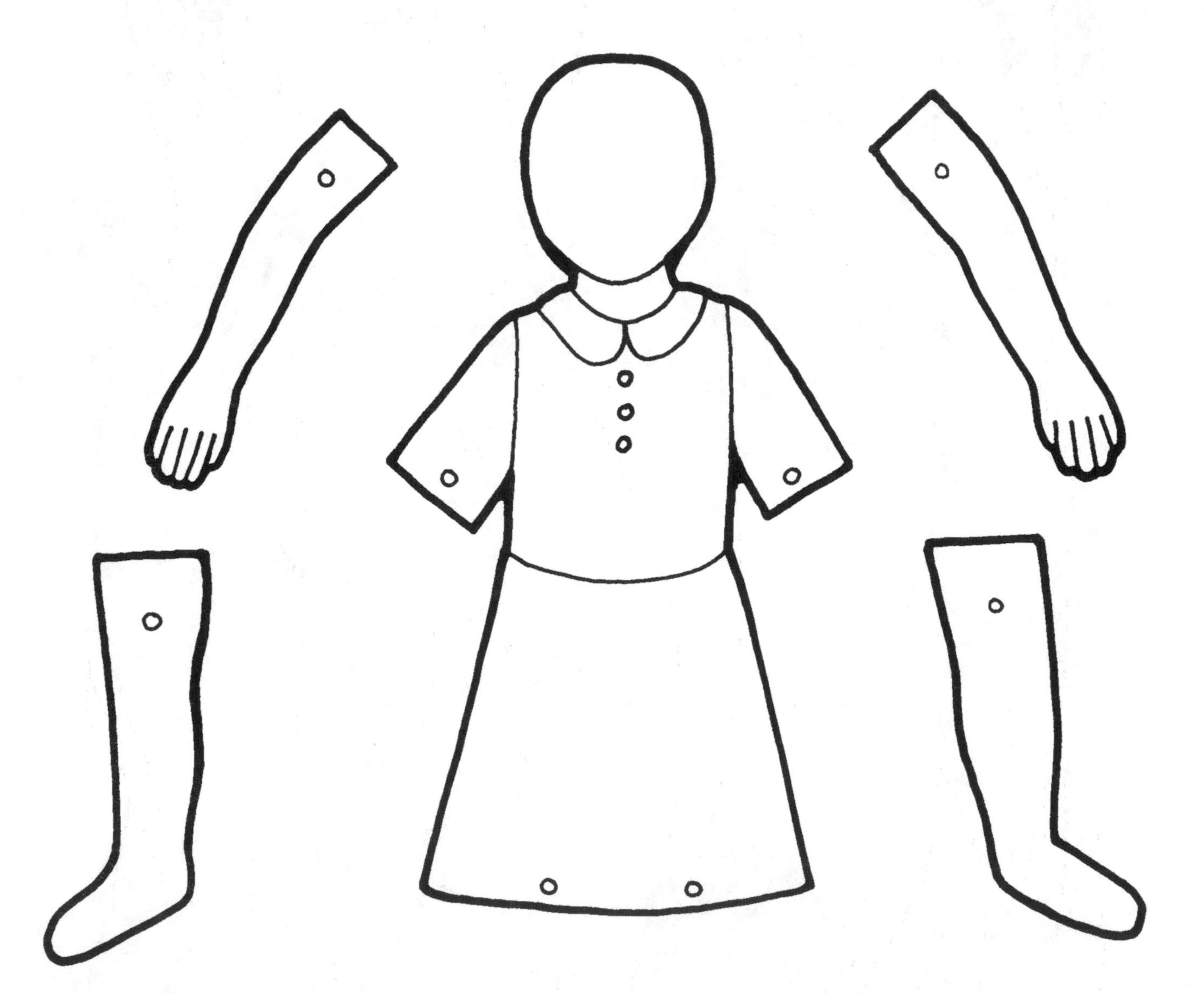

A person may have trouble moving arms and legs. In what other ways can people get around?

Fire Safety

Fire Safety

Objectives:

Each child will learn . . .

- how fire can help us.
- how fire can hurt us.
- about firefighters and their jobs.
- fire safety at home, at school, and in the wild.

Discussions:

As a class, the group can discuss . . .

- how fire helps.
- how fire hurts.
- home fire safety in regards to appliances, matches, fireplaces, fire escapes, and fire hazard areas.
- firefighters and their jobs, clothing, tools, and training.
- how and why to be careful in the wild.
- school fire safety.
- fire drills (procedure and importance).

Activities:

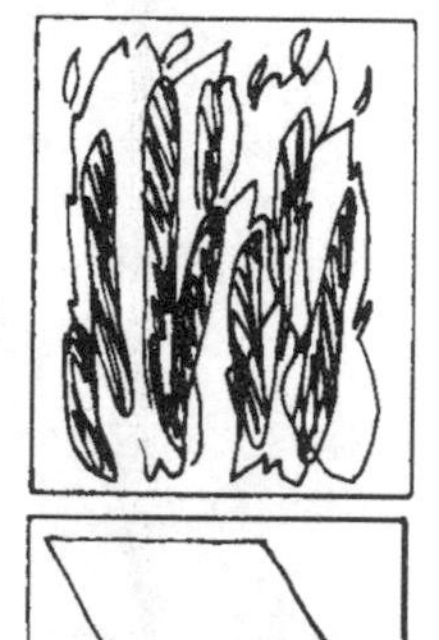

Give each child a roll-on deodorant bottle or other bottle filled with red, yellow, or orange tempera paint and a copy of page 51. Children can take turns using the paint to make a "fire" design for the book cover. Alternatively, a 12" x 18" (30 cm x 45 cm) folded sheet of manila paper can be used to paint on freehand. Use the paper for the cover. (Painting with roll-on bottles is easy for children to do. Wash the "ball" before storing.)

Each child is given an assembled matchbook with matches (page 53) and crayons. The child can color and decorate the matchbook cover and the tips of the matches. Glue the matchbook to a sheet of construction paper and glue the sentence strip below it.

Provide each child with a copy of page 54, yarn (for the fire hose), and crayons. Children can color the firefighter and attach his arm with a paper fastener. Paste the firefighter and hydrant onto a separate sheet of paper. Thread the yarn through his hand so that he holds the hose. Buildings and other scenery can be drawn to complete the picture. Glue the sentence strip below it.

Let the children color and cut out the animals (page 55), gluing them in the nature scene. Add the sign to the picture as well.

Provide each child with page 56, crayons, a cotton ball for smoke, and glue. Direct the children to color the building. They can then draw a face in the window and a ladder below the window. Spread glue around one or more sides of the window and stretch the cotton across the glue to make smoke.

Do Not Play with Matches

Color the matchbook and matches. Cut them out and glue them together. Glue the matchbook to another sheet and paste the sentence strip below it.

Close Cover Before Striking.

fold

fold

Matches are useful, but children should not use them.

Firefighters

Color and cut out the firefighter, arm, and hydrant. Attach the arm to the fire-fighter with a paper fastener. Punch a hole in the hand. Glue the firefighter and hydrant to another paper with the sentence strip below the picture. Add yarn from the hydrant through the hand to make a fire hose.

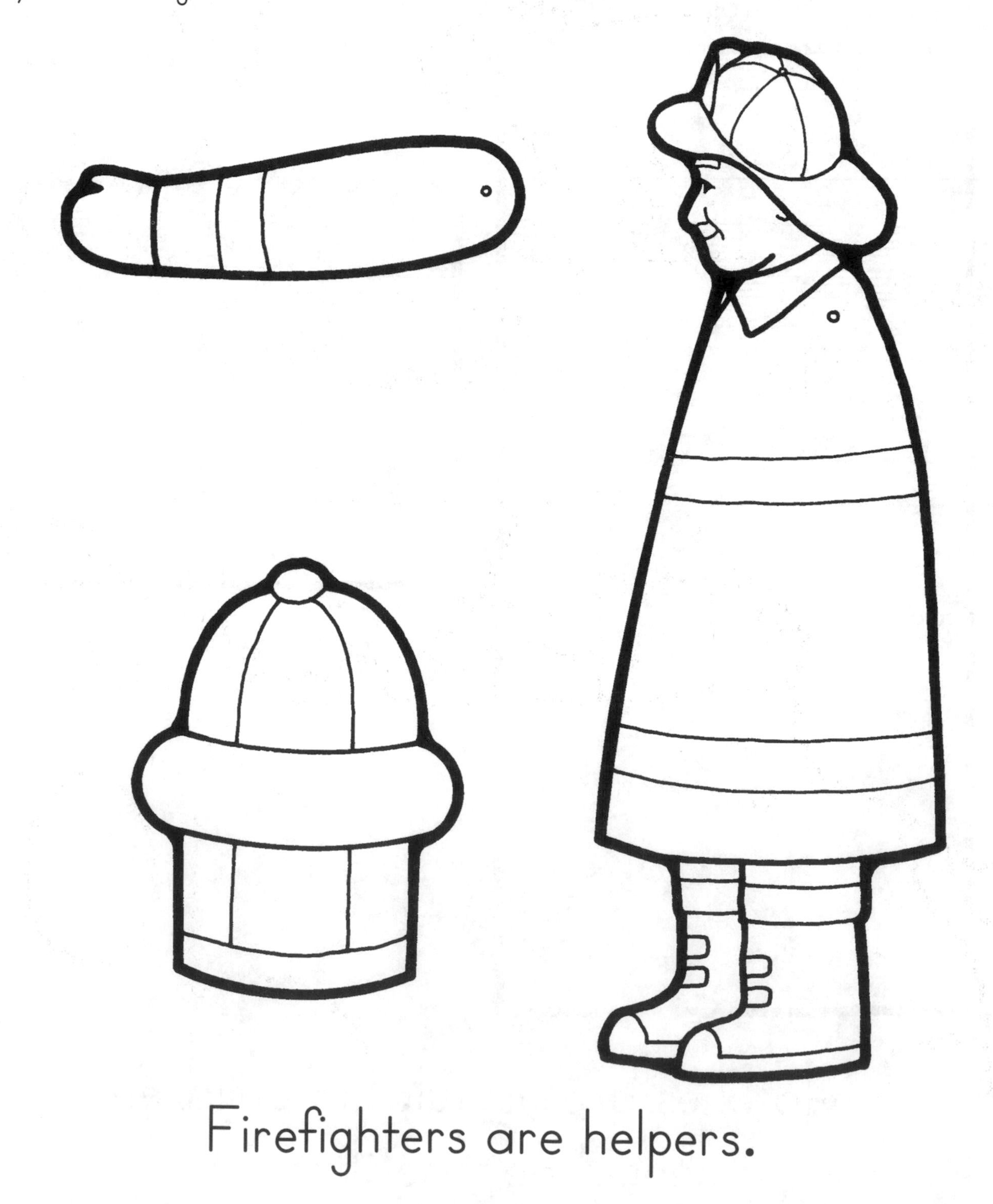

Protecting Our Wilderness

Color and cut out the animals and sign. Color the scene. Glue the animals and sign into the scene.

Keeping Safe

Color the building. Add a ladder below the window and a person inside the window. Glue cotton around the window to make smoke.

Know how to leave safely in case of fire.

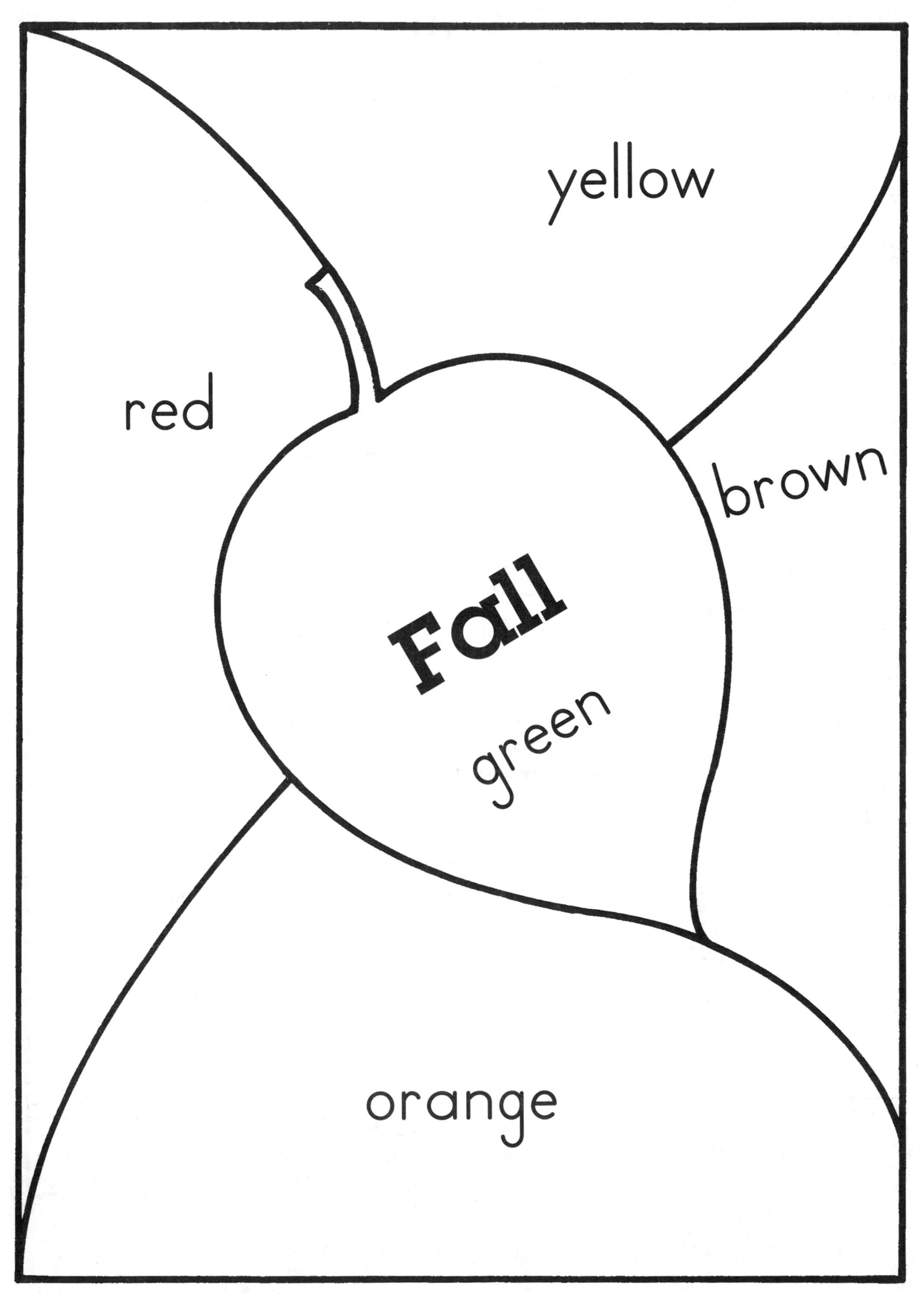
yellow
red
brown
Fall
green
orange

Fall

Objectives:

Each child will learn about . . .

- natural things of fall.
- fall clothing.
- fall activities.
- fall weather.
- animal habits during fall.

Discussions:

As a group, the class can discuss . . .

- how trees change.
- how leaves change and fall.
- how grass changes.
- fall weather.
- kinds of clothing worn for the weather.
- reasons for fall changes.
- activities to do in the fall.
- how animals prepare for cold weather.

Activities:

Let the children color page 57 as directed to make their folder covers.

Let each child color page 59. With a small piece of dry sponge dipped in tempera paint, the children can add leaves of various colors to the picture.

Provide each child with a copy of page 60, crayons, and some type of nut or seed. Let the children color their pictures. Then add a drop of glue to the squirrel's paws and place the nut or seed. Let dry.

Provide each child with a scarecrow sheet (page 61), glue, and bits of yarn in straw colors. The children can color the scarecrow, add birds, and paste short pieces of yarn at the ends of the pant legs and sleeves to represent straw.

Instruct each child to add warm fall clothing to the drawing on page 62. If desired, let them glue on a piece of fabric to make a warm scarf around the figure's neck. As an extension, provide cold weather dress-up clothes for the children to use in their play.

Tear bits of fall-colored tissue paper. Provide each child with a copy of page 63 and a pile of paper bits. Also provide liquid starch in plastic cups and paintbrushes. Let the children color the picture and then add colored leaves by painting on the bits of tissue with liquid starch. To do so, paint a thin layer of starch in the area to be covered. Add the tissue-paper bits. Apply another thin layer of starch on top of the tissue paper. Let dry.

Color the tree. Add leaves with dabs of paint.

Leaves fall from trees.

Getting Ready

Color the squirrel. Glue a seed or nut in its paws.

Animals prepare for winter.

Harvest

Color the scarecrow. Add birds around him. Paste yarn at the end of his legs and arms to make straw.

Garden crops are gathered.

Keeping Warm

Draw warm clothes on the person to keep warm.

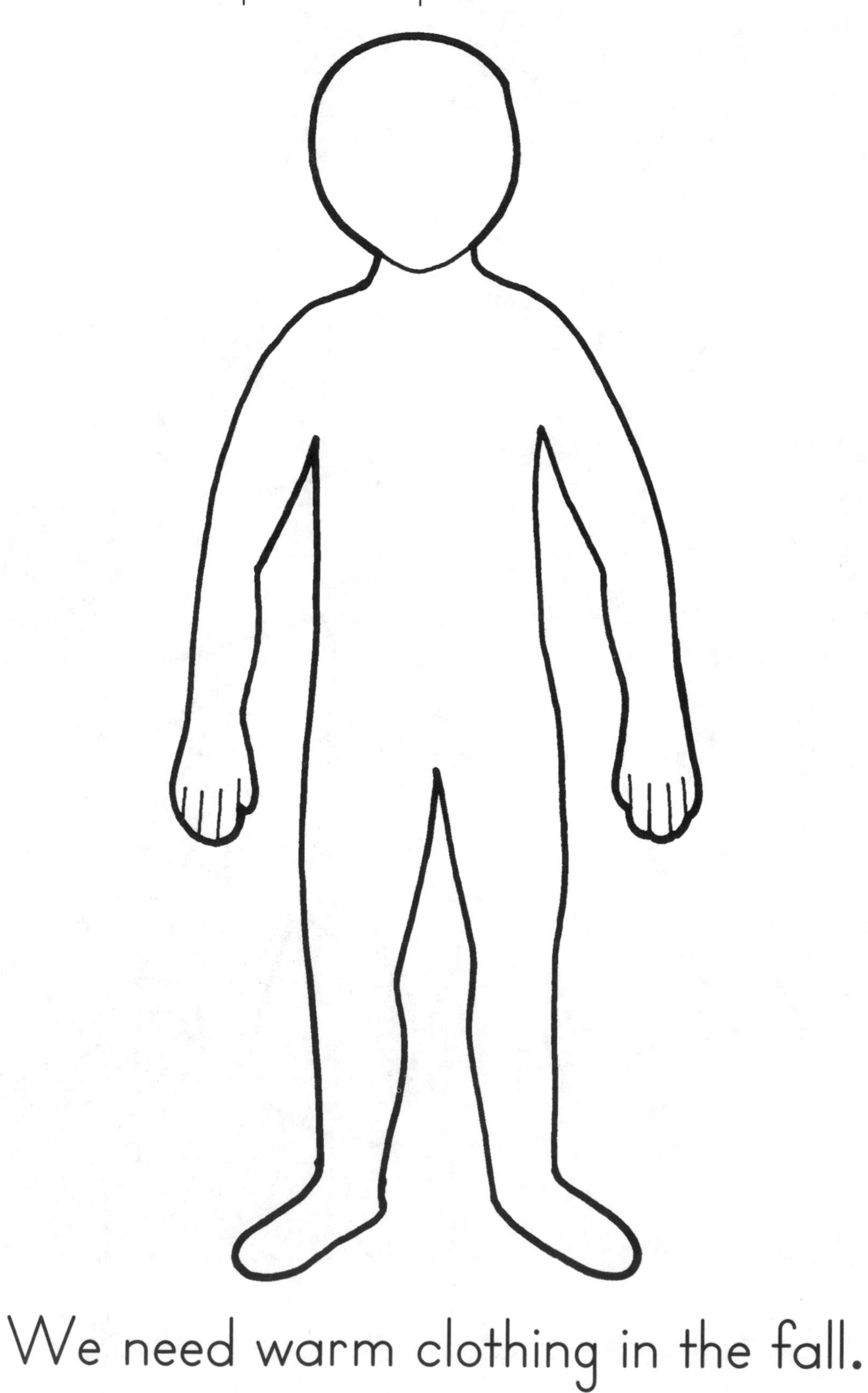

We need warm clothing in the fall.

Fall Leaves

Color the picture. Paste bits of colored paper on the picture to make fall leaves.

People rake leaves in the fall.

The President

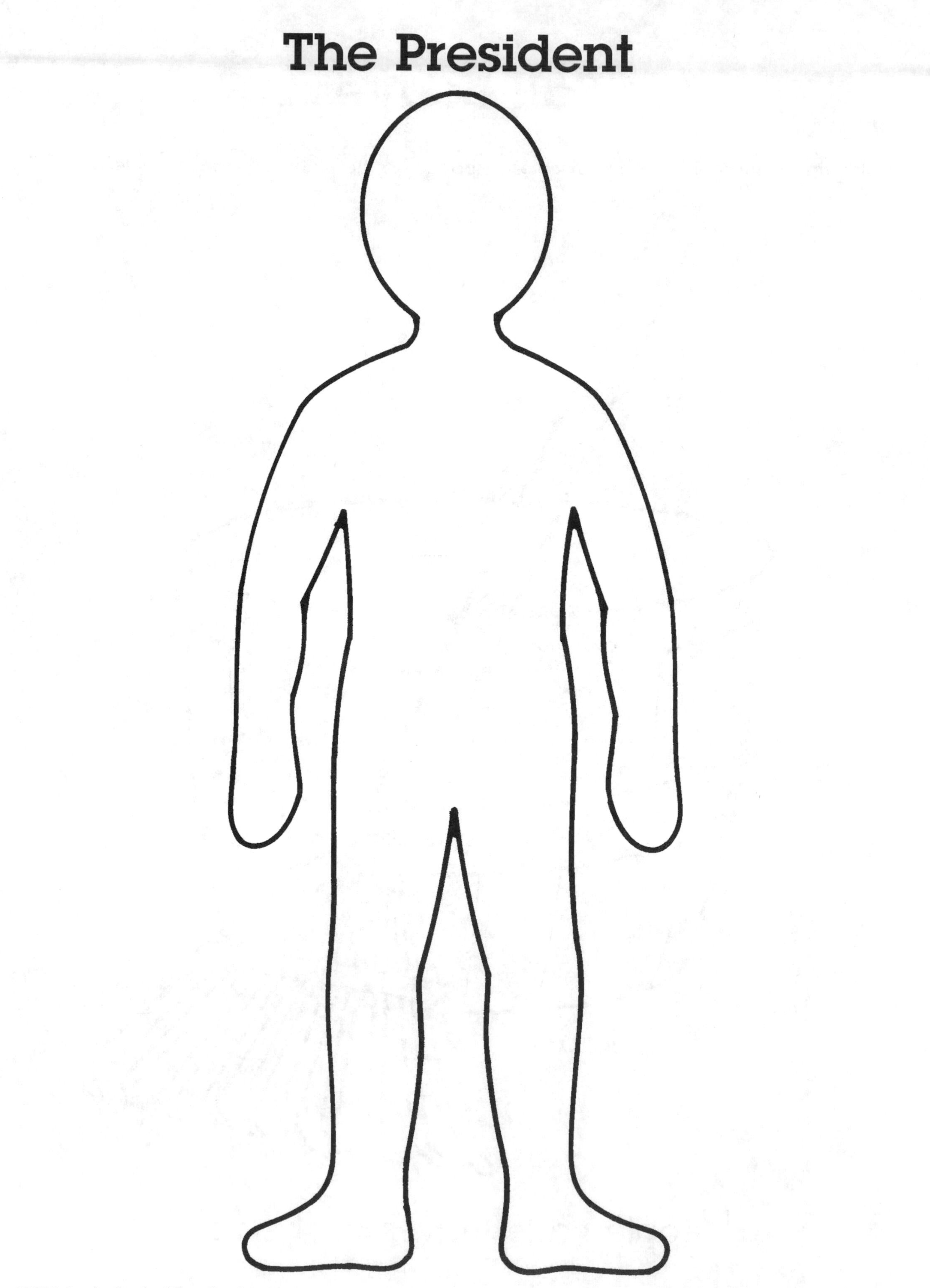

The President

Objectives:

Each child will learn . . .

- why we have presidents.
- about current and former presidents.
- what jobs the president does.
- where the president lives and works.
- how the president is chosen.

Discussions:

As a group, the class can discuss . . .

- how the United States was started.
- why we have a president.
- names for leaders in other countries.
- who has formerly been president in our country and who is president today.
- what jobs the president does.
- the president's daily schedule.
- the president's family life.
- the White House.
- who works in the White House.
- how and why the president is chosen.
- what voting means and why we vote.
- who can vote.

Activities:

Let the children color page 64 as directed to make their folder covers.

Provide each child with a copy of page 66. After discussion, the children can draw and color different faces to complete the picture.

Give each child a copy of page 67. Let the child draw what he or should would like to do as president of the country. Complete the sentence for the child. Let the children share their ideas with the class.

Provide each child with page 68. After discussing the president's many jobs, help the child to cut on the dotted line and fold up the sheet to make a briefcase. (An adult will need to cut out the handle.) The back of the folded-up sheet can be colored brown. Draw in a line and other marks to make the flap and clasp of the briefcase. When folded, the briefcase will "hold" the president's work.

After talking about the White House, instruct the children to color page 69, adding windows, trees, and more to complete the picture.

Color the ballot on page 70.

For the People

Draw many faces to show all the people for whom the president works.

The president works for all the people of our country.

If I Were President

Write what you would do if you were president.

The President's Work

Cut out the briefcase. Fold it up where shown. Color the briefcase.

What jobs does the president have?

The White House

Color the White House. Add details.

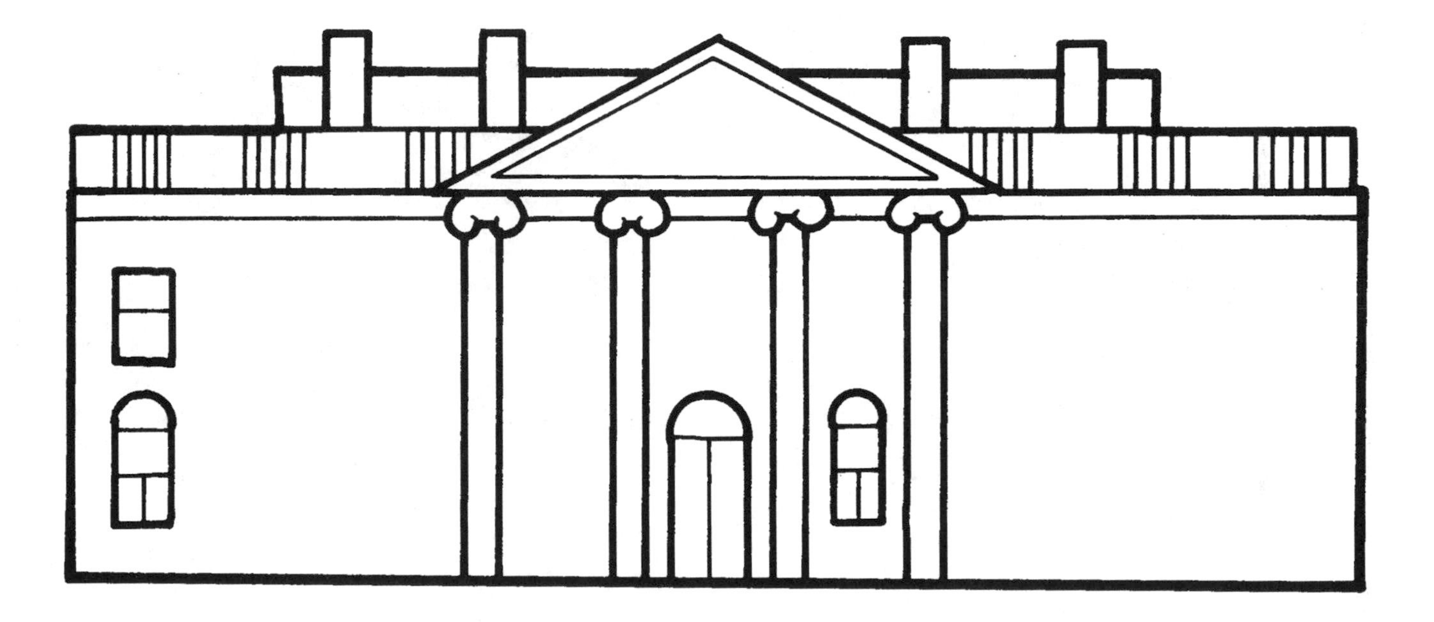

The White House is the president's home.
The White House has many rooms.
Many people work in the White House.
We can visit the White House, too.

How Do We Vote?

Color the ballot, hand, and pencil. Mark your vote.

Many grownups in our country vote to choose the president.

Being Healthy and Happy

Being Healthy and Happy

Objectives:

Each child will learn about the . . .

- need for good food.
- need for exercise.
- need for rest.
- need for keeping clean.
- need for proper clothing.

Discussions:

As a group, the class can discuss . . .

- why we need food.
- the kinds of good food and snack food.
- why we need exercise.
- various kinds of exercise.
- why we need rest and when to rest.
- how we act without enough rest.
- why we need to keep clean.
- how we can keep clean.
- why we need proper clothing.
- kinds of clothes and when to wear them.

Activities:

After discussing how healthful foods keep us fit and strong, give each child a fruit pattern (page 73). Paste the fruit to another paper. Let the child color it, adding a face, arms, and legs to make a "person."

Give each child the cutout parts of the figure (page 74), paper fasteners, and crayons. The child can color the figure and fasten it together with the paper fasteners. Staple the figure at the head to a separate sheet. Glue the sentence strip below it.

Supply children with page 75 and crayons. They can color the sheet, adding a window, rug, etc., to complete the picture. (If desired, tell them to add details of their own rooms at home.)

Each child is given a bathtub sheet (page 76) and crayons. The child can color the picture. Then, make soap suds by mixing equal parts of Ivory Snow and water with an electric mixer. Put a small amount of the suds on the water in the tub. Let dry.

Provide the children with page 77 and crayons. Let the children draw themselves in the raincoat on a rainy day. Discuss how clothing is used for protection.

Eating Right

Color a piece of fruit and glue it to another paper. Add a face, arms, and legs to make a fruit person. Glue the sentence strip below it.

Exercising

Draw the person's face. Color and cut him out. Hook the person together with paper fasteners and make the figure exercise.

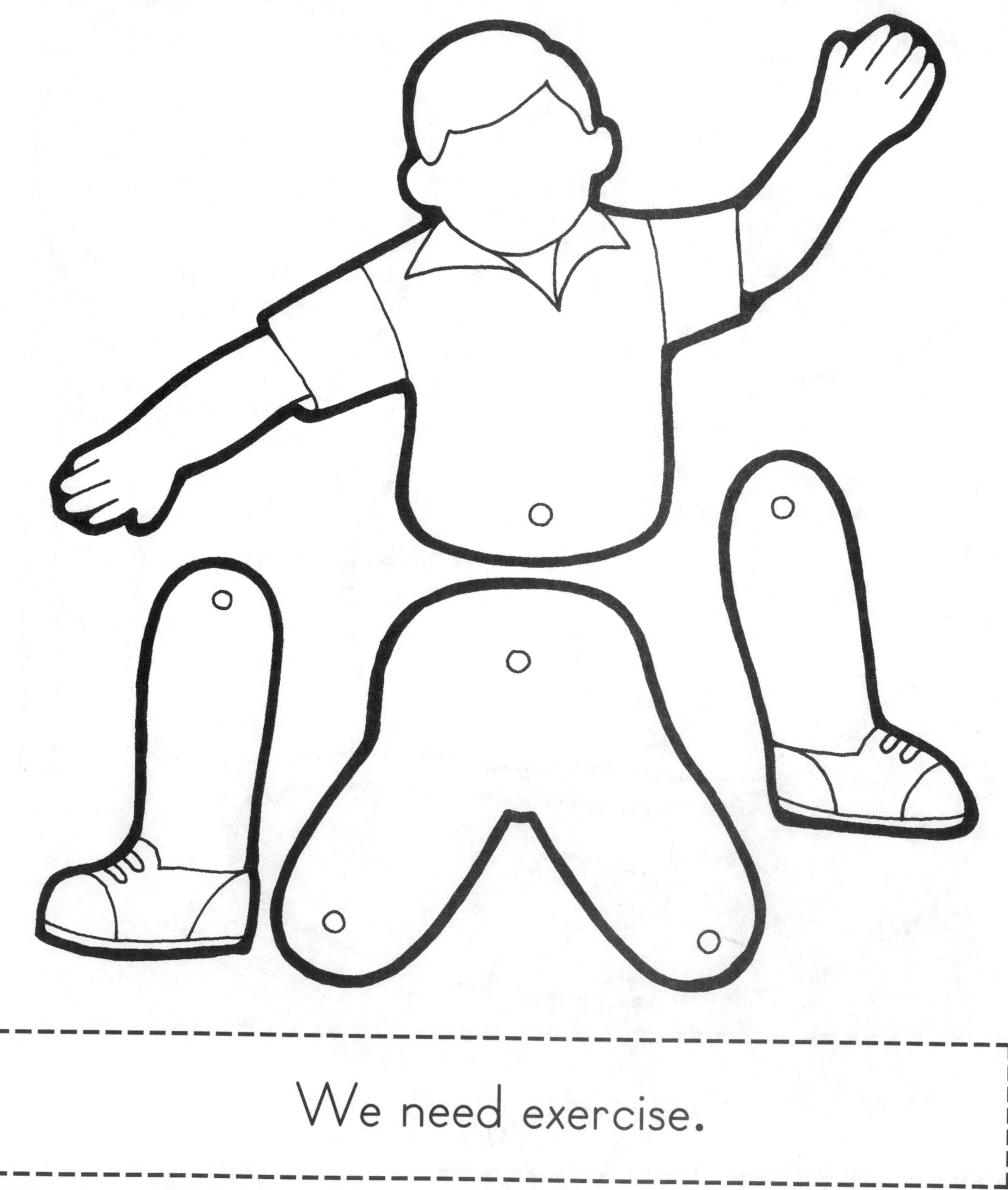

We need exercise.

Resting

Draw details in the picture to make a bedroom.

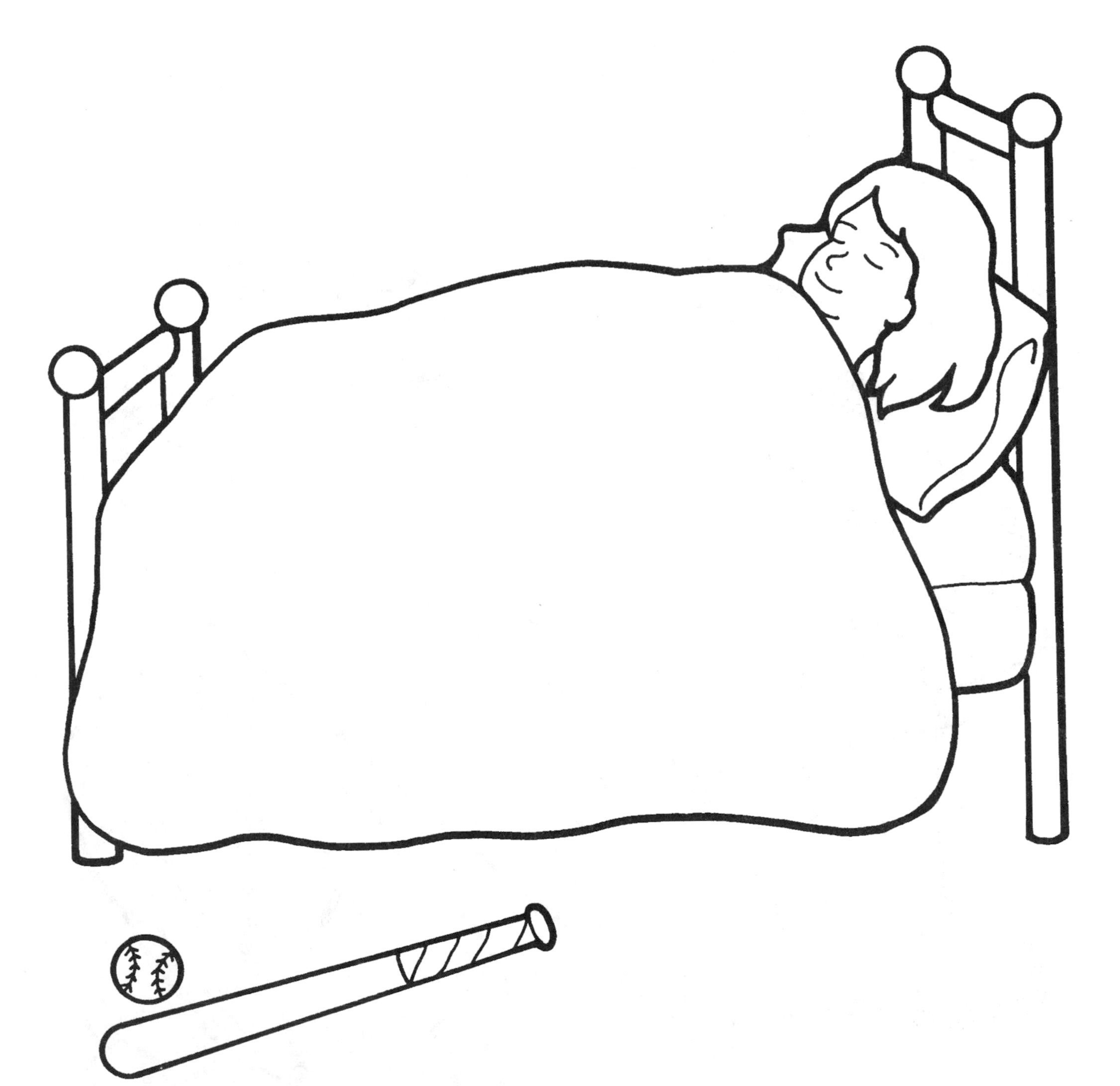

We need rest.

Keeping Clean

Draw yourself and your bath toys in the tub.

We can wash ourselves.

Clothing That Protects Us

Draw yourself in the raincoat. Add raindrops and an umbrella.

Raincoats keep us dry. What other clothes do we wear to protect us?

Native Americans

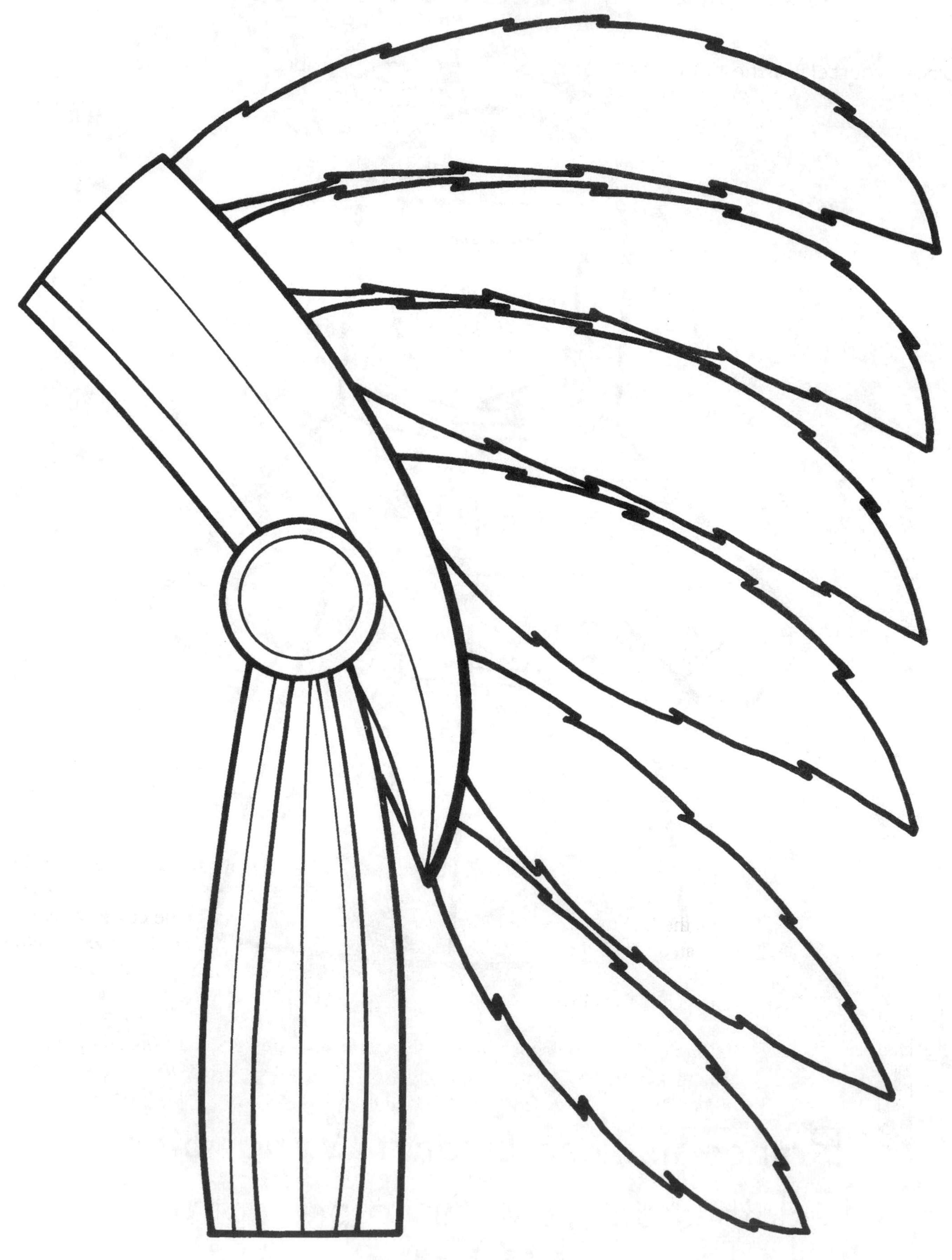

Native Americans

Objectives:

Each child will learn about . . .

- the general locations of various Native American tribes.
- Woodland Indians.
- Plains Indians.
- Pueblo Indians.
- River Indians.

Discussions:

As a group, the class can discuss . . .

- how Native Americans are treated today and in the past.
- what various Native American tribes wore in the past and today.
- Native American homelands.
- Woodland Indian homes, habits, and food.
- Plains Indian homes, habits, and food.
- Pueblo Indian homes, habits, and food.
- River Indian homes, habits, and food.

Activities:

After coloring the cover sheet (page 78), children can add feathers with glue for a three-dimensional look.

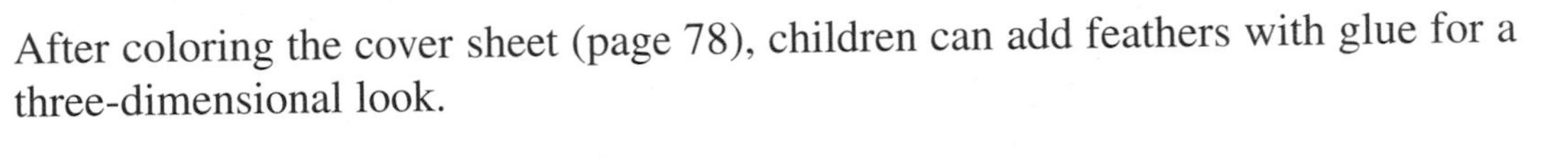

Provide the children with a copy of page 80, crayons, scissors (if they are able to cut), and glue. Discuss how Woodland hunters wore their hair, and allow the children to color the picture, drawing in a face and adding a necklace or other accessory. Help the children to color the feather strip in many colors, fold it on the center line, and cut it like a feather. Glue the feather to the hair to complete the picture.

Provide each child with a teepee pattern (page 81). The child can color the teepee. Cut it out as well as the door flap and glue it to another paper. Color a scene around the teepee.

Supply each child with the five-slitted panel and five strips of paper (page 82) in another color. With help, the child can weave the strips through the slits. Also, trace the leaf pattern onto brown paper. Glue a cotton ball in the center where indicated. Fold the leaf up on both sides to make a cotton boll. Staple the cotton boll to the woven "cloth" and glue both to another sheet of paper with the sentence strip below it.

Let the children color the totem pole pattern on page 83. Cut it out and glue it around a cardboard tube (from a paper towel or toilet paper roll). Alternatively, let the children draw their own totem pole design on a piece of paper and glue that to the tube.

The pictures on pages 84–88 can be used for student booklets. Use page 78 for a booklet cover or let the children create their own.

Woodland Hunter

Color the hunter and his feather. Cut out the feather and glue it in the hunter's hair.

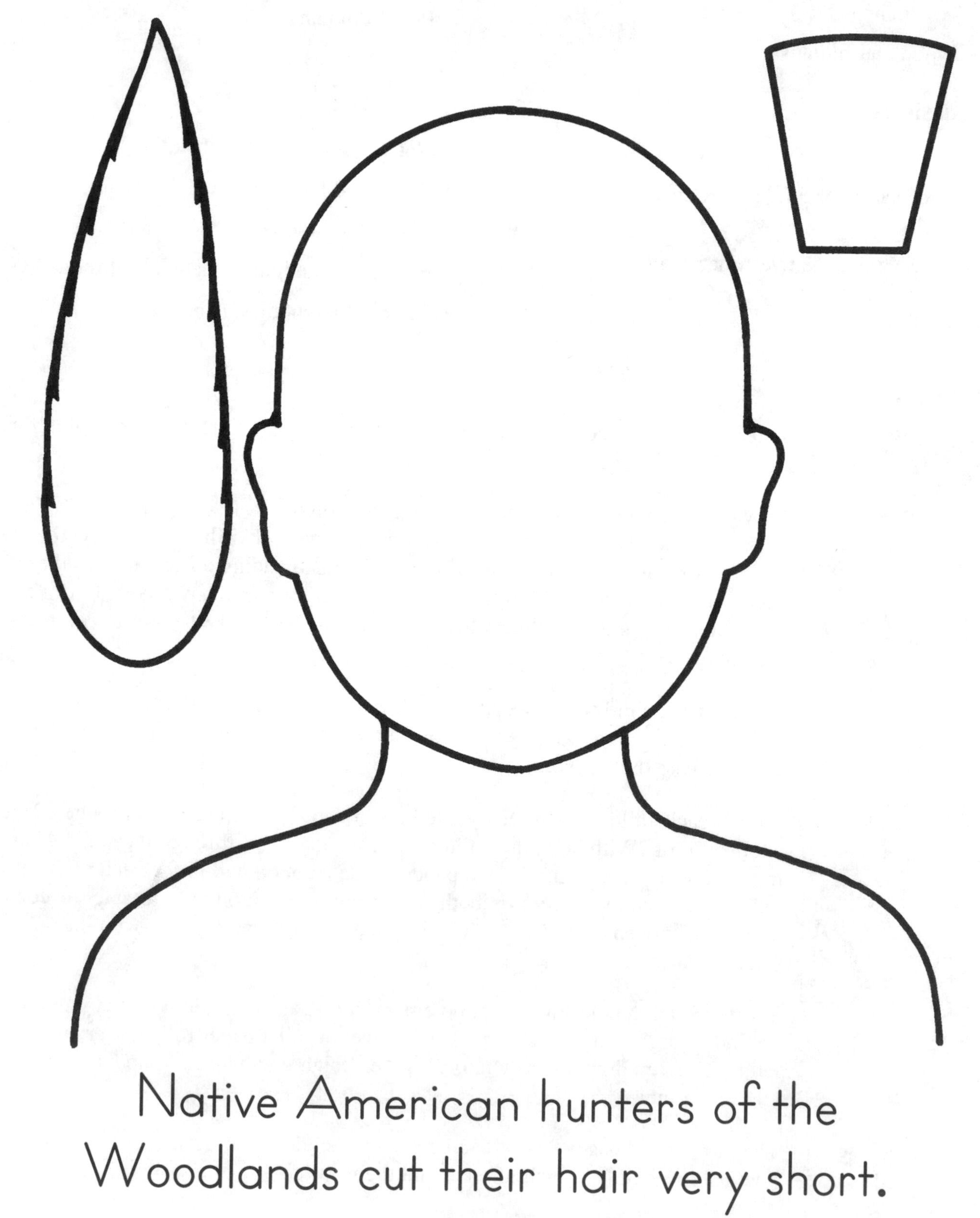

Native American hunters of the Woodlands cut their hair very short.

Teepees of the Plains Indians

Color and cut out the teepee. Cut and fold the door flap. Glue the teepee to another paper and color a scene where a Plains Indian might have lived long ago.

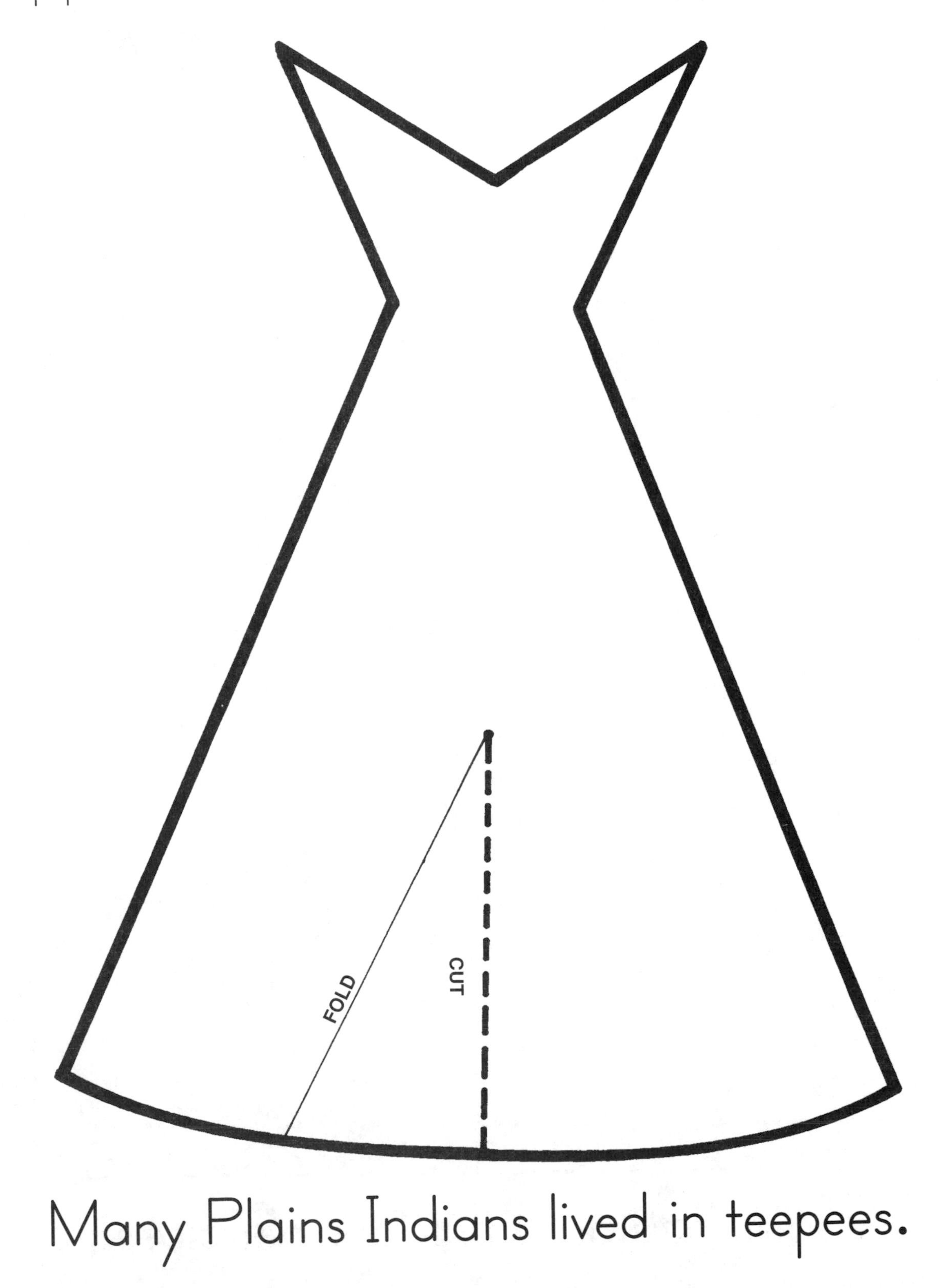

Many Plains Indians lived in teepees.

Weaving Cloth like the Pueblo Indians

Weave five colored strips of cloth through the slits of the larger pattern. Glue cotton inside the cotton boll and fold the leaves over it. Glue the cotton boll to the woven cloth.

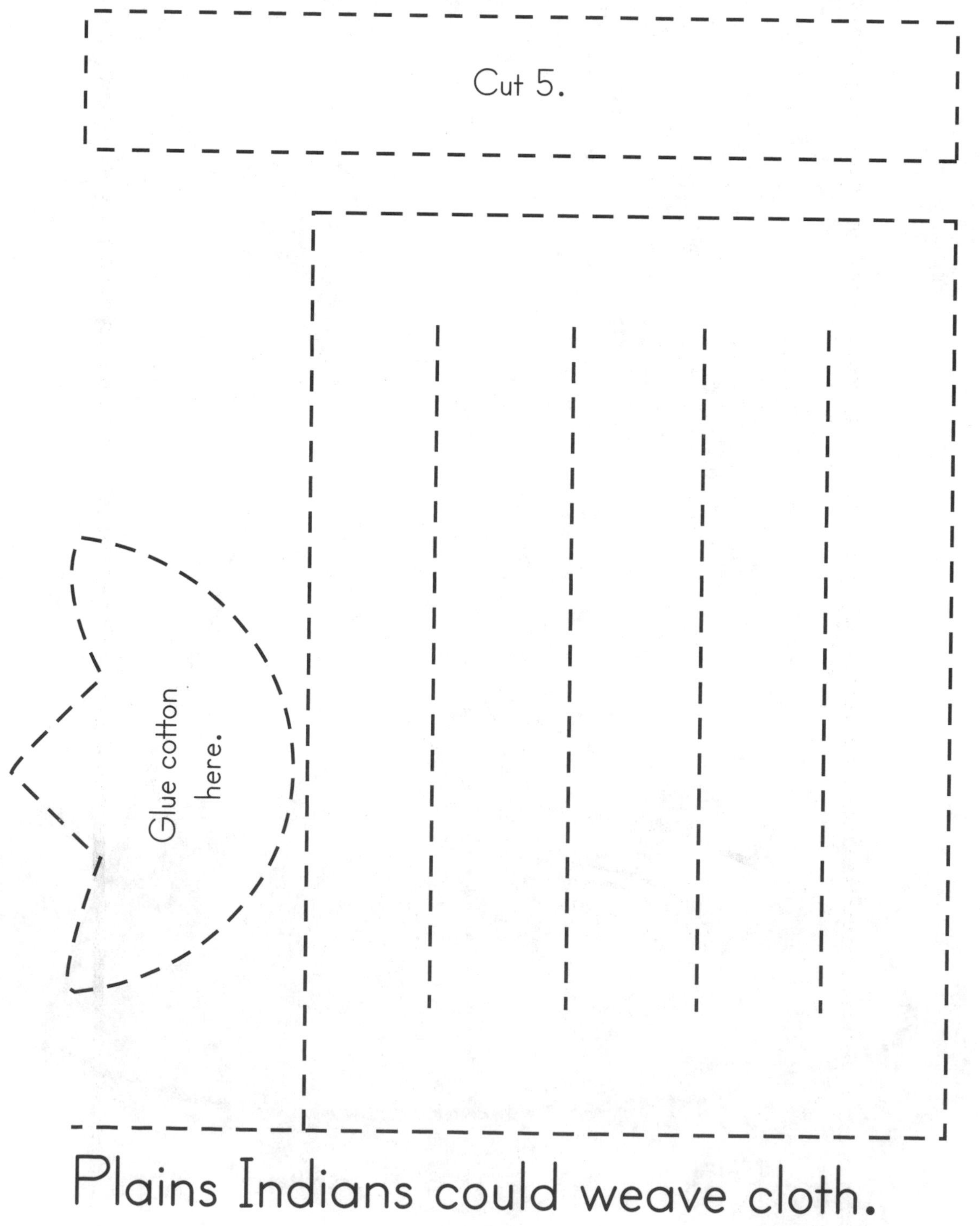

Totem Pole of the River Indians

Color the totem pole. Cut it out. Glue it around a cardboard tube to make a pole.

Indians of America

Color the map. It shows where the Woodland, Plains, Pueblo, and River Indians lived.

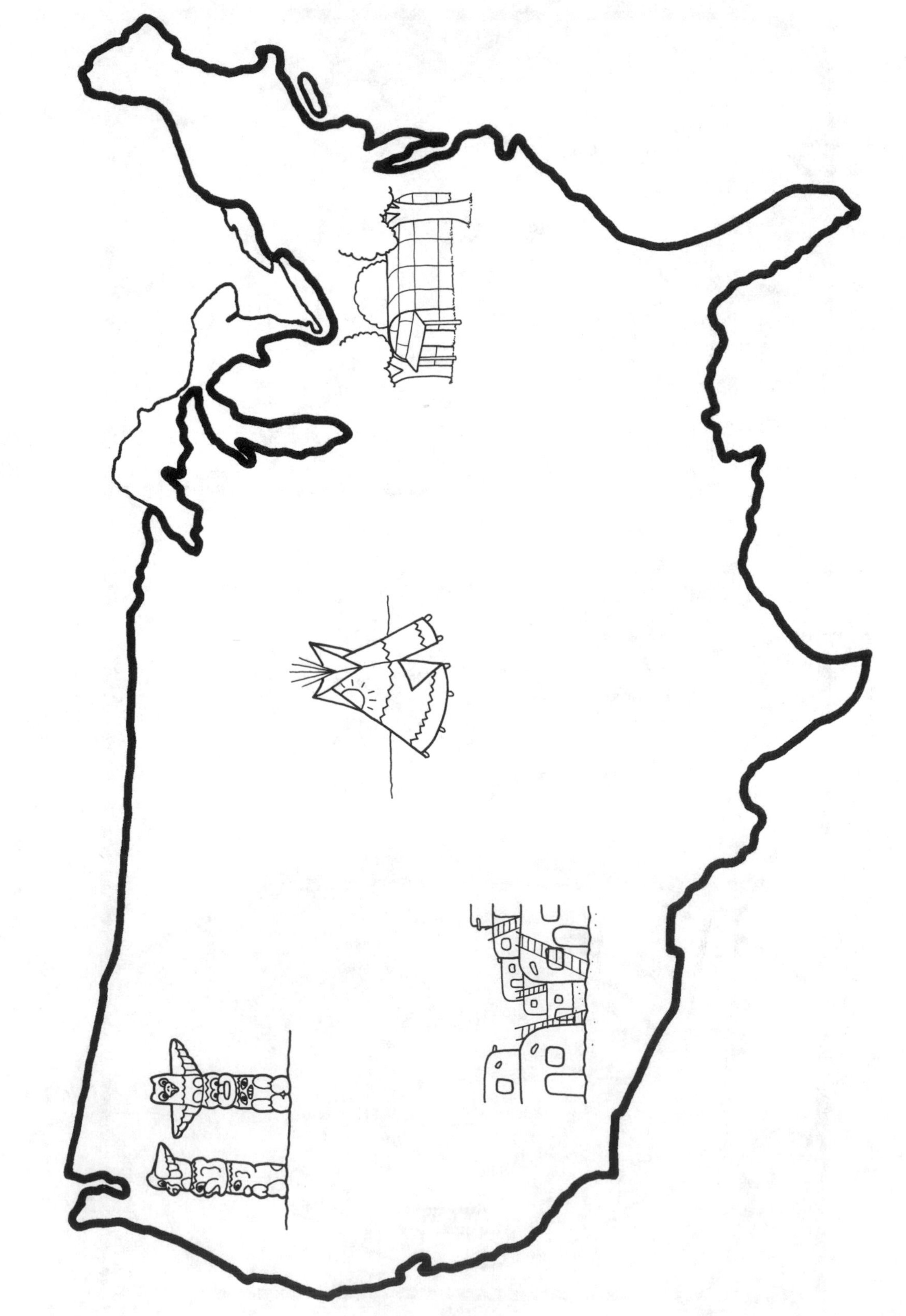

Woodland Indians

Color the pictures. They tell about the Woodland Indians.

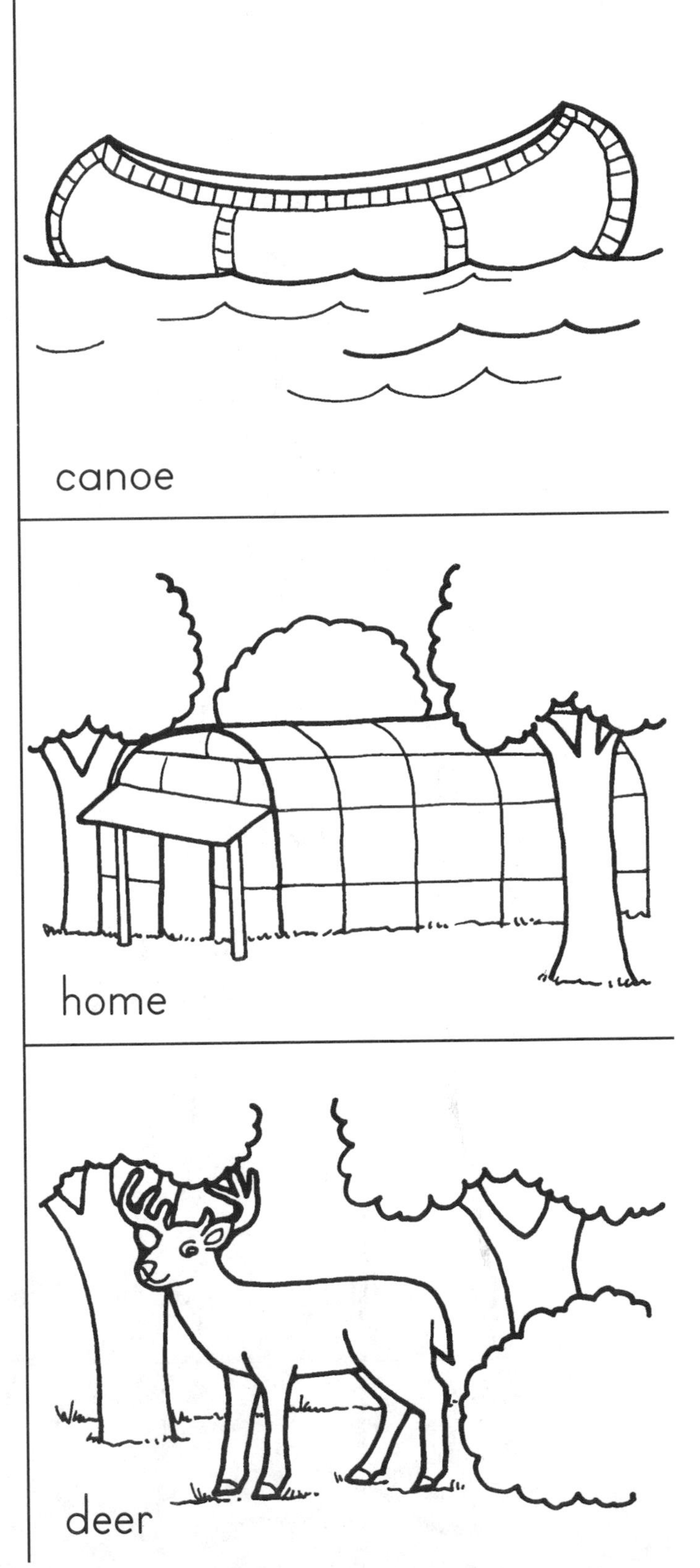

Plains Indians

Color the pictures. They tell about the Plains Indians.

Pueblo Indians

Color the pictures. They tell about the Pueblo Indians.

River Indians

Color the pictures. They tell about the River Indians.

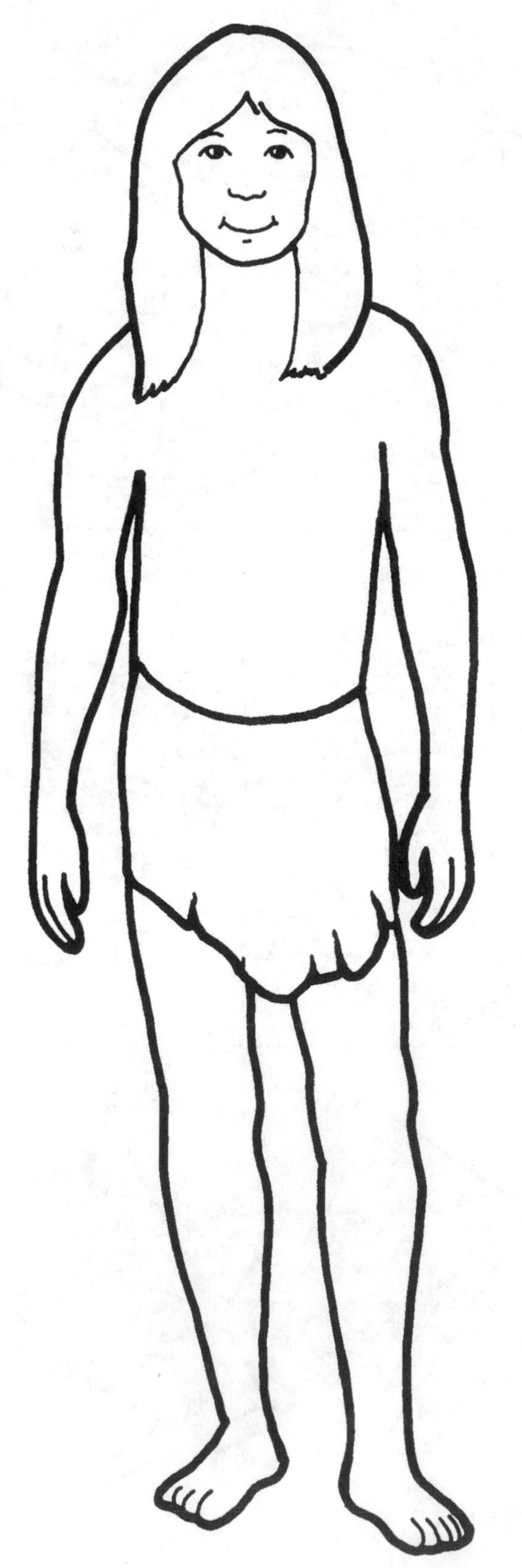

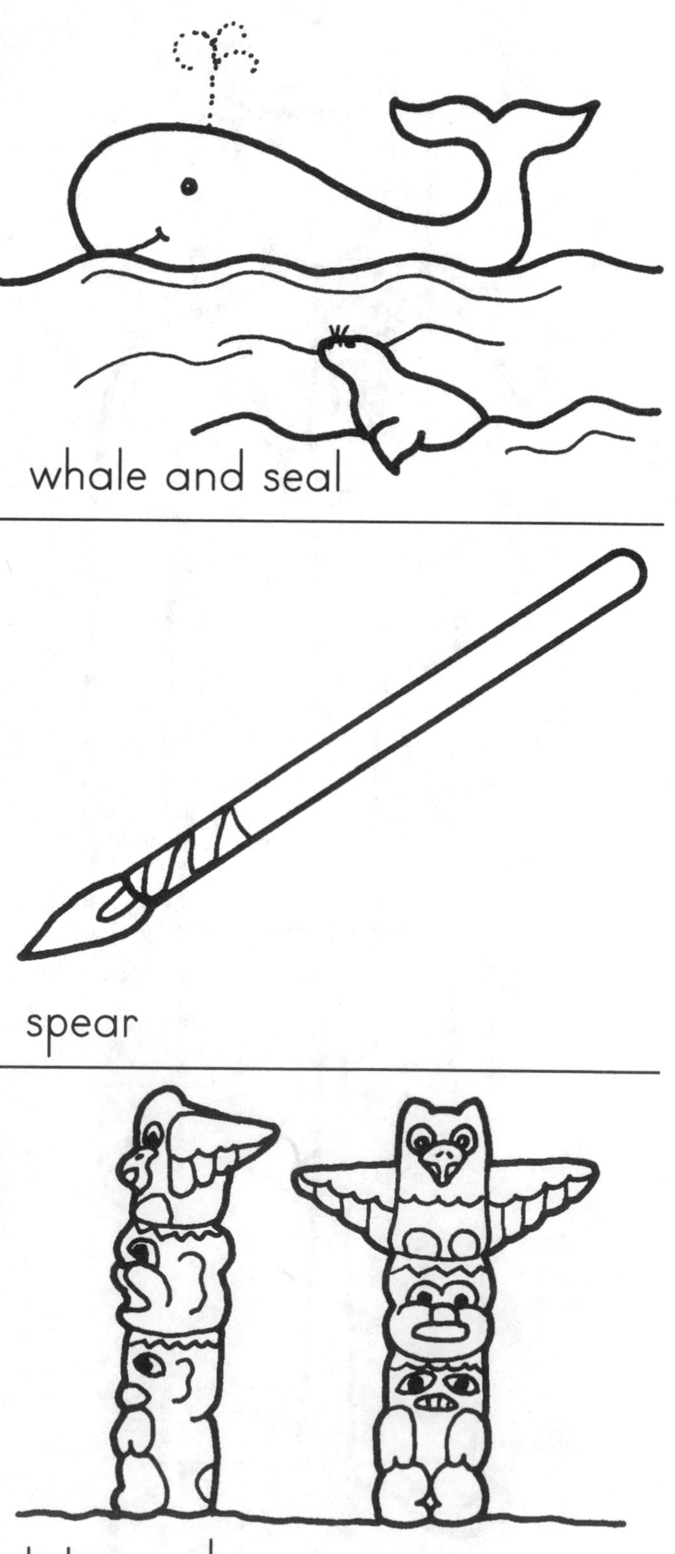

Pilgrims

Pilgrims

Objectives:

Each child will learn . . .

- who the Pilgrims were.
- why the Pilgrims wanted a new home.
- about the journey on the *Mayflower*.
- about the first year in the New World.
- about the first Thanksgiving.

Discussions:

As a group, the class can discuss . . .

- who the Pilgrims were.
- where the Pilgrims lived.
- why the Pilgrims wanted a new home.
- coming to the New World.
- winter in the New World.
- the first Thanksgiving.
- Thanksgiving today.

Activities:

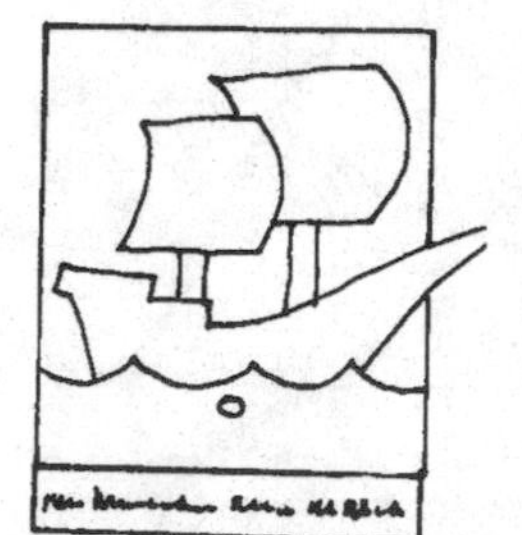

Give each child a light-blue paper (8.5" x 11"/21.25 cm x 27.5 cm) and blue, green, and purple crayons. Let them color "water" on the paper with the crayons. Scallop a short edge of the paper and fold up the scalloped edge about four inches (10 cm). With a paper fastener, attach a boat (page 91) inside the water fold. Paste sails in place and draw masts to make the Mayflower. Paste the sentence strip below the ship.

Provide each child with a blue sheet, three green hearts (page 92), white snow, crayons, and white chalk. Instruct the children to paste the hearts upside down on the blue sheet to make an evergreen tree. Draw a leafless tree beside the evergreen and add snow with the chalk. Paste the sentence strip below the picture.

Provide each child with a pattern for an ear of corn (page 93) and two corn husks cut from brown paper. Instruct the children to color the corn kernels in various colors. (It may be helpful to show them real corn that is grown in these bright colors. Such varieties are usually available around the time of autumn harvests.) Attach the husks to one end of the ear with a paper fastener. In this way, the husks can be opened to reveal the corn.

Using the hand pattern (page 94), place the wrist edge on the fold of a sheet of index paper and trace around the hand. Cut out the image, leaving the bottom fold intact. Next, fold where indicated on the pattern. Show the children how to draw and color a turkey on one hand. On the other hand, help them to write what they are thankful for. (The teacher can write what the child dictates.) The child can draw features of the hand (knuckles, nails, etc.) around the writing. Prop up the turkey/hand for display. If necessary, tape or staple the turkey/hand at the top to keep it standing.

Mayflower

Cut two white sails for the ship. Cut the *Mayflower* from brown paper. Glue the ship onto blue paper. Draw masts. Color the water.

The *Mayflower* sailed on the water.

Winter for the Pilgrims

Use the patterns to make snow and an evergreen tree. Stack the hearts upside down to make the tree and paste them onto the snowy field. Glue the snow and tree to a blue background and draw other details to make the winter scene.

Winter for the Pilgrims was cold and snowy.

Corn

Color the corn in bright colors. Make two husks from brown paper. Use a paper fastener to attach the husks to one end of the ear. Open and close the husks to show the corn.

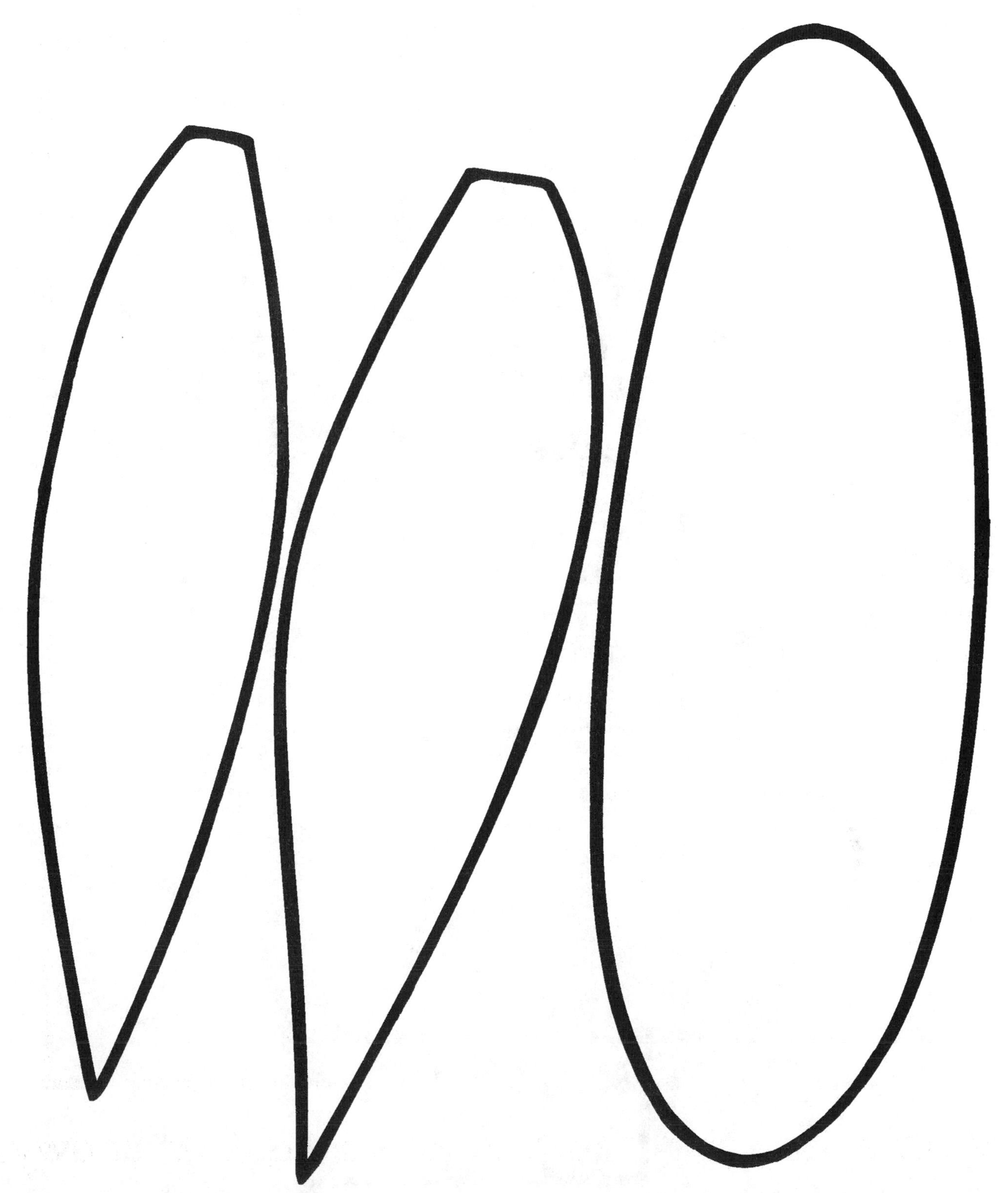

Thankful Turkeys

Fold heavy paper and trace the hand pattern on the fold. Draw a turkey on one hand and write what you are thankful for on the other hand. Glue one fold on top of another to make a stand.

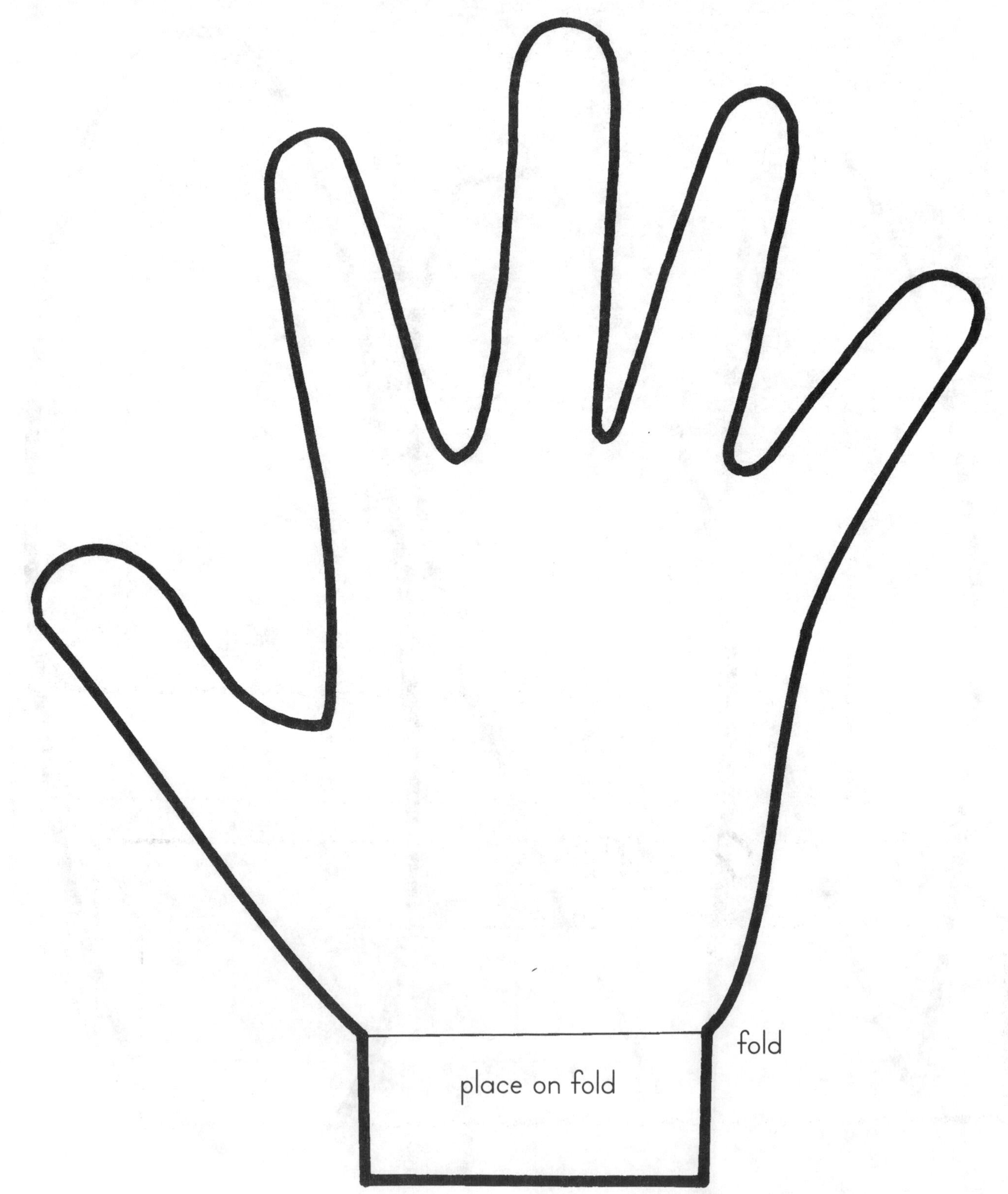

Winter Holidays

Winter Holidays

Objectives:

Each child will learn about . . .

- Christmas decorations and traditions.
- celebrating other winter holidays.
- giving and receiving gifts.

Discussions:

As a group, the class can discuss . . .

- holiday decorations.
- holiday meanings and purposes.
- kinds of gifts people might receive.
- a special gift each child would like.
- ways to thank people for gifts.
- different ways to celebrate special days.

Activities:

Give each child a copy of page 97 and crayons. After discussing the reasons for decorating trees at Christmas, the child can color the tree, adding details of garland, ornaments, and presents beneath it. If desired, dot white glue on the tree and sprinkle glitter over it to make the tree shimmer as though it were lit.

Provide each child with a fireplace, stocking, and boot pattern (page 98). With help, each child can draw lines to form fireplace bricks. Let them decorate the stocking and color the boots, attach the stocking to the mantle, and place the boots inside the fireplace opening (as if Santa were ascending or descending). For an interesting look the children will enjoy, trace the fireplace pattern onto corrugated "brick" paper (sold in general stores during the holiday season) and trace the stocking and boots onto red and black felt, respectively.

Provide each child with the patterns on page 99. The children can color Santa and attach him to a labeled sheet (sentence strip) with the chimney and rooftop. Leave the chimney open (like a pocket) so Santa can move up and down.

Complete the sentence (page 100) for each child with "receive" or "give." Instruct the children to color a special gift on the pattern where indicated. Cut out the full pattern and fold it over. Tell the child to color wrapping paper on the cover (the part that has been folded over). Color a bow as well or tape an actual bow and ribbons to the "package." Glue the package and sentence strip to another paper.

Discuss the various holidays that take place at the end of the year, especially Hanukkah, Kwanzaa, and Christmas. Explain the importance of candles in the celebrations. Then, provide the children with page 101 to color. Alternatively, enlarge any of the three patterns on a photocopy machine and let the children decorate them with bits of colored tissue and liquid starch (see page 58) to make vibrant holiday flames and a glittering menorah, Advent wreath, or kinara.

Christmas Trees

Color the tree. Add decorations and presents.

Decorating a tree is fun.

Stockings

Cut out the patterns. Make the fireplace and stocking red. Make Santa's boots black. Glue the pieces onto another paper and add details to make a picture.

Here Comes Santa Claus

Color Santa and the chimney. Glue the chimney to another paper around the sides and bottom, but leave the top open. Make Santa go down the chimney.

Santa Claus comes down the chimney.

Holiday Gifts

Complete the sentence with "give" or "receive." Draw the gift. Cut out the package. Fold down the lid and color wrapping paper and a bow. Glue the package and sentence to another paper.

Fold here.

Draw your gift here.

What special gift would you like to ____________?

Celebrations of Light

Color the pictures.

Some people celebrate Hanukkah.

Some people celebrate Christmas.

Some people celebrate Kwanzaa.

Star Helpers

Star Helpers

Objectives:

Each child will learn . . .

- ways to help.
- the rewards of helping.

Discussions:

As a group, the class can discuss . . .

- reasons to help.
- the importance of safety and permission from adults.
- readiness to help.

(Note: Teachers, please stress safety and permission from adults in all situations.)

Activities:

After coloring the star (pages 102), help the children to cut it out. Attach the star to a bit of yarn and move it from page to page in the folder as the activities are completed. The stars can also be hung around the room for decorations.

Encourage children to talk about things to do in each room mentioned on page 104. Then instruct them to draw a picture for each square. As an extension, act out helping situations that the children discuss and draw.

Let the children color all the items on the page (105), cut them out (with help as needed), and glue them where they belong to make a neat and tidy room.

Instruct the children to color themselves in a helping situation after discussing how they can help outside (page 106).

Provide each child with a copy of page 107. Instruct them to color the sheet. Then let them glue bits of trash in the trash can as well as trash being thrown away by the person in the picture.

Let the children color the picture and arm on page 108, writing letters or numbers (or their versions of them) on the "chalkboard." Cut out the arm and affix it with a paper fastener at the O. Move the arm to show it erasing the chalkboard.

Helping at Home

Color a picture to show how you help in each room.

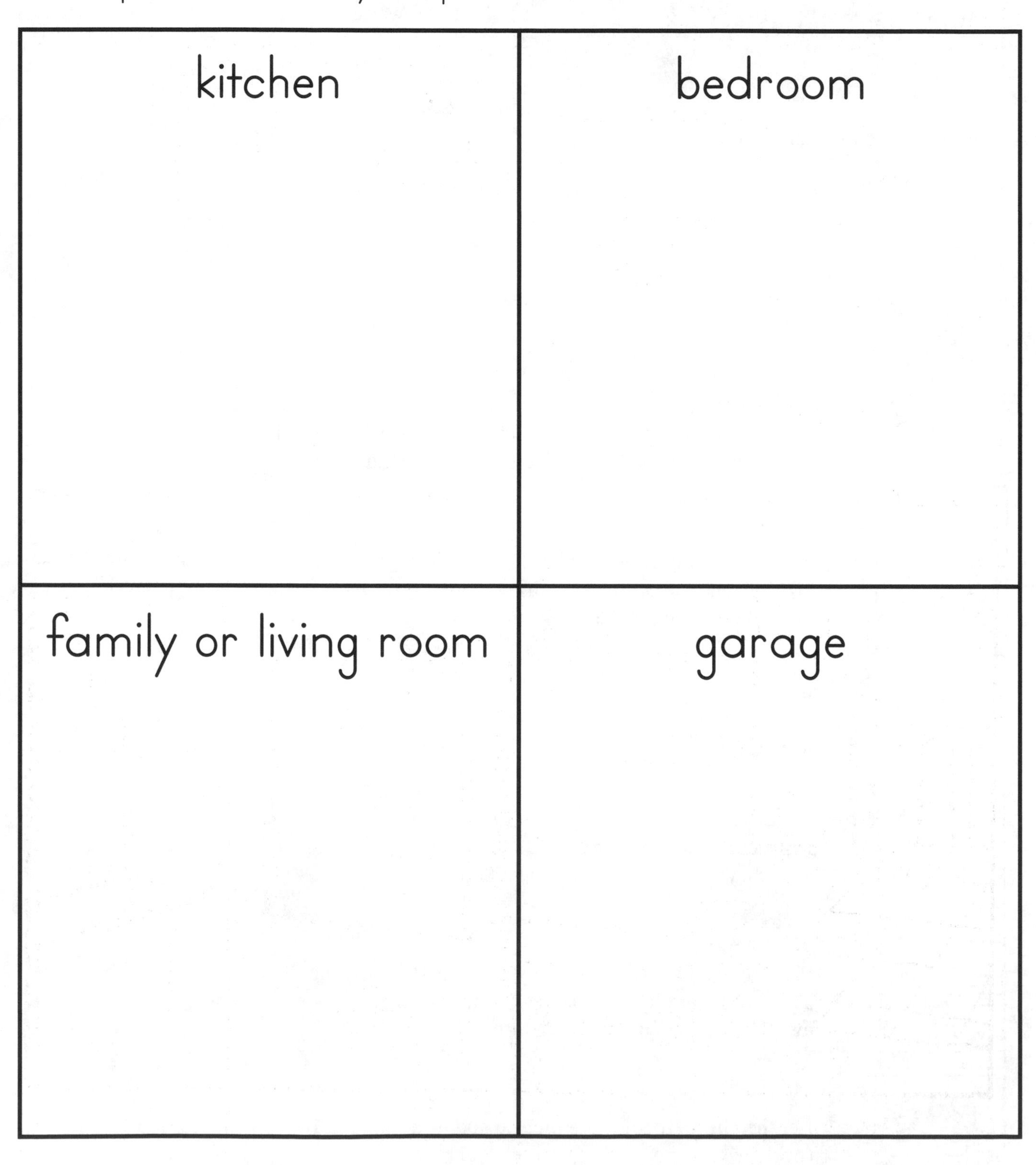

I can help in the house.

In My Room

Color the pictures. Cut out the items below, and glue them where they belong in the room.

I can keep my room neat and tidy.

Helping Outside

Draw a picture of yourself helping to take care of the yard.

I can help in the yard.

Keeping My Neighborhood Clean

Color the picture. Glue trash in the trash can. Glue trash for the person to throw away, too.

I help to keep my neighborhood clean.

At School

Color the picture. Cut out the arm. Attach it to the child with a paper fastener. Move the arm to erase the board.

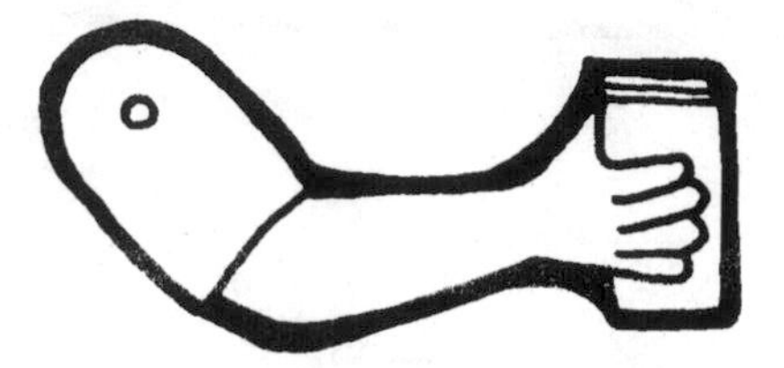

I can help at school.

Weather

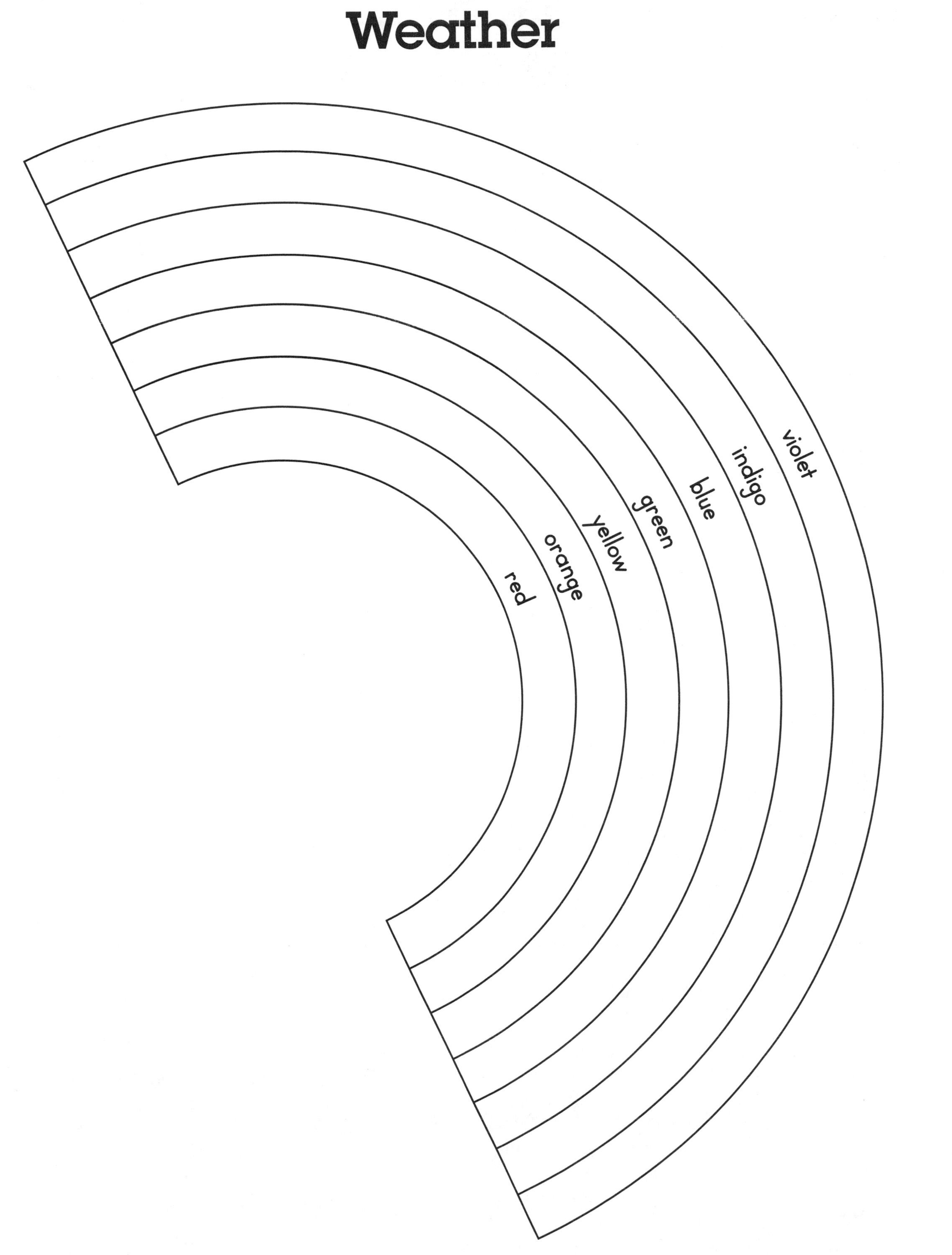

Weather

Objectives:

Each child will learn . . .

- what weather is.
- the characteristics of different kinds of weather.
- causes and effects of weather.
- how a thermometer helps us.

Discussions:

As a group, the class can discuss . . .

- what weather is.
- weather words.
- what the sun is and how it helps us.
- types of clouds and what they are.
- wind and its effects.
- what rain is and how it helps us.
- what snow is and its effects.

Activities:

Instruct the children to color half of the thermometer strip (page 111) red and to color the thermometer itself lightly in a different color. Cut slits on the thermometer as indicated. Insert the strip and let the children move it up and down to change the temperature reading. (It is helpful to fold the ends of the strip to keep it from pulling through.) The completed thermometer can be attached to a sheet with the sentence strip below it.

Provide each child with a copy of page 112. Let the children paint the sun, making vivid rays around it. This is an excellent watercolor activity since the blending of colors will not matter. In fact, blended reds, yellows, oranges, and blues will have a beautiful effect.

Give each child a copy of page 113 to color, adding birds or even a kite in the sky. Then, use glue and stretched cotton balls to make the clouds.

Children will enjoy coloring a picture of their own faces (page 114) with messy hair blowing in the wind. To make the hair, cut appropriate lengths of yarn in the general colors of the children's hair. Let the children glue the hair onto the heads, attaching it in unusual directions as though it is being blown in the wind.

Provide each child with a labeled sheet (page 115), crayons, scissors (if able to cut), a 4" (10 cm) white circle, and a 2" (5 cm) colored circle. Have the children color a blue background in the top triangle and a blue sky with green grass in the bottom triangle. Fold the white circle into halves and fourths and cut it to form a snowflake (or let the child do it). Glue it in the top triangle. Fold the colored circle into fourths and cut around the edges. Glue it in the bottom triangle, letting the child draw a stem and leaves below it to make a flower. Add raindrops above the flower.

Thermometers

Color the thermometer lightly. Color one strip red. Cut and glue together. Cut out the thermometer and the slits on the thermometer. Put the strip through the slits and fold down the ends of the strip. Glue the thermometer and sentence strip to another paper. Move the strip to change the temperature.

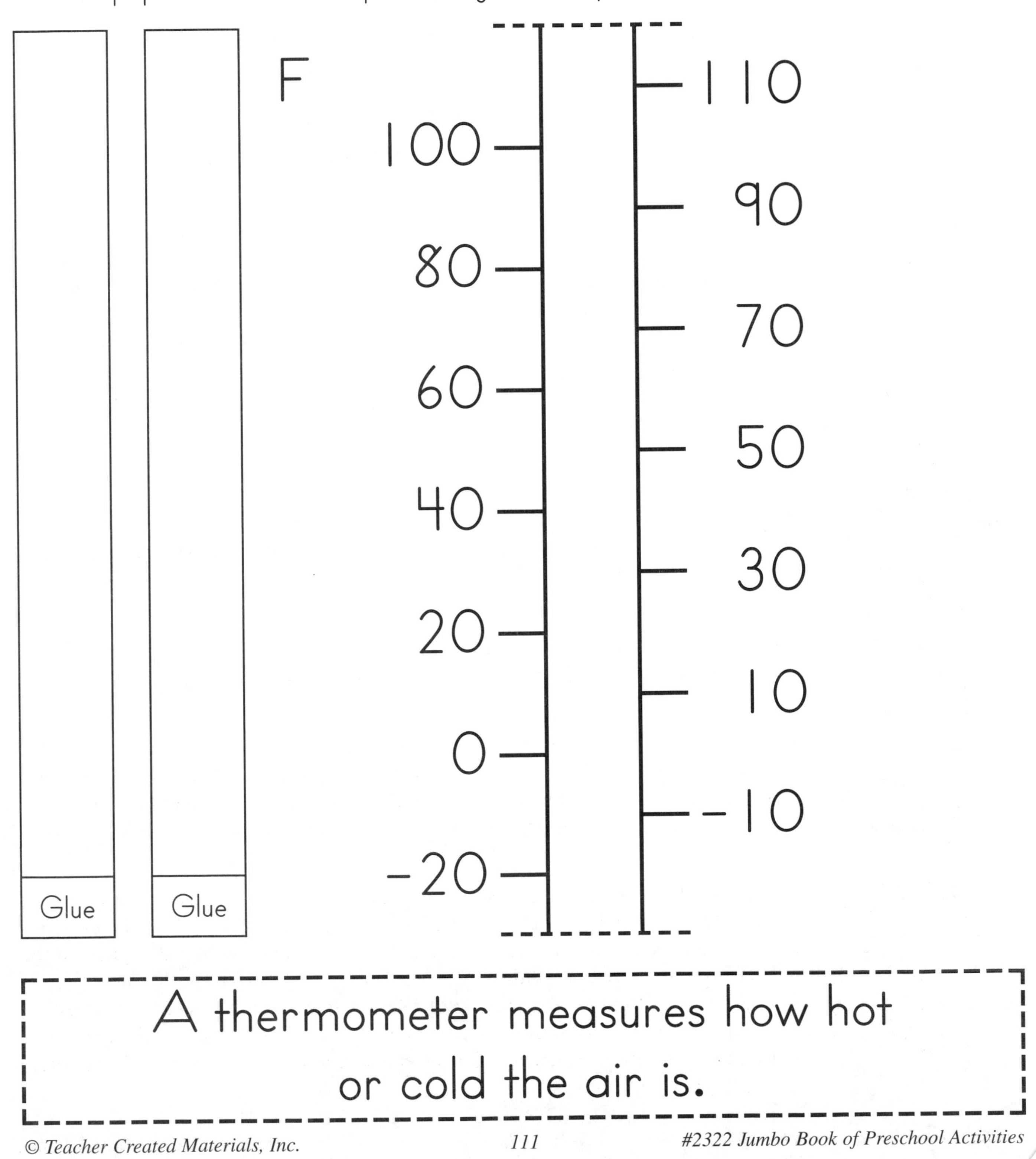

The Sun

Paint the sun. Paint bright rays around the sun, too.

The sun is a superstar.
It gives us heat and light.

Clouds

Draw the sky. Stretch and glue cotton balls over the sky to make the clouds look fluffy.

Clouds are pretty.
Clouds are not soft and fluffy.
Clouds are wet and cold.

Wind

Color a picture of your face. Glue yarn to your head to make hair. Make the hair blow in the wind.

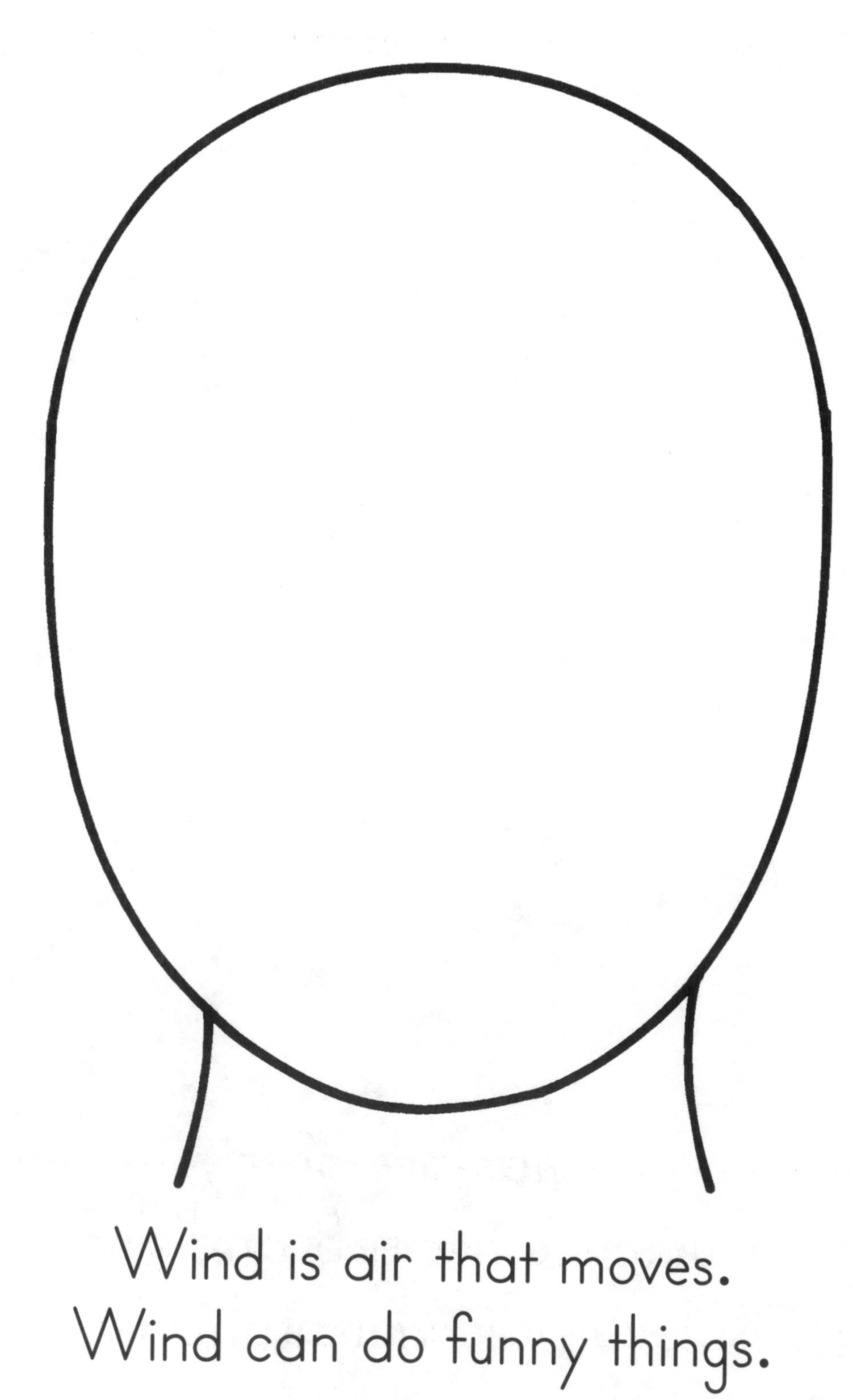

Wind is air that moves.
Wind can do funny things.

Snow and Rain

Color the top triangle blue. Cut a snowflake and glue it in the top triangle. Color the bottom triangle with blue sky and green grass. Cut a flower and glue it in the bottom triangle. Add raindrops above the flower.

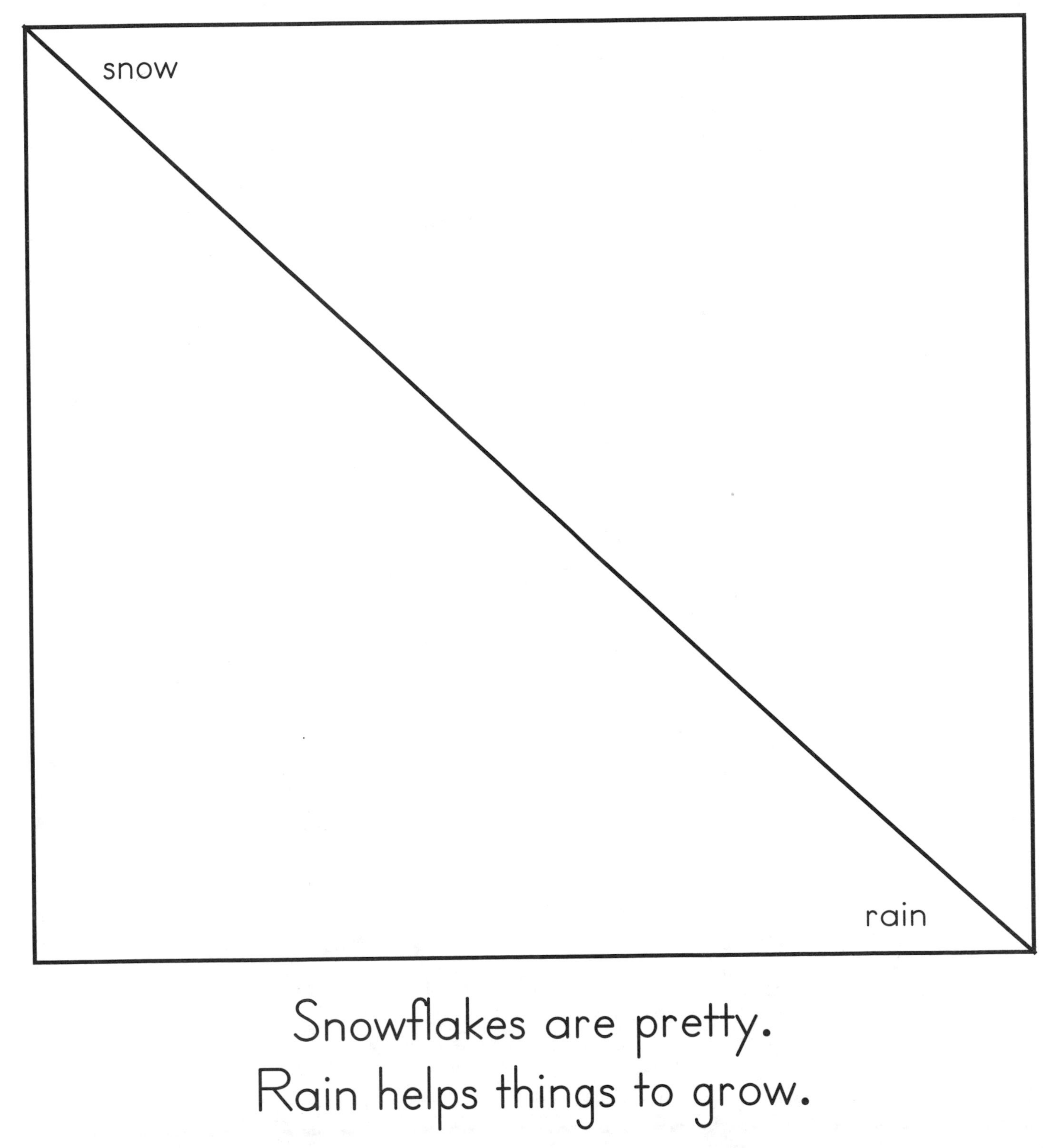

Snowflakes are pretty.
Rain helps things to grow.

Winter

Winter

Objectives:

Each child will learn . . .

- why we have seasons.
- of changes in weather.
- of changes in activities.
- animals that hibernate.

Discussions:

As a group, the class can discuss . . .

- names of seasons.
- reasons for seasons.
- how the weather changes in winter.
- how activities change in winter.
- animals that hibernate.
- what hibernation means.

Activities:

Provide each child with the patterns and sentence strip on page 118. Discuss with the children how the position of the earth changes our seasons. Instruct the children to color the earth and sun patterns. Glue the sun to a sheet of blue paper. Attach the earth to the paper with a paper fastener. Glue the sentence strip below the two. Show the children how to move the earth to change the seasons.

Each child is given the clothing sheet (page 119). After some discussion about dressing for cold weather, the child can add a hat, mittens, scarf, and facial features. Ask the children to draw a "cold" sky around the person, too. It will be interesting to see how they interpret the directions. (Instead of coloring, you might allow the children to paste bits of fabric to make the clothing.)

Discuss hibernation with the children. Distribute page 120. Ask the children to add hibernating animals in the cave and burrow. If desired, cut animals from brown, black, gray, and white felt or fake fur and let the children glue the animals in their dens for a tactile experience.

Provide each child with a copy of page 121. After discussing how animals search for food in the winter, let the children color the mouse, adding a tail, and gluing seeds and nuts to the paper to provide the mouse with some food.

Distribute page 122 to the children. Let them color the squirrel, drawing a nut or seed in the hiding place the squirrel has found. Then, provide the children with felt or fake fur so they can cut (with help, if needed) a bushy tail to glue to the squirrel's back end. If desired, the tail can be colored or painted instead, although the children will enjoy the feel of a fabric tail.

Changing Seasons

Color the earth and sun. Glue the sun to another paper. Attach the earth to the paper with a paper fastener. Glue the sentence strip below the sun and earth. Tip the earth to show the changing seasons.

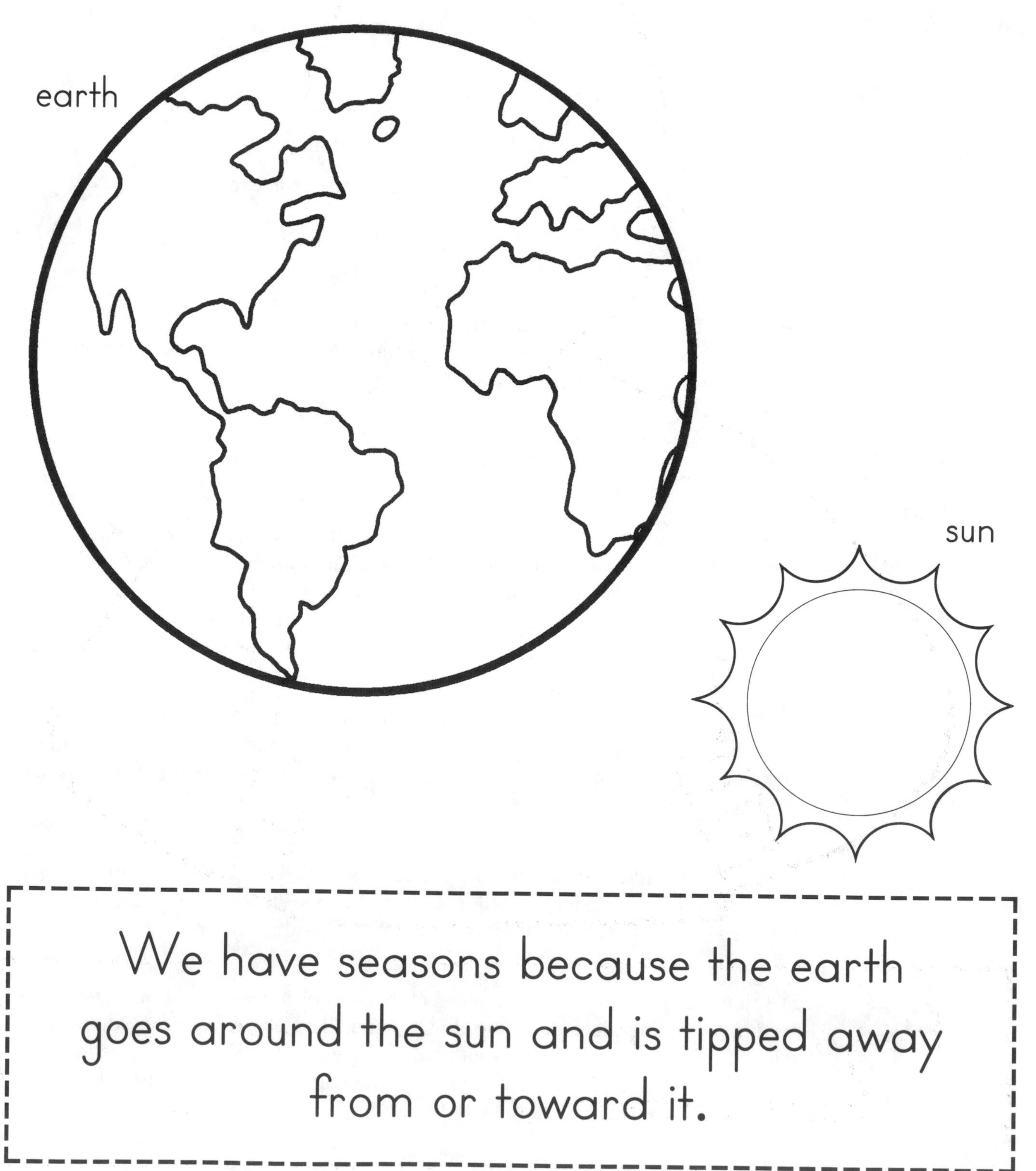

Dressing Warmly

Add a winter hat, scarf, and mittens to the child. Color a face, too!

People wear warm clothes in the winter.
Some animals grow thick fur, too.

Hibernation

Color the picture. Add hibernating animals in the cave and burrow.

Bears and some other animals hibernate in their homes through most of the winter.

Searching for Food

Help the hungry mouse find some food. Color the picture and draw a tail on the mouse. Glue nuts and seeds around him so that he can eat.

Some animals do not hibernate or store food for the winter. They search for food in cold weather.

Hiding Food

Color the picture. In the hole, draw a nut for the squirrel to hide. Give the squirrel a big, furry tail, too.

Squirrels and some other animals gather and store food for when the weather turns cold.

Teeth

Teeth

Objectives:

Each child will learn . . .

- why teeth are important.
- about the different kinds of teeth.
- about good care of teeth.
- about a dentist's job.

Discussions:

As a group, the class can discuss . . .

- why teeth are important.
- kinds of teeth (which teeth do what jobs).
- care of teeth.
- food that helps to keep teeth healthy.
- how dentists help us.
- the kind of training dentists have.

Activities:

Each child is given a puppet person (page 125) to cut out, scissors, and crayons. Help the child to draw a face, hair, etc., onto the person and to cut it out. Fold back the side tabs and tape or staple them. The puppet can stand on its own, or the child can hold it with his/her fingers inserted through the back. As an extension, have the children make their puppets tell about good oral hygiene.

Explain to the children what the different kinds of teeth do. Then distribute page 126 which will illustrate the jobs. Let the children color the page. As an extension, allow the children to do each of the things shown while naming the different kinds of teeth.

Discuss "Healthy Teeth" (page 127) and let the children color the page.

Each child is given a copy of page 128, torn red and yellow paper, and paste. The child can paste the small pieces of torn paper within the fruit outlines.

Distribute page 129 to each child. Let them color more candy in the jar, or collect a variety of candy wrappers ahead of time and let the children paste the wrappers in the jar.

Healthy Teeth Puppet

Color and cut out the puppet. Fold back the tabs and tape or staple them. Let the puppet stand or put your fingers through the opening to make the puppet move.

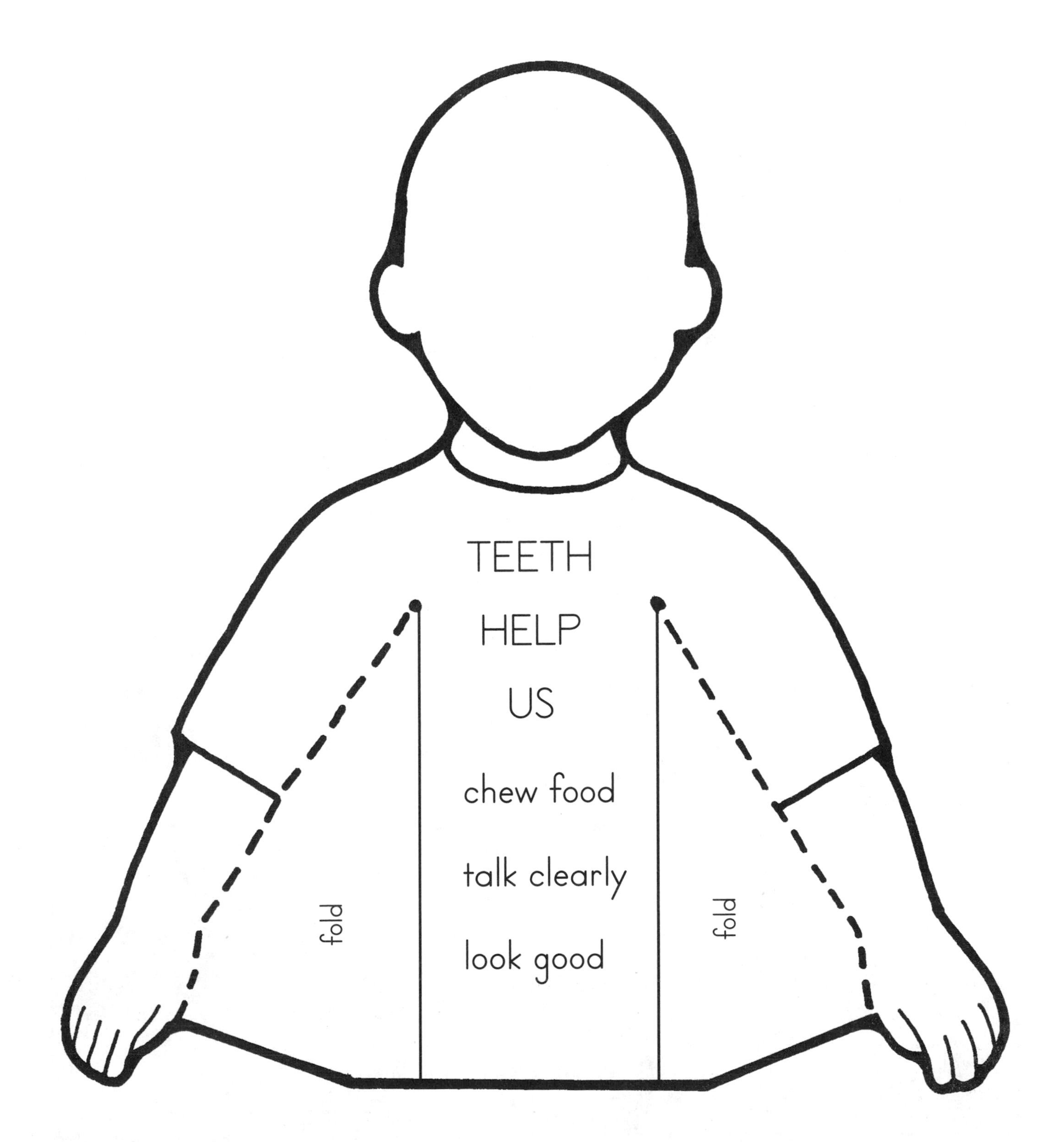

Kinds of Teeth

Color the pictures. Learn what teeth do.

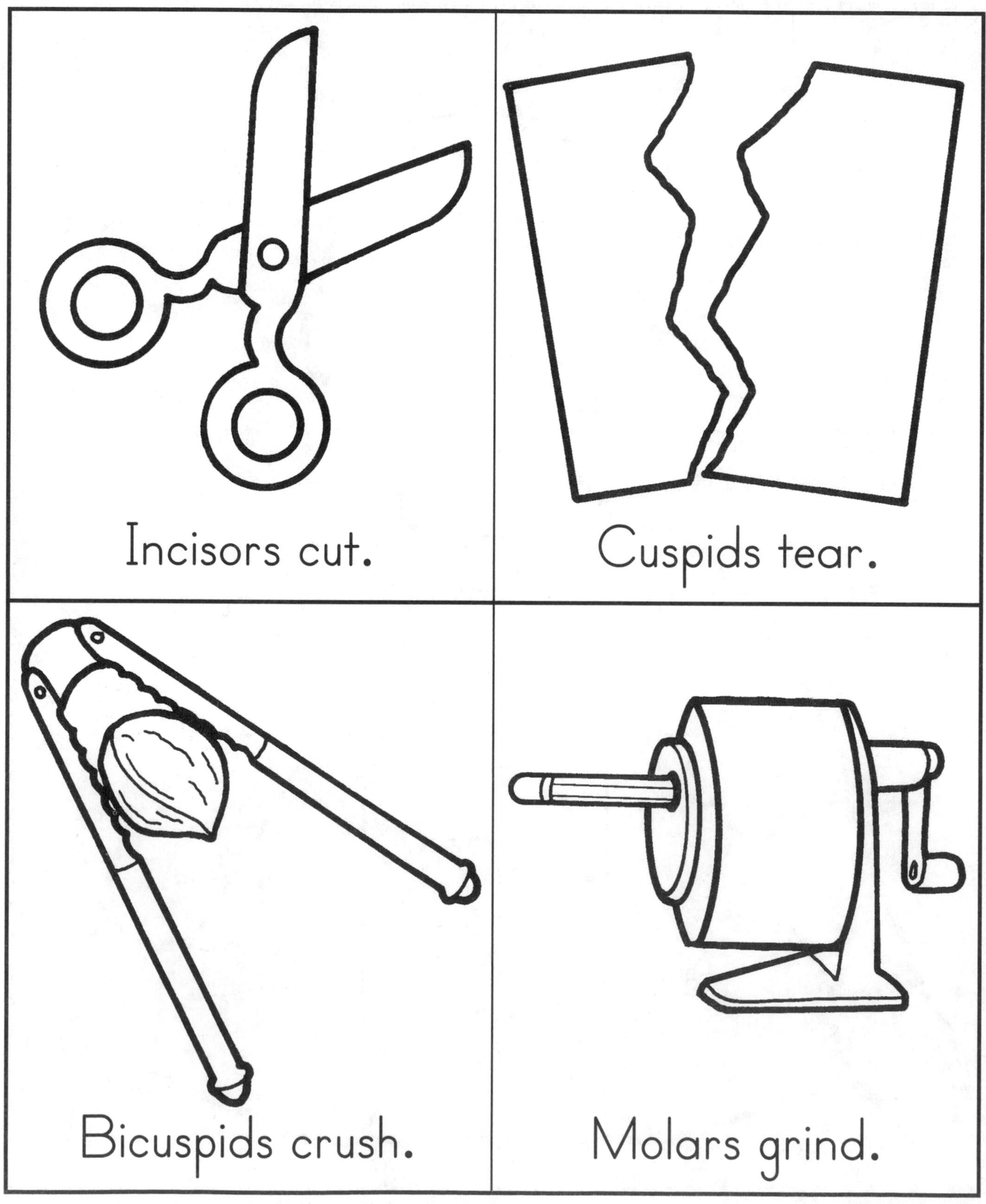

Healthy Teeth

Color the pictures. Learn how to take care of your teeth.

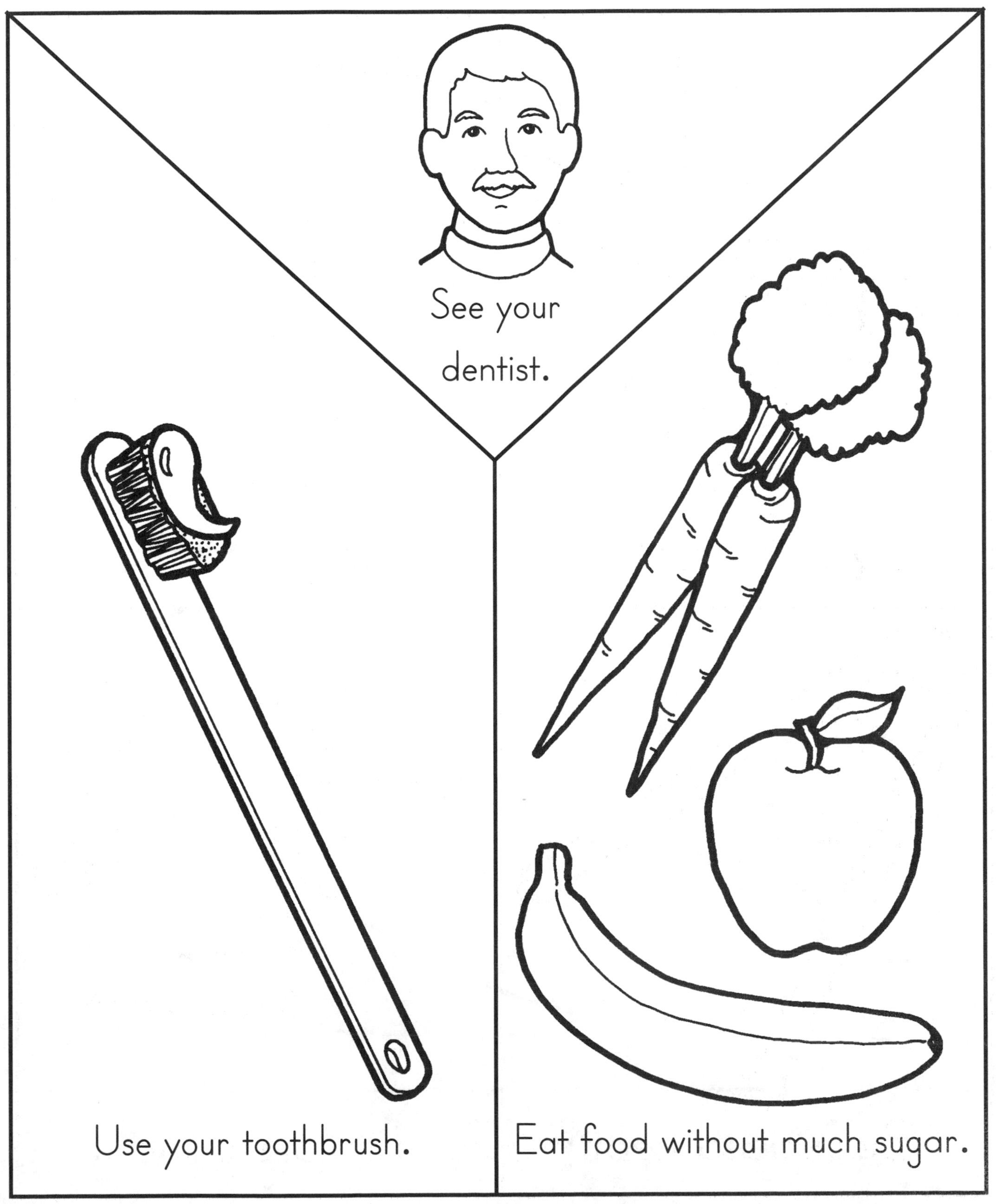

Healthy Eating

Tear red and yellow paper. Glue the pieces in the apple and banana to color them.

Teeth need healthful food to stay strong.

Sugar Alert!

Paste candy wrappers inside the candy jar. Be careful not to eat too many sweets!

Eat only a little sugar.

Post Office

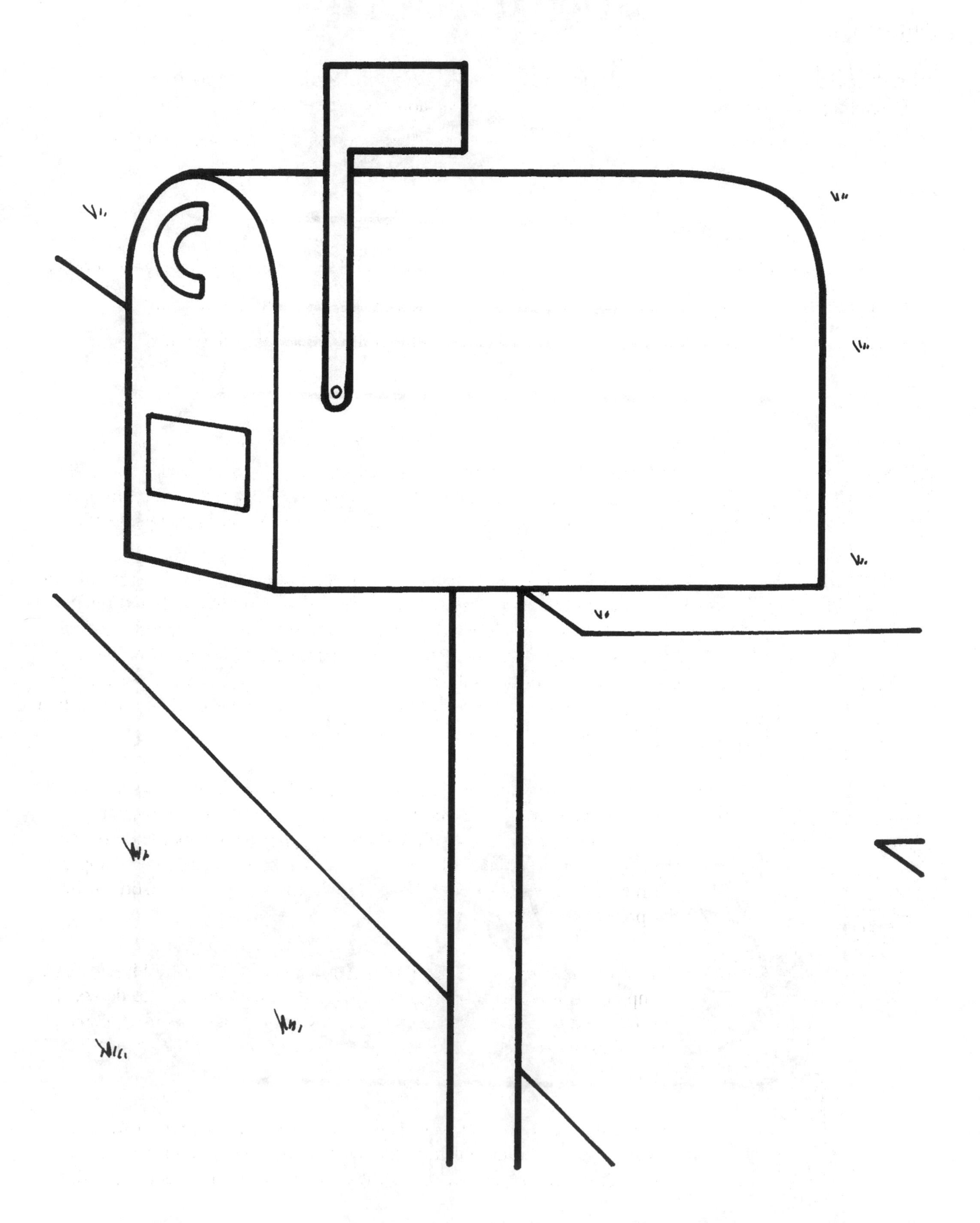

Post Office

Objectives:

Each child will learn . . .

- what a post office is.
- why the post office is helpful.
- about workers in the post office.
- about addressing letters and packages.

Discussions:

As a group, the class can discuss . . .

- what a post office is.
- where post offices are located.
- why post offices are helpful.
- the work done at and away from the post office.
- addressing letters and packages.
- things to be sent through the mail.

Activities:

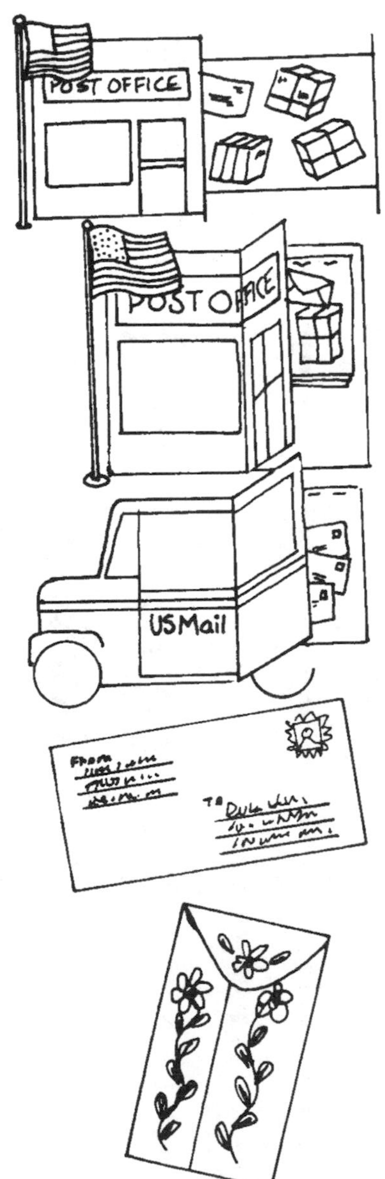

Provide each child with page 132 and the mail strip on page 304. Let the children color the pictures, adding additional packages and letters to the mail strip. Cut the indicated slits on page 132. Insert the strip through the slits. Move the strip so the mail goes into and out of the post office.

Supply the children with page 133 and the corresponding pictures on page 304. Instruct the children to color both pages. Cut on the dotted lines of the building and fold open the right section (the door). Glue the rest of the page (keeping the door free) to another sheet of paper. Then have the children color the four job squares. Cut apart the jobs and staple them at the top into a little book. Paste the book under the post office door so that when the door is opened, the jobs can be read.

Give the mail truck sheet (page 134) to the children as well as the mail jobs from page 304. Instruct the children to color the truck and job pictures. Cut on the truck's dotted lines and paste the paper (except for the flap) to another sheet of paper. Cut apart the job squares and staple them together. Paste the squares under the truck's flap (as described in the previous activity).

Give each child a copy of page 135. Show them where the addresses and stamp go. Allow them to write the addresses if they are able to do so. If not, let them write whatever squiggles they choose in the correct areas. The children can also color a stamp or place a sticker in the appropriate place.

Provide the children with page 136. Cut and fold the pattern inward as shown. Let the children design and color a greeting card on the inside and an envelope on the outside. A sticker can be used to secure the flap.

At the Post Office

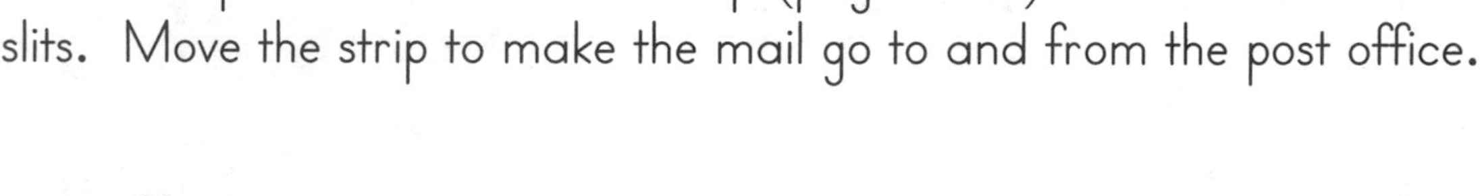

Color the picture and the mail strip (page 304). Cut the slits. Place the strip through the slits. Move the strip to make the mail go to and from the post office.

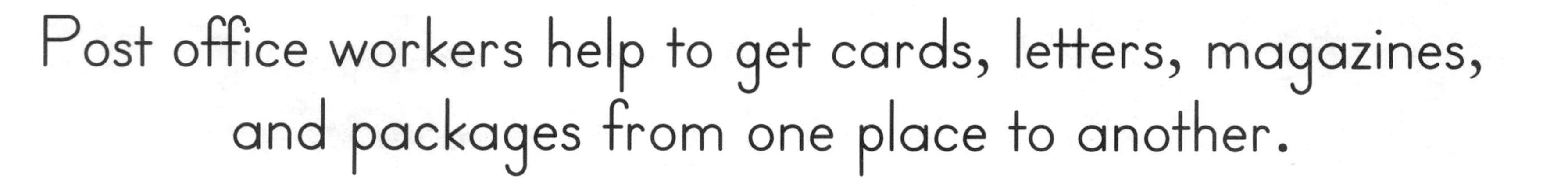

Post office workers help to get cards, letters, magazines, and packages from one place to another.

Post Office Jobs

Color the picture and the post office jobs (page 304). Cut the dotted lines of the post office. Glue this page to another sheet, keeping the cut flap free. Cut apart the jobs and staple them into a booklet. Paste the booklet behind the post office flap.

Workers at the post office have many jobs to do.

Mail Truck

Color the picture and the mail truck jobs (page 304). Cut the dotted lines of the truck. Glue this page to another sheet, keeping the cut flap free. Cut apart the jobs and staple them into a booklet. Paste the booklet behind the mail truck flap.

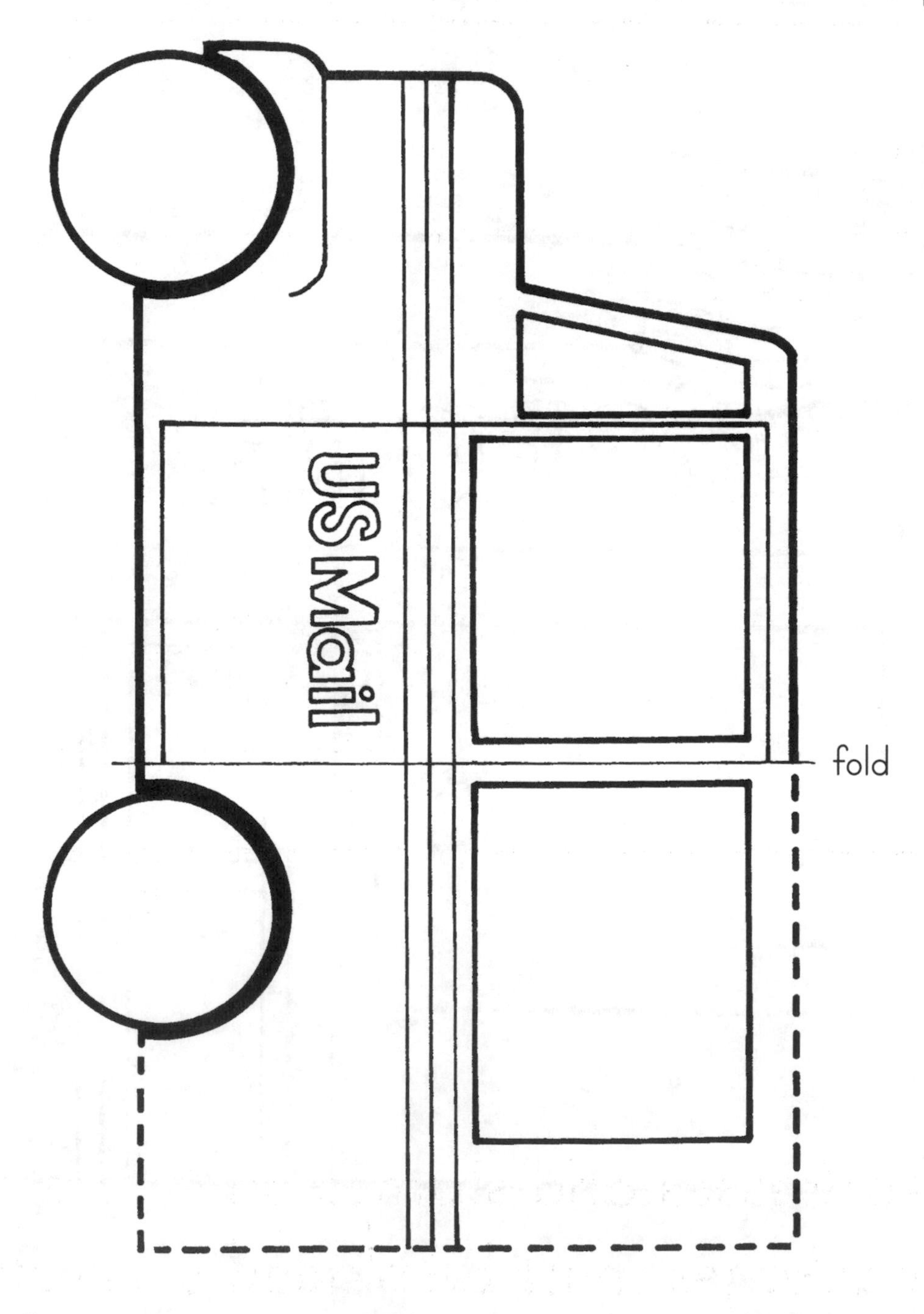

Some post office workers take the mail in trucks to deliver it.

Letters

Write an address and return address on the envelope. Color a stamp, too.

From

____

____

____

To

____

____

____

Addresses and stamps on letters and packages must be placed correctly.

Sending Special Messages

Cut along the bold lines. Fold inward at the fold lines. Color a special greeting inside the folds. Decorate an envelope on the outside of the fold.

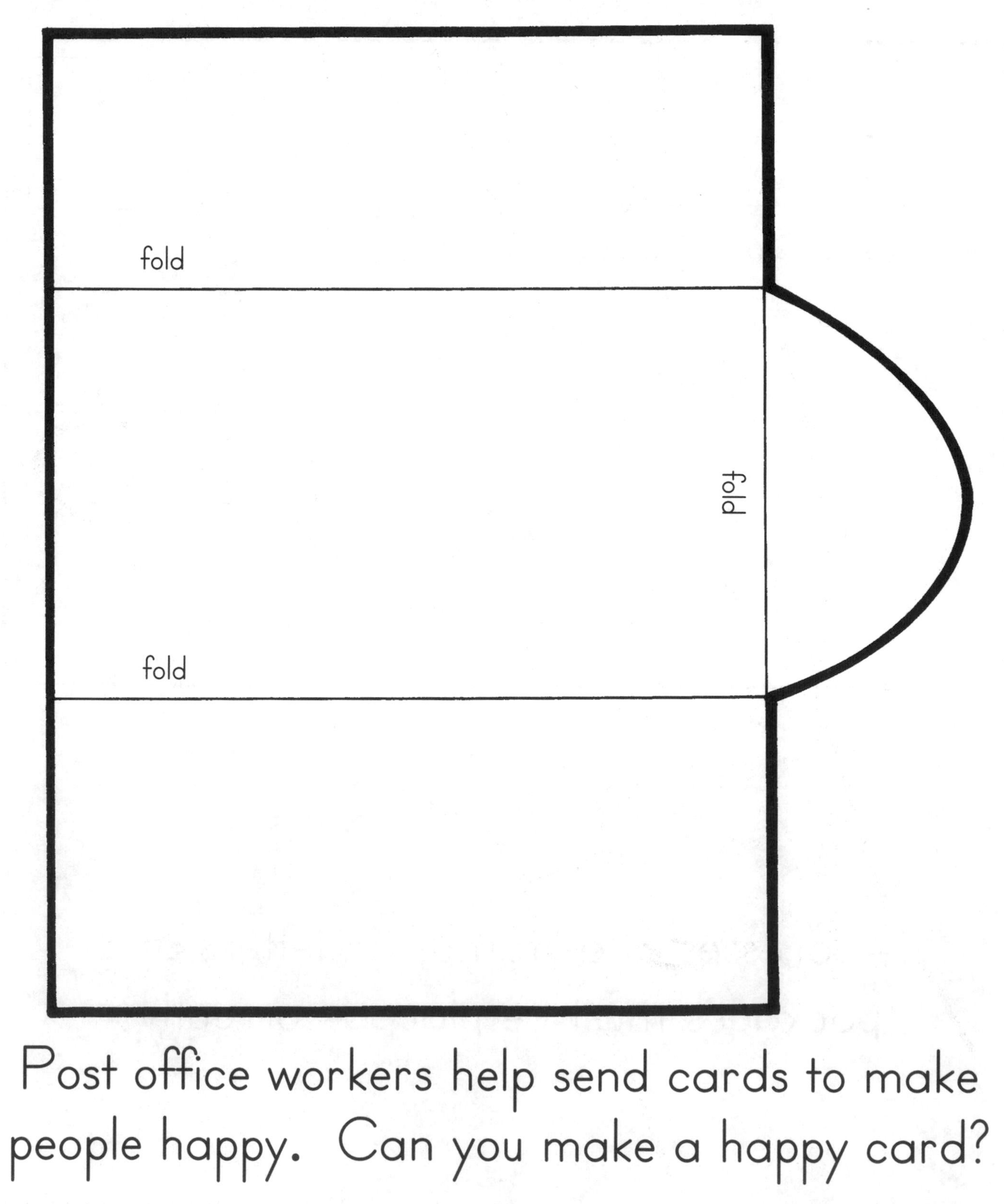

Post office workers help send cards to make people happy. Can you make a happy card?

Time

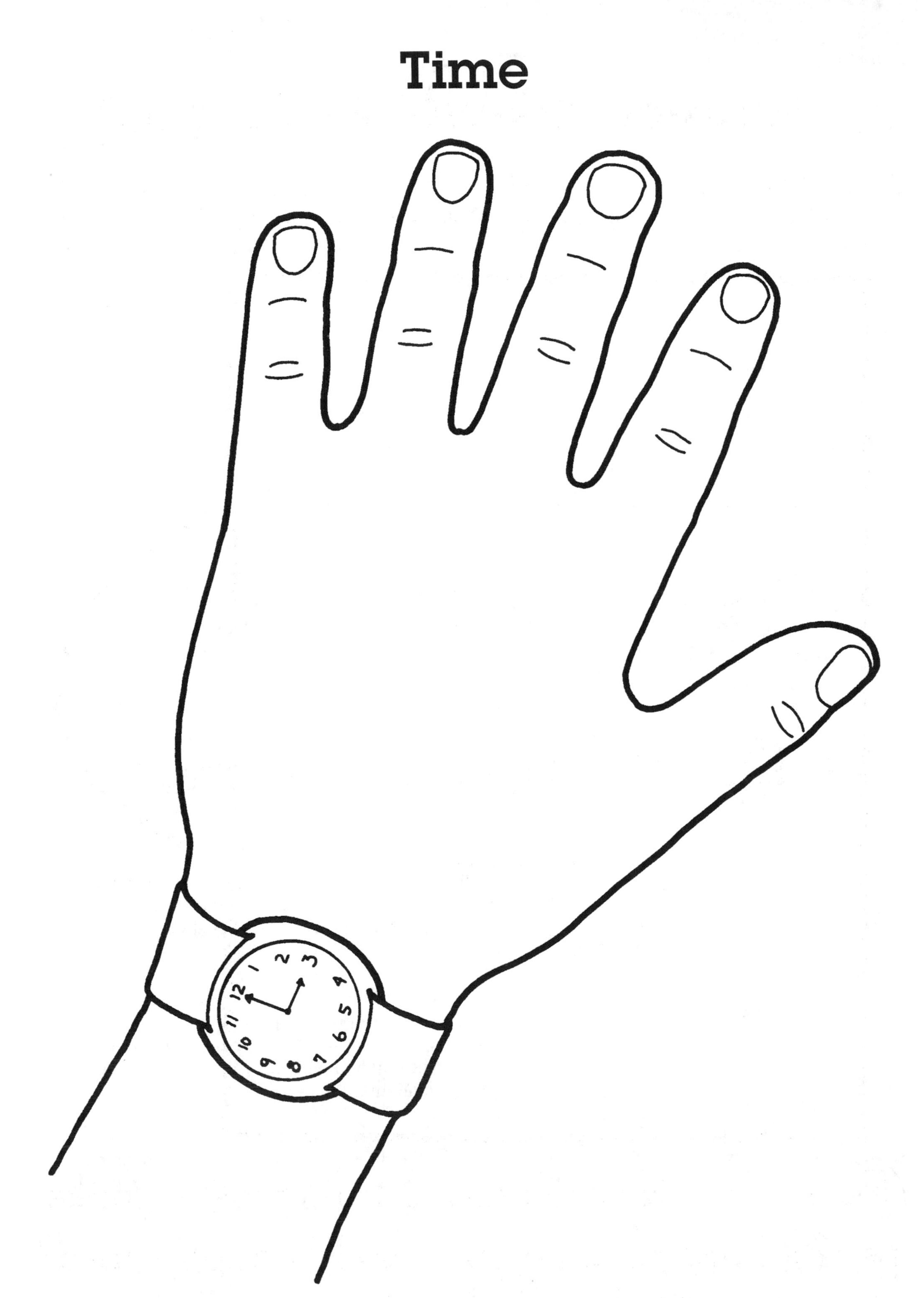

Time

Objectives:

Each child will learn . . .

- time words.
- reasons for learning to tell time.
- how to make clock faces.
- how to tell time "on the hour."
- about different types of clocks.
- about "half past."

Discussions:

As a group, the class can discuss . . .

- time words.
- why we need to know about time.
- how a clock face looks.
- "on the hour" (o'clock) times.
- "half past" times.
- kinds of clocks.

Activities:

Give each child the "Day and Night" sheet (page 139) and crayons. After discussing the differences between daytime and nighttime, ask the children to draw the same scene in each space, showing only the differences of day and night.

Provide each child with page 140 and a crayon. Help the child to write numerals (or the child's version of them) around the circle to form a clock face (12 at the top, 6 at the bottom, etc.). The lines will help with placement of the numbers. The child can add hands to the clock as well.

Provide each child with page 141 and a paper plate. Help the child to cut out the circle, numbers, and hands. Glue the circle onto the plate. Help the child to glue the numbers in sequence around the clock face on the dots. Attach the hands in the center, using a paper fastener.

Let the children color page 142. Cut out the pendulum. Attach the pendulum to the grandfather clock at the O. Move the pendulum back and forth "to keep time." The children will enjoy making the "tick-tock" sound as they swing the pendulum in rhythm.

Let the children color and cut out the alarm clock pieces. Glue them together onto a separate sheet of paper. Glue the sentence strip beneath the clock. Bring an alarm clock into the classroom so the children can hear how it sounds.

Day and Night

Color a daytime scene in the day section. Color the same scene at night in the other section.

day	night

Sunlight is the biggest difference between day and night.

Clock

Write the numbers on the clock. Also draw the clock hands.

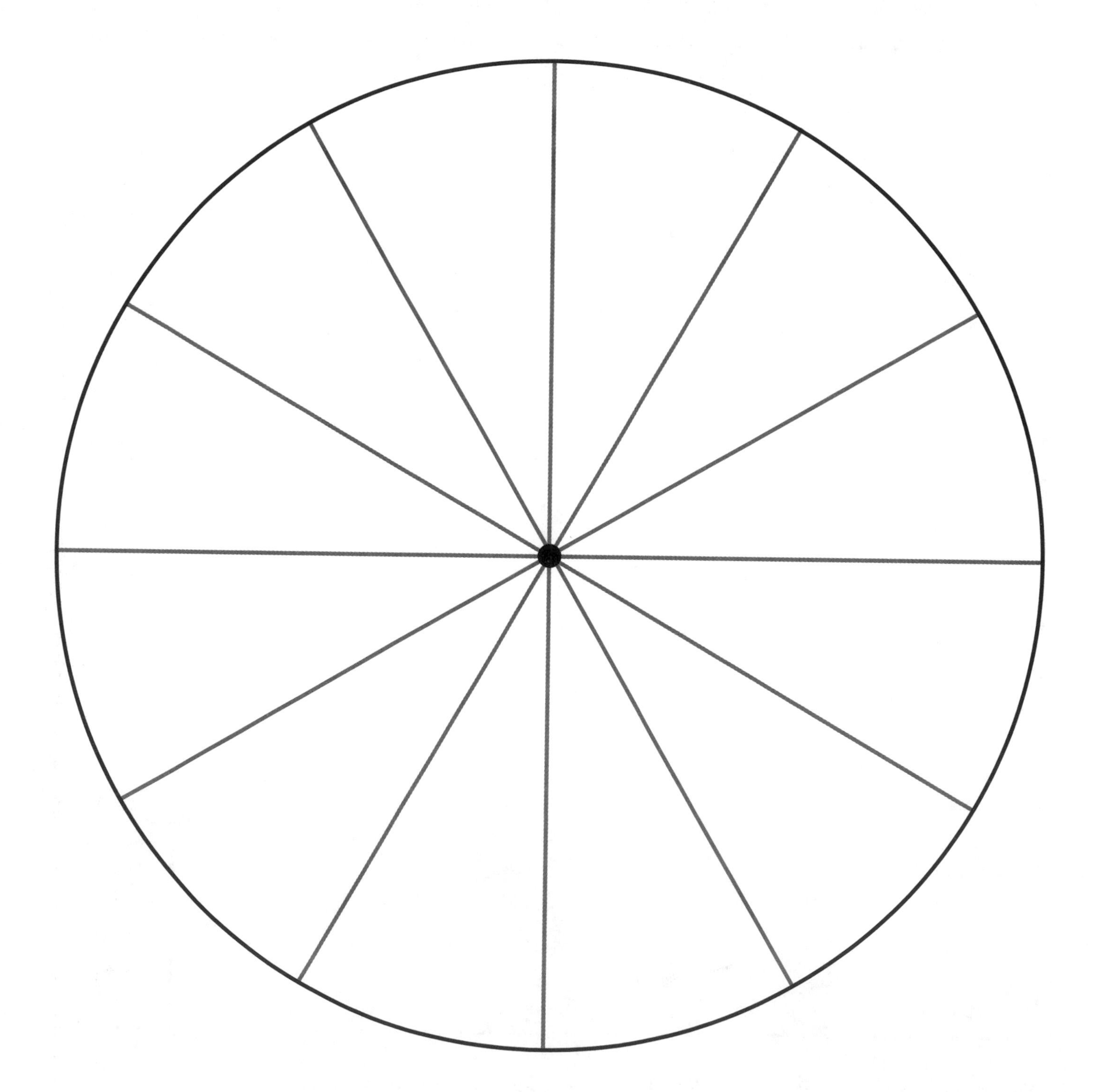

What time is it?

Clockmaker

You can be a clockmaker! Cut out the circle, numbers, and hands. Glue the circle to a paper plate. Glue the numbers onto the dots. (Be sure to keep them in order with 12 at the top and 6 at the bottom!) Attach the hands at the X with a paper fastener. Set the clock to your favorite time of day.

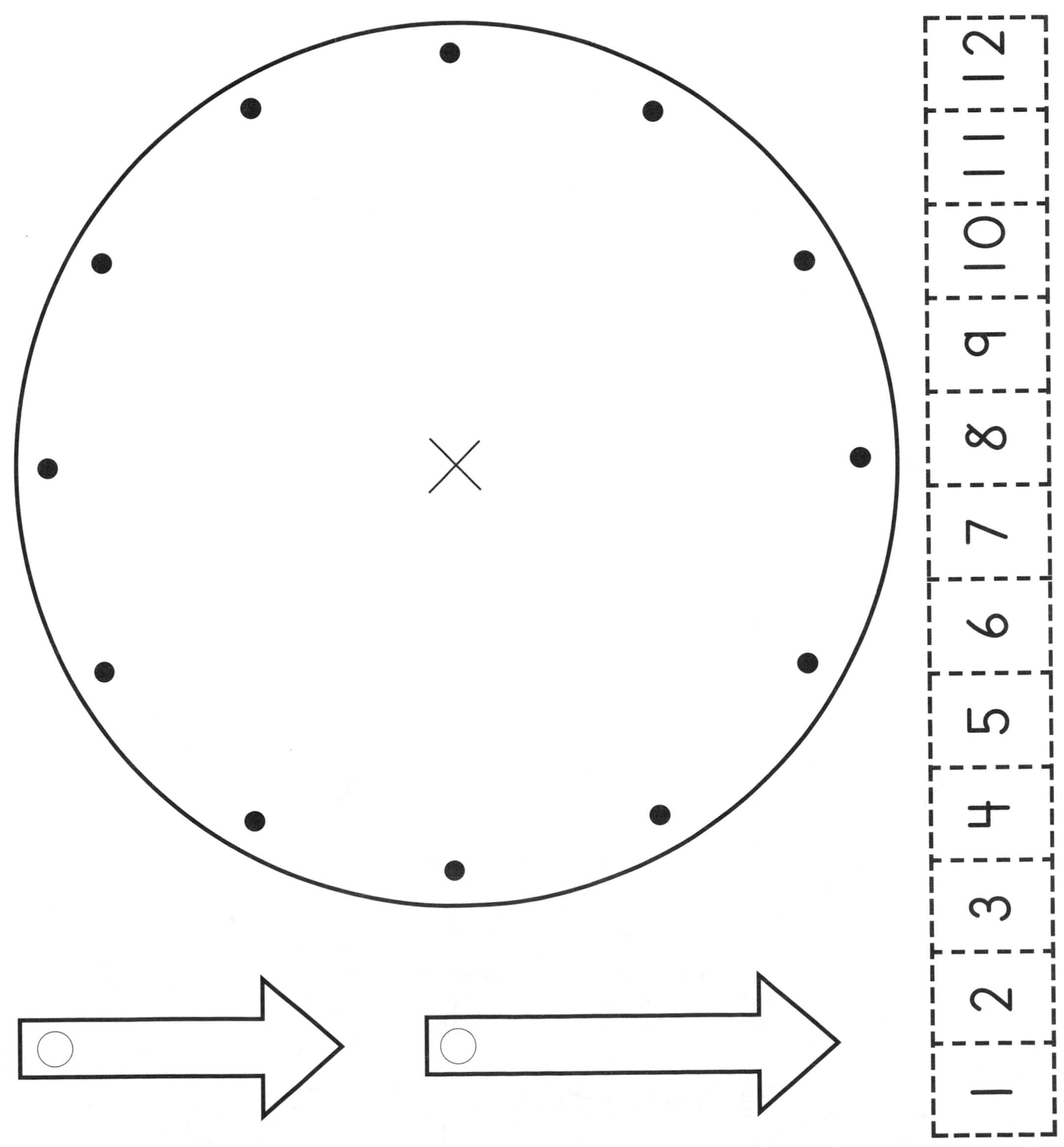

Grandfather Clock

Color the clock and pendulum. Cut out the pendulum. Attach it to the clock with a paper fastener at the O. Move the pendulum back and forth to keep time.

What sound does the grandfather clock make?

Alarm Clock

Color and cut out the pieces to the alarm clock. Glue them together onto another sheet of paper. Glue the sentence strip below the clock.

An alarm clock tells us when to get out of bed.

Good Manners

Good Manners

Objectives:

Each child will learn . . .

- the reasons for using good manners.
- about good manners at all times and places.

Discussions:

As a group, the class can discuss . . .

- why good manners are important.
- what good manners tell about us.
- manners at home, school, the table, and away from parents.

Activities:

Discuss with the children how using good manners is a way of following directions. Then instruct them to color page 146 according to the directions. (Help them as needed.)

Let the children color page 147. Afterwards, instruct the children to cut a food picture from an old magazine and glue it onto the plate. A piece of paper napkin or paper towel can be glued to the left of the plate as well.

Direct the children to add numerals to the phone (page 148) and to color both the earpiece and the handset. (If the children are unable to write numerals, write the numbers for them.) Glue twine, ribbon, or yarn between the two pieces of the phone to make a cord.

Instruct the children to color both pictures on page 149. Help them to cut out the top flap. Cut the slit where indicated. Insert the flap through the slit, laying the flap picture onto the other picture. Move the flap to the right to show how the children take turns.

Tell the children to color the faces, hair, and hands of the two children sharing the book (page 150). Let the children dictate a title for the book which the teacher or classroom aide can write.

Following Directions

Follow the directions to color this page.

2	1	2	1	2	1	2	1
G	O	O	D	1	2	1	2
2	M	A	N	N	E	R	S
1	2	A	R	E	2		2
2	1	2	N	I	C	E	1
1	2	1	W	A	Y	S	2
2	1	O	F	2		2	
1	D	O	I	N	G	1	2
T	H	I	N	G	S.	2	1
1	2	1	2	1	2	1	2

Color 1 red.
Color 2 blue.
Color the letter boxes yellow.

Table Manners

Color the picture. Cut a picture of food from an old magazine and glue it onto the plate. Fold a paper napkin and glue it to the left of the plate.

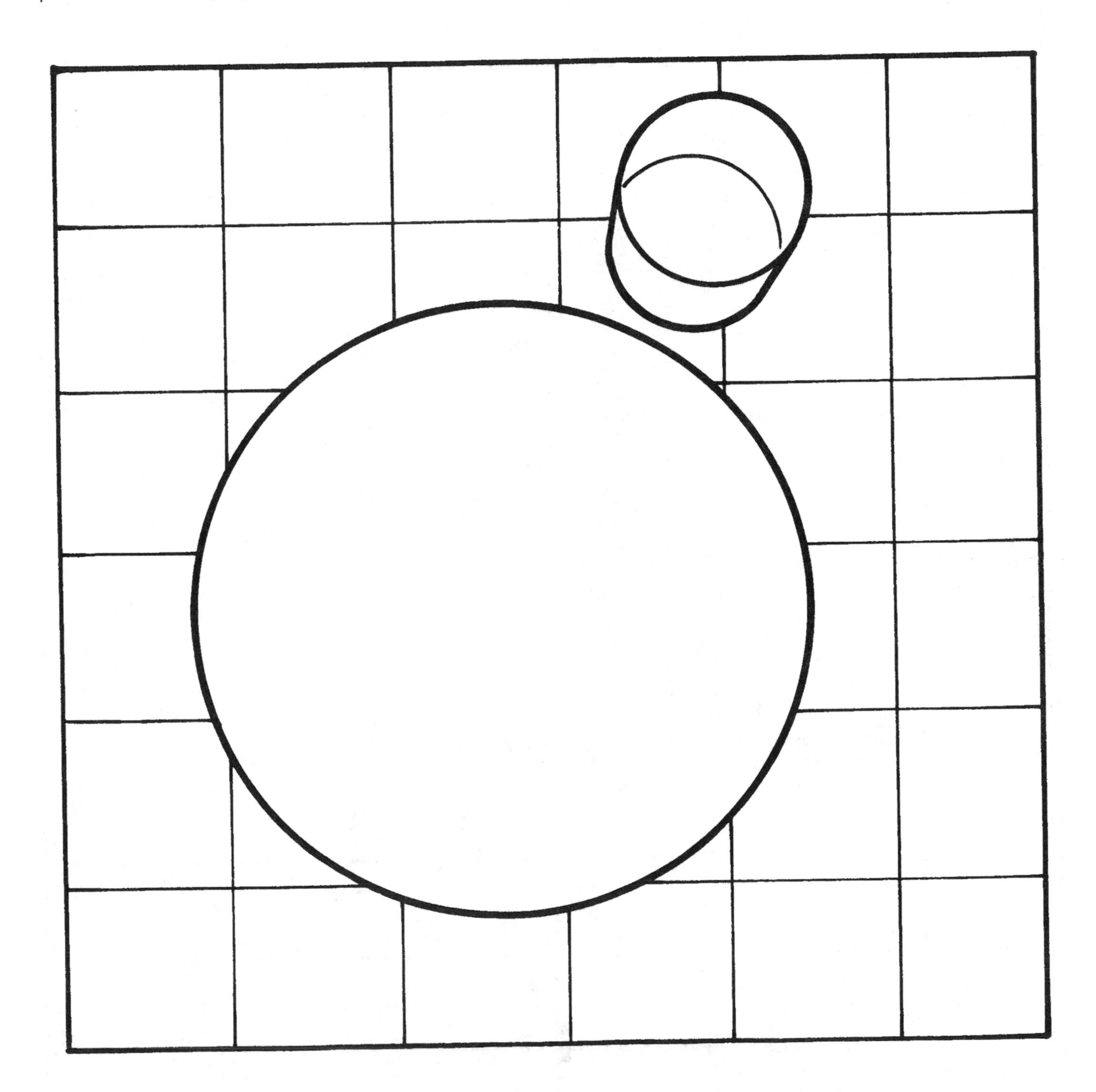

Try to eat neatly.

Telephone Manners

Color the phone. Fill in the numbers on the phone in order. Glue a string between the two phone sections to make a cord.

Talk clearly on the telephone and be polite.

Taking Turns

Color both pictures. Cut out the boy. Cut the slit at the bottom. Insert the flap through the slit and lay the flap picture over the other picture. Move the flap to the right to show the boy taking his turn.

It is good manners to wait patiently for your turn.

Sharing

Draw faces and hair on the children. Show them enjoying the book together.

Using good manners means we can share.

Measurement

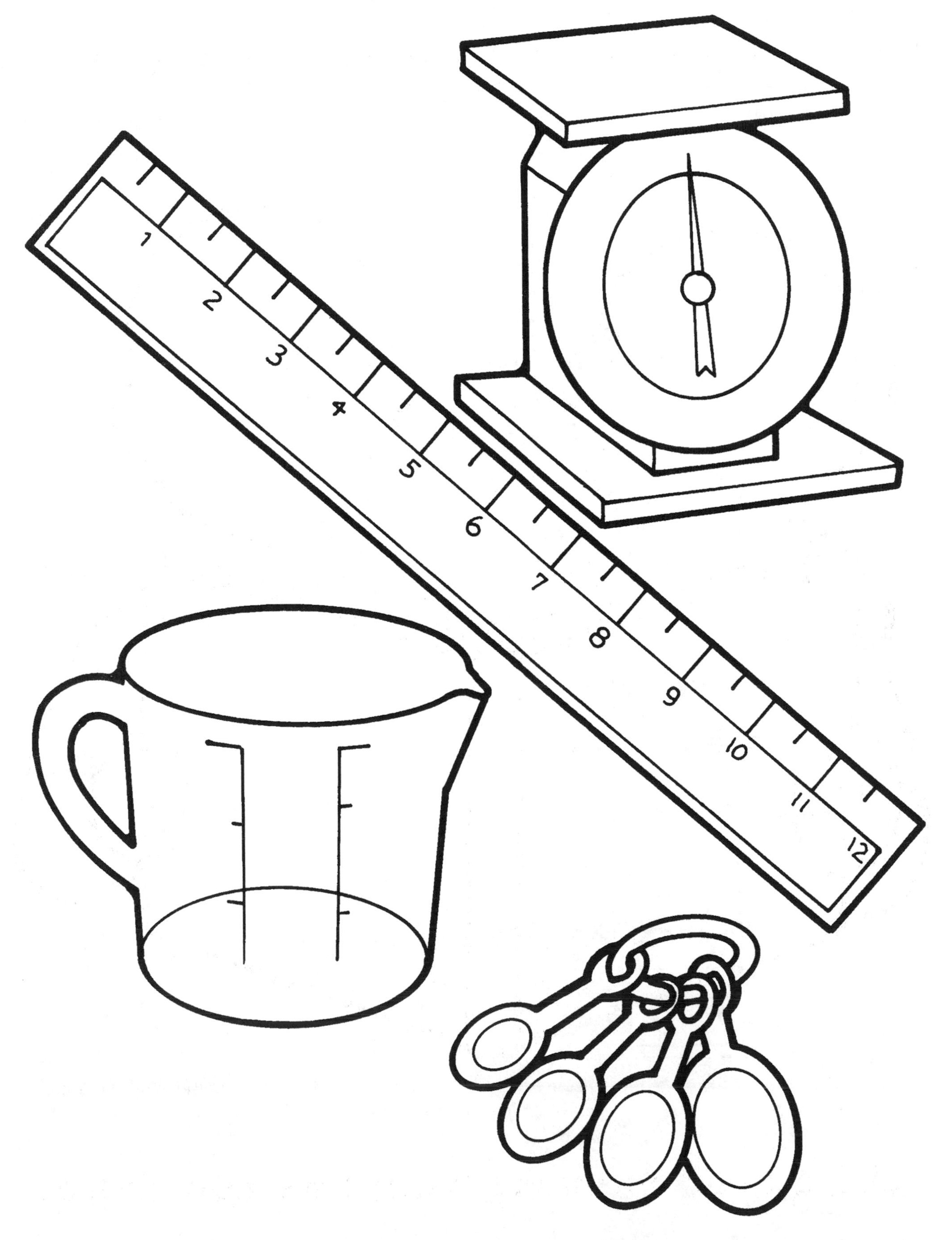

Measurement

Objectives:

Each child will learn about. . .

- kinds of measurement.
- measuring liquids.
- measuring solids.

- measurement words.
- weighing and measuring people and things.
- rulers in both inches and centimeters.
- one half.

Discussions:

As a group, the class can discuss . . .

- how things are measured.
- why there is a need for measuring.
- measurement words.
- using a ruler.
- weighing and measuring children and what this tells us.
- measuring liquids.
- measurements in recipes.

Activities:

Give each child the body outline (page 153) and crayons. Let the children color the person. Then help them to fold the paper under at the lines, thereby shortening the figure. Staple the picture at the top to another page. Fold the paper up and down to show the person growing and shortening.

Provide each child with pages 154 and 155. Cut out the ruler on page 154. Let the children use the ruler to measure the items on pages 154 and 155. Help them to write the numbers in the blanks. Then measure other things in the classroom.

Read the directions on page 156 to the children. Instruct them to draw an item that fits the description in each square. Help them to write the words in the blanks.

Discuss halves. Then help the children to cut around the dotted halves of the shapes on page 157. Fold the halves over and trace around them. Open the halves. Instruct the children to color half of each shape.

Growing Up

Color the person. Cut out the box and sentence strip. Fold the person on the lines so the body is shortened. Staple the person at the top to another paper. Glue the sentence strip below it.

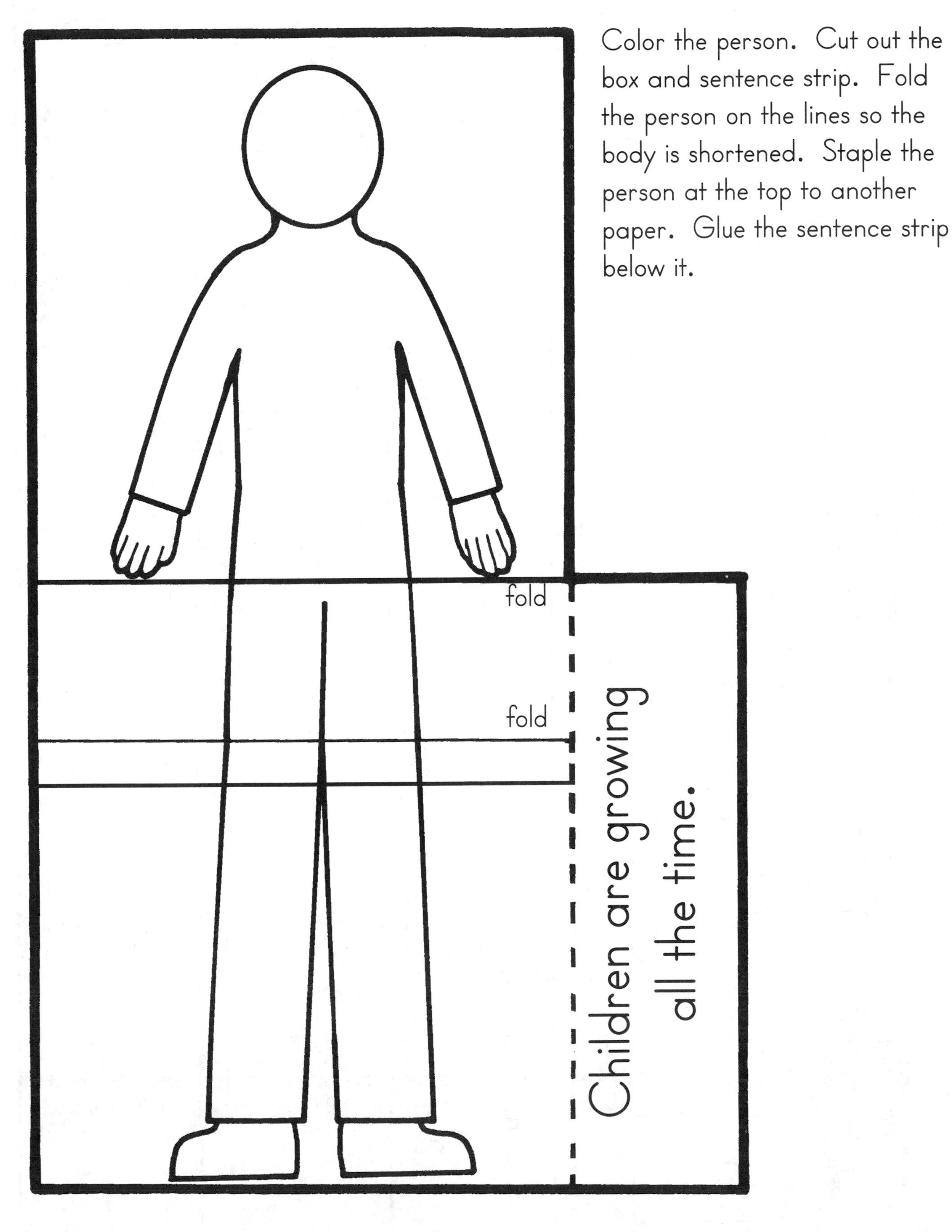

Using a Ruler

Color the ruler and cut it out. Color the other pictures, too. Use your ruler to measure the items on this page and the next one. Trace the correct numbers in the blanks.

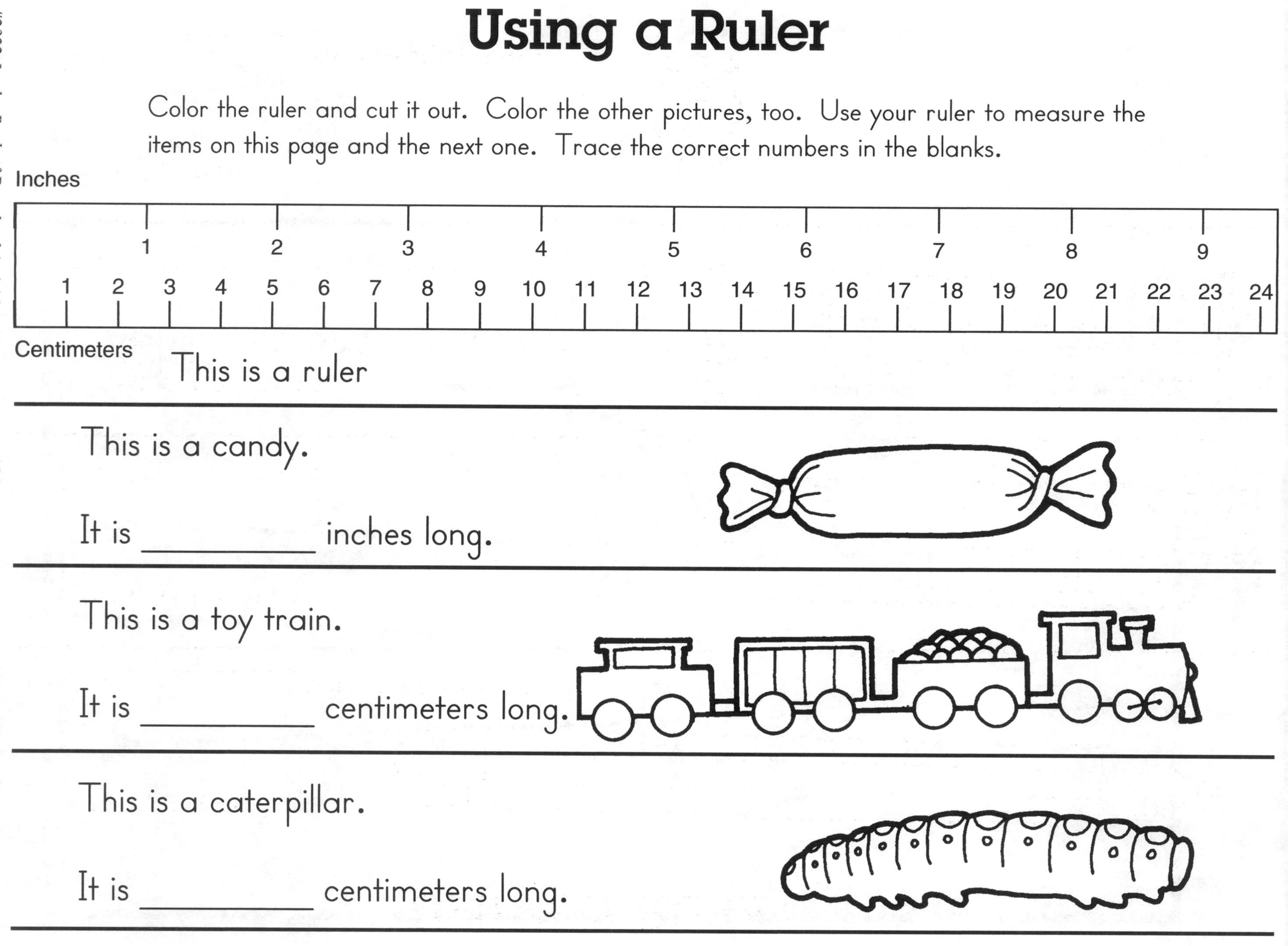

This is a ruler

This is a candy.

It is __________ inches long.

This is a toy train.

It is __________ centimeters long.

This is a caterpillar.

It is __________ centimeters long.

Using a Ruler *(cont.)*

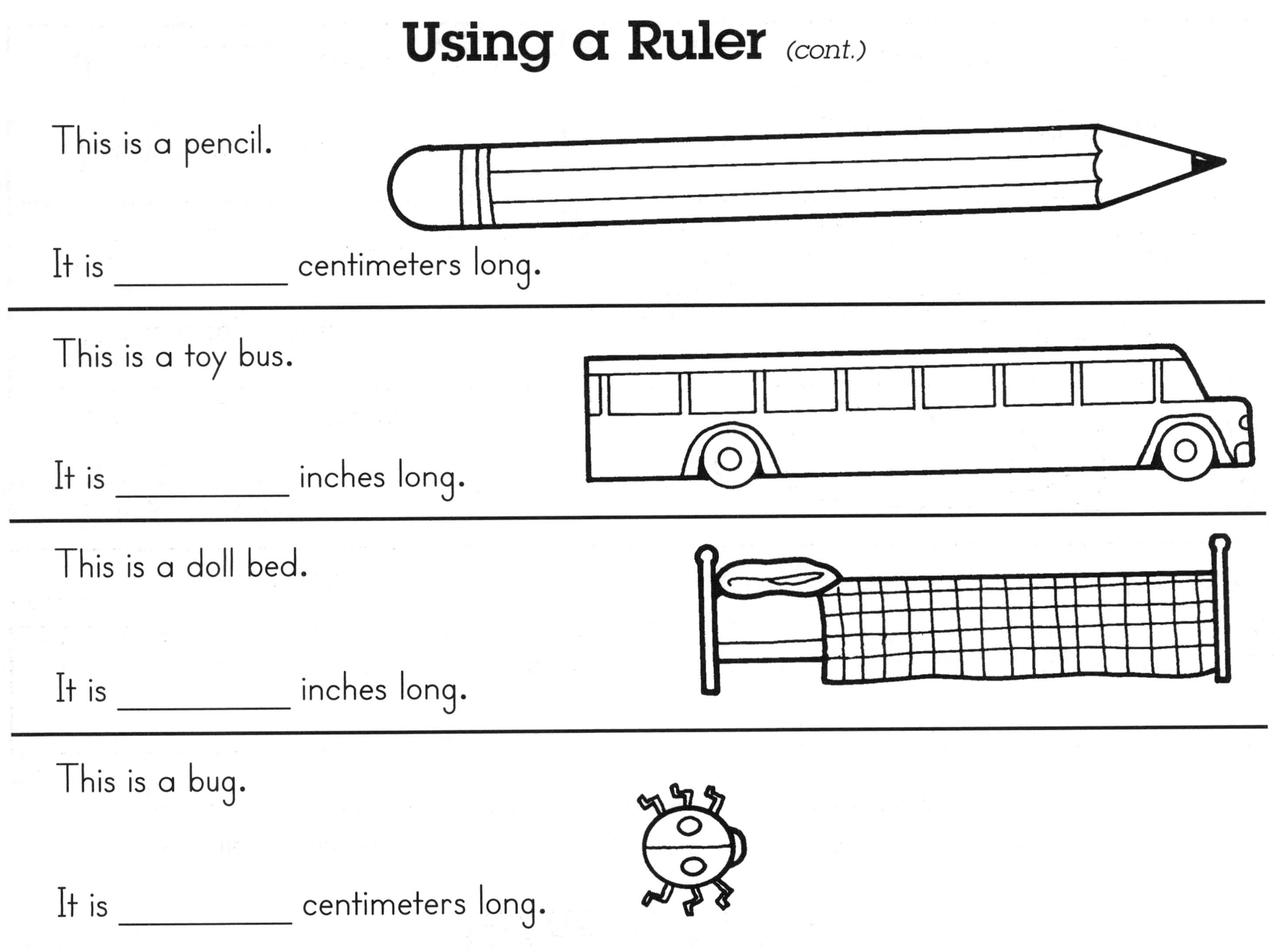

This is a pencil.

It is __________ centimeters long.

This is a toy bus.

It is __________ inches long.

This is a doll bed.

It is __________ inches long.

This is a bug.

It is __________ centimeters long.

Sizes

Read the words. Draw pictures to match the words. Fill in the blanks.

This is heavy. It is ____________________.	This is light. It is ____________________.
This is little. It is ____________________.	This is big. It is ____________________.

Halves

Cut out the shapes along the dotted lines. Fold over each shape at the solid lines. Trace around the halves to make the other half of each. Open the folds. Color half of each shape.

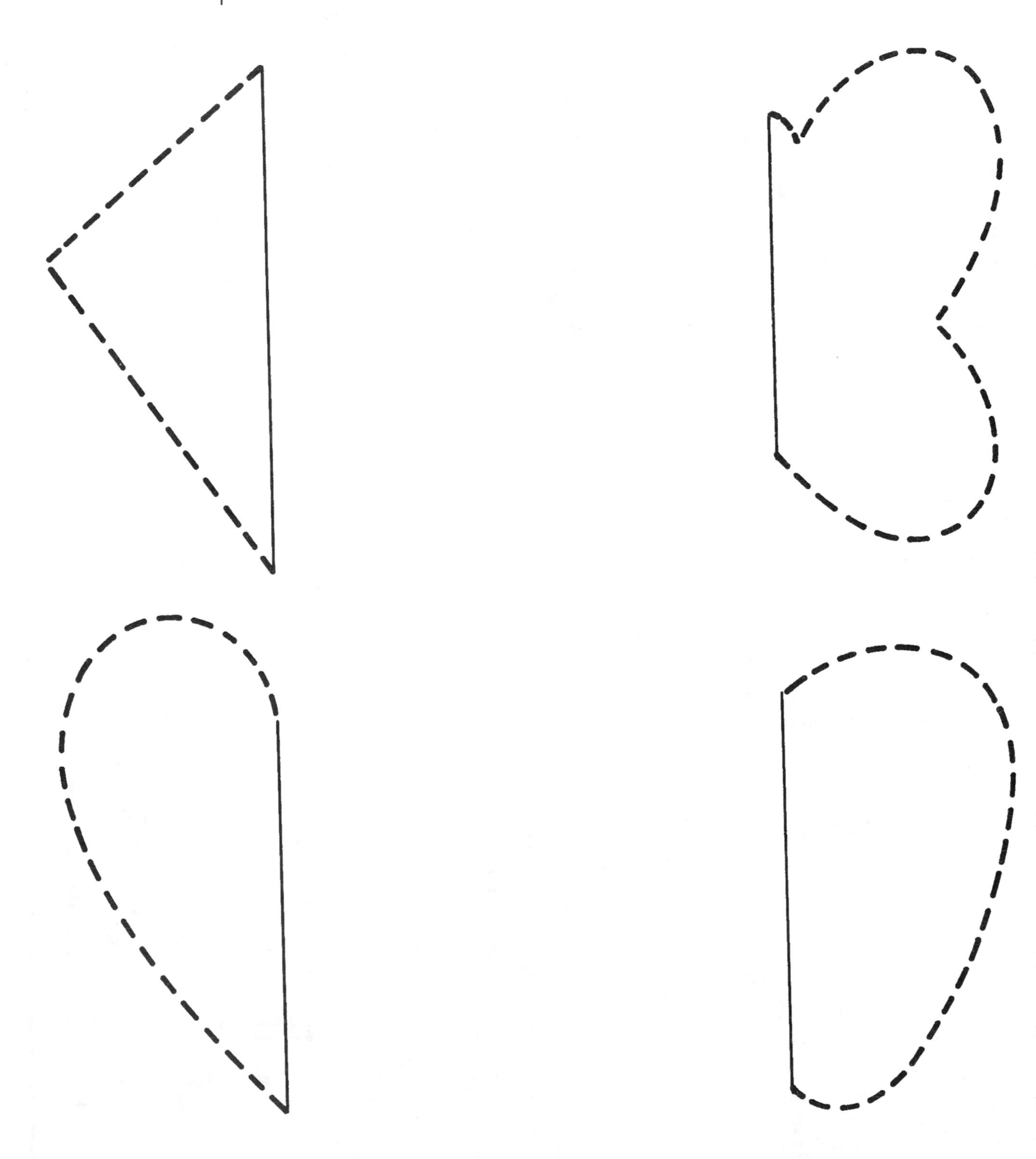

Homes

Homes

Objectives:

Each child will learn about . . .

- kinds of homes.
- reasons for homes.
- locations for homes.

Discussions:

As a group, the class can discuss . . .

- the meaning of home.
- why homes are important.
- why homes are different.
- homes on land, in or near water, above land, and underground.

Activities:

Give the children the patterns and poem on page 160. Let them color the turtle and turtle shell. Glue the shell onto the turtle and glue them both to another paper. Glue the poem above or below the turtle.

Let the children draw a home for each of these ground dwellers (page 161). Color the pictures. Attach a piece of yarn to make the mouse's tail.

Let the children draw a home for each of these water dwellers (page 162). Color the pictures. Glue bits of torn brown paper to make the beaver's tail.

Let the children draw a home for each of these above-ground dwellers (page 163). Color the pictures. Glue tissue paper wings to the butterfly.

Let the children draw a home for each of these underground dwellers (page 164). Color the pictures. Fat yarn can be pasted to the worm after the sheet is colored.

All Kinds of Homes

Color and cut out the patterns. Glue the shell onto the turtle. Glue the turtle to another paper. Glue the poem to the paper, too. Ask someone to read the poem to you.

On the Ground

Draw a home for each of these creatures who live on the ground. Color the pictures. Draw a face on the person, and glue a piece of yarn to the mouse to make a tail.

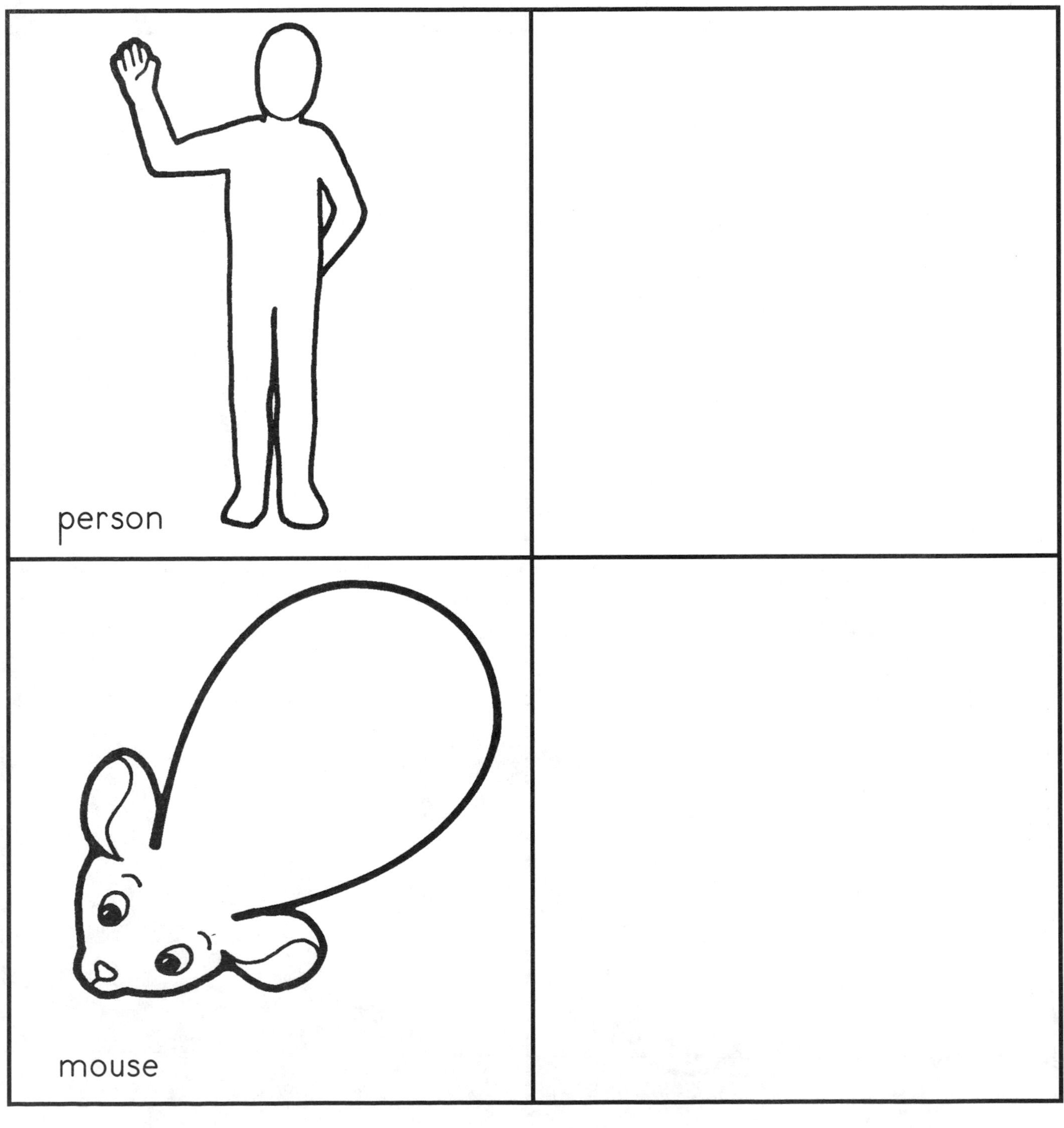

Some homes are best on the ground.

On the Water

Draw a home for each of these creatures who live in or near the water. Color the pictures. Glue bits of torn brown paper to the beaver's tail to make it thick and rough.

Some homes are best in or near the water.

Above the Ground

Draw a home for each of these creatures who live above the ground. Color the pictures. Glue tissue paper onto the butterfly's wings to make them colorful.

Some homes are best high above the ground.

Under the Ground

Draw a home for each of these creatures who live underground. Color the pictures. Glue brown yarn onto the worm to make it roly-poly.

Some homes are best under the ground.

The Five Senses

The Five Senses

Objectives:

Each child will learn about . . .

- tasting.
- touching.
- smelling.
- hearing.
- seeing.

Discussions:

As a group, the class can discuss . . .

- what the senses are.
- how the eyes, ears, nose, mouth/tongue, and hands/skin look.
- how each of these organs help us.
- care and safety of our sensory organs.

Activities:

Let the children choose a pair of eyes from those on page 167. They can then glue the eyes to a paper plate and draw a face to go with them. Let the children know that the eyes can belong to a person, animal, or even an imaginary being. After the children draw faces, paste the sentence strip on the other side of the plate.

Distribute the patterns from page 168, copied onto gray paper. (Trace the trunk pattern onto a fold in the paper so that the trunk is twice the length of the pattern.) Let the children glue the elephant to another sheet of paper with the sentence strip below it. Show them where to draw eyes on the elephant, also. Then, instruct them to accordion-fold the elephant's trunk and glue it to the center of its face.

Provide each child with the rabbit patterns from page 169, a paper fastener, crayons, and paste. The child can paste the pieces to another sheet to make a rabbit, attaching the ears to the head with a paper fastener so they can be wiggled. Instruct the children to draw and color additional details and to glue the sentence strip below the rabbit.

Distribute to each child a hippo and four teeth patterns (page 170), crayons, and paste. The child can add eyes, color the hippo, and glue the teeth in place. Fold the hippo as shown and glue it to another paper. Glue the sentence strip below it.

Provide each child with two hands (page 171), skin-toned crayons, and a sentence strip. Instruct them to color the hands (adding details such as fingernails, rings, etc.) and to staple or glue the hands at the wrists to the sides of a sheet of paper (so the hands meet in the center). Underneath where the hands meet, the children can draw an object that might be held in the hands.

The Eyes Have It

Choose a pair of eyes to color and cut out. Glue the eyes to a paper plate. Color the rest of the face.

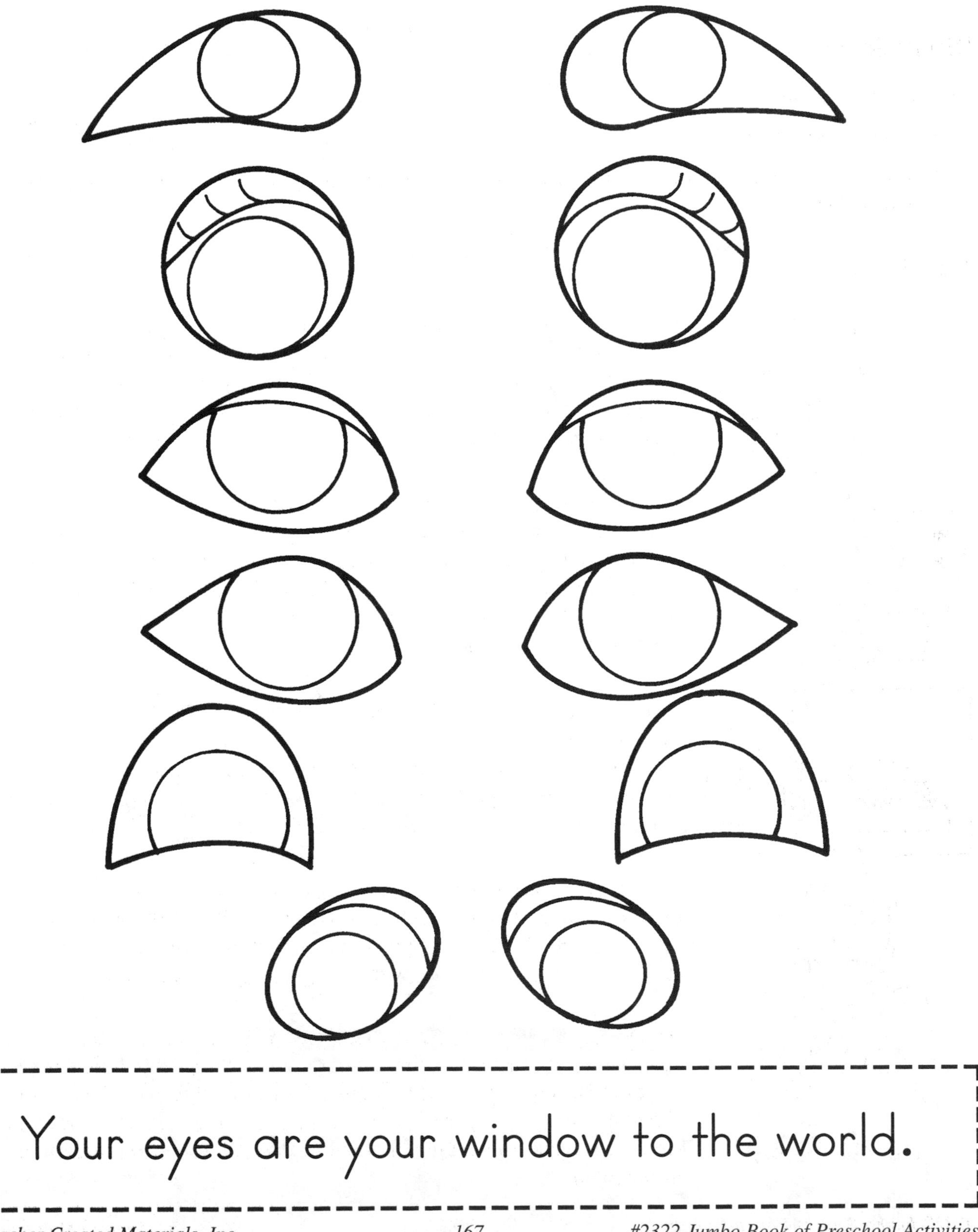

Your eyes are your window to the world.

Your Nose Knows

Cut out the elephant. Trace the trunk onto another paper so the end of the trunk pattern is on the paper's fold. Cut out the trunk (which is now twice as long as the pattern). Fold the trunk like an accordion. Glue the trunk to the elephant's face. Draw eyes on the elephant. Glue the elephant and sentence strip to another paper.

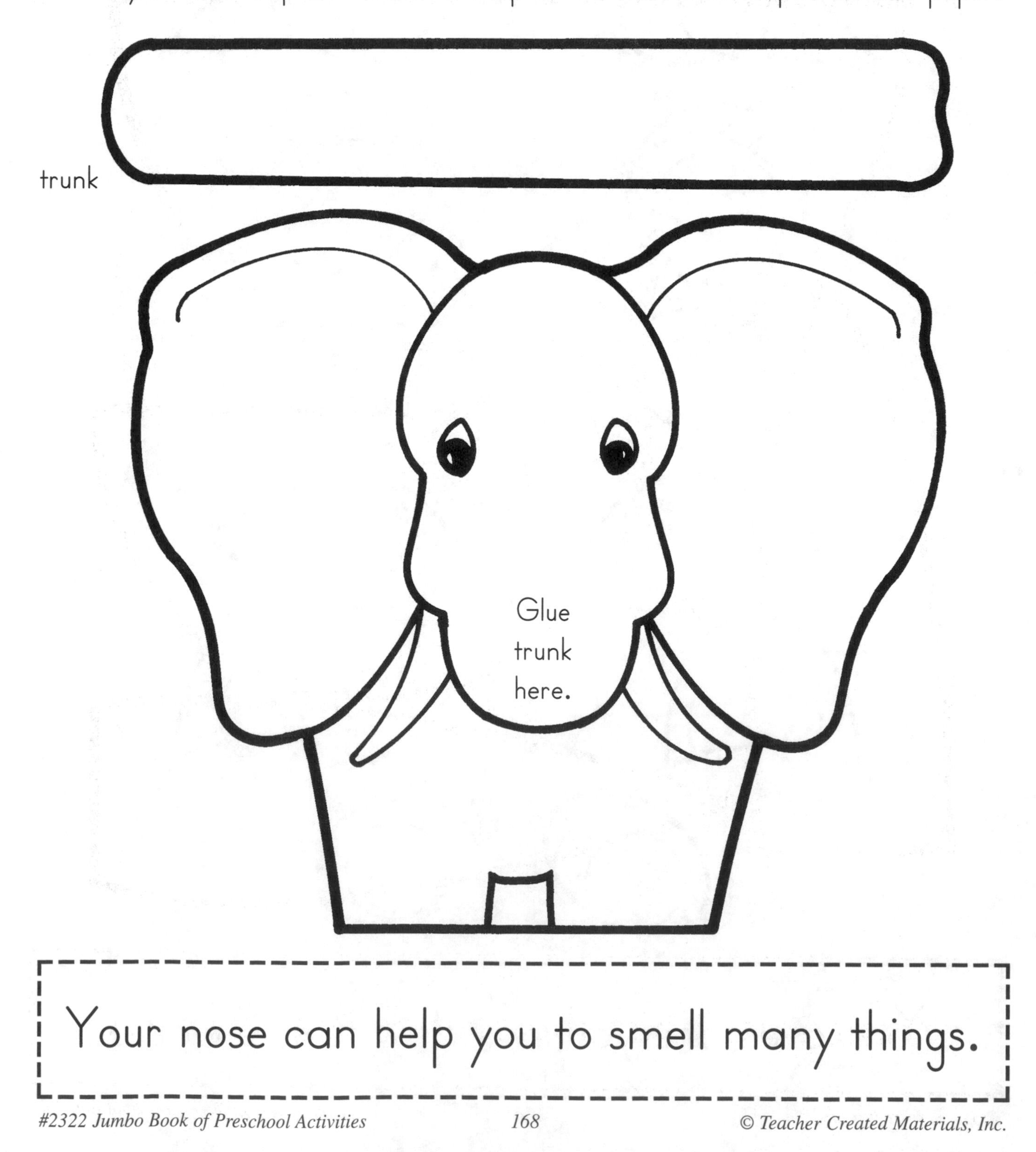

Your nose can help you to smell many things.

Rabbit Ears

Cut out the patterns. Glue the head and body patterns at the X to another paper to make a rabbit. Attach the ears to the head with a paper fastener at the X. Draw a scene around the rabbit. Glue the sentence strip below the rabbit.

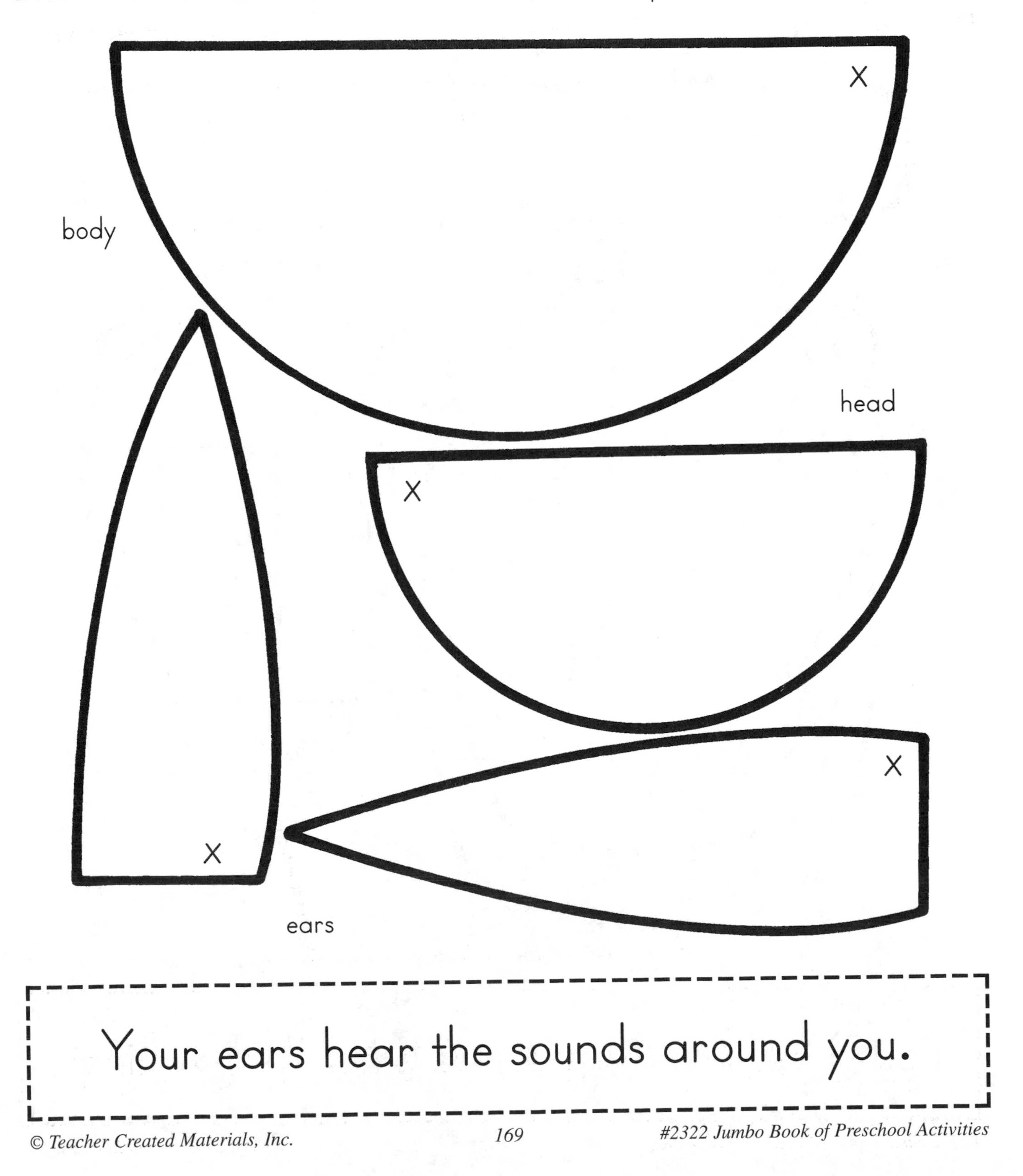

Open Wide

Color and cut out the hippo and four teeth. Glue the teeth to the mouth. Color the eyes on the hippo. Fold the hippo's mouth as shown. Glue the folded hippo to another paper and glue the sentence strip below it.

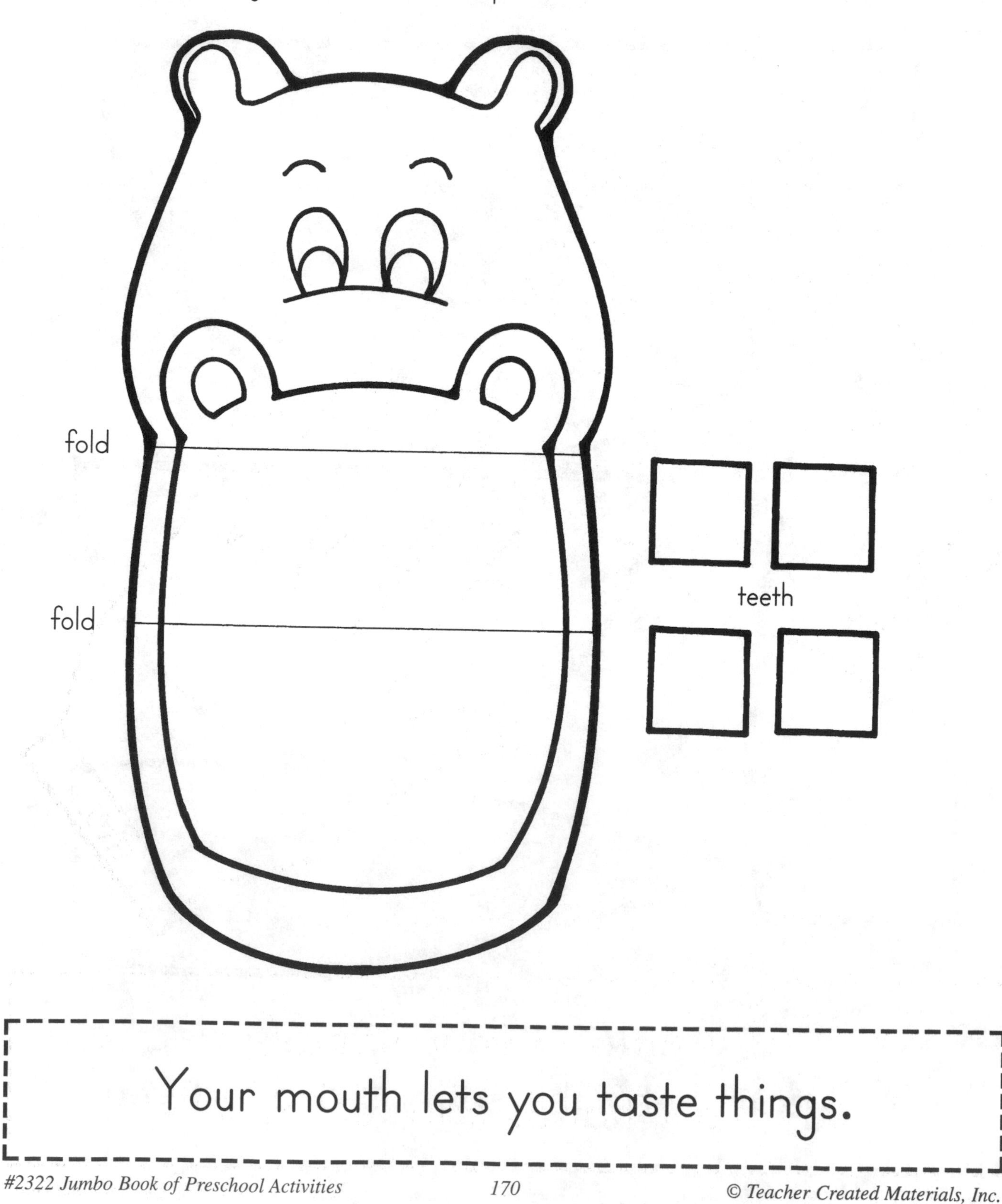

Your mouth lets you taste things.

I've Got to Hand It to You

Color and cut out two hands. Glue the hands at the wrists to the edges of a piece of paper so the hands cross over in the middle. Draw underneath the hands an object that they might be holding. Glue the sentence strip below the hands and object.

Cut 2 hands.

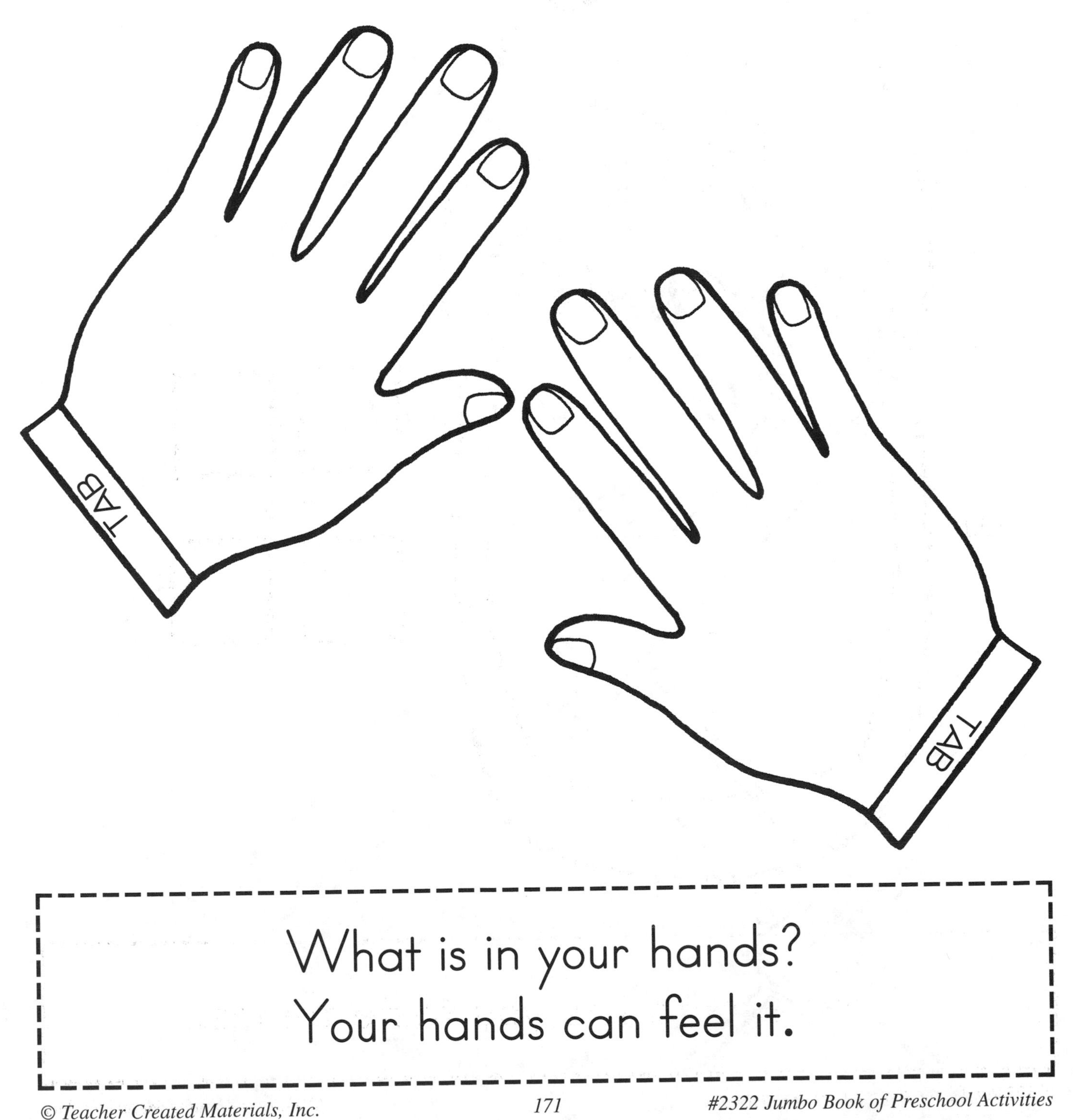

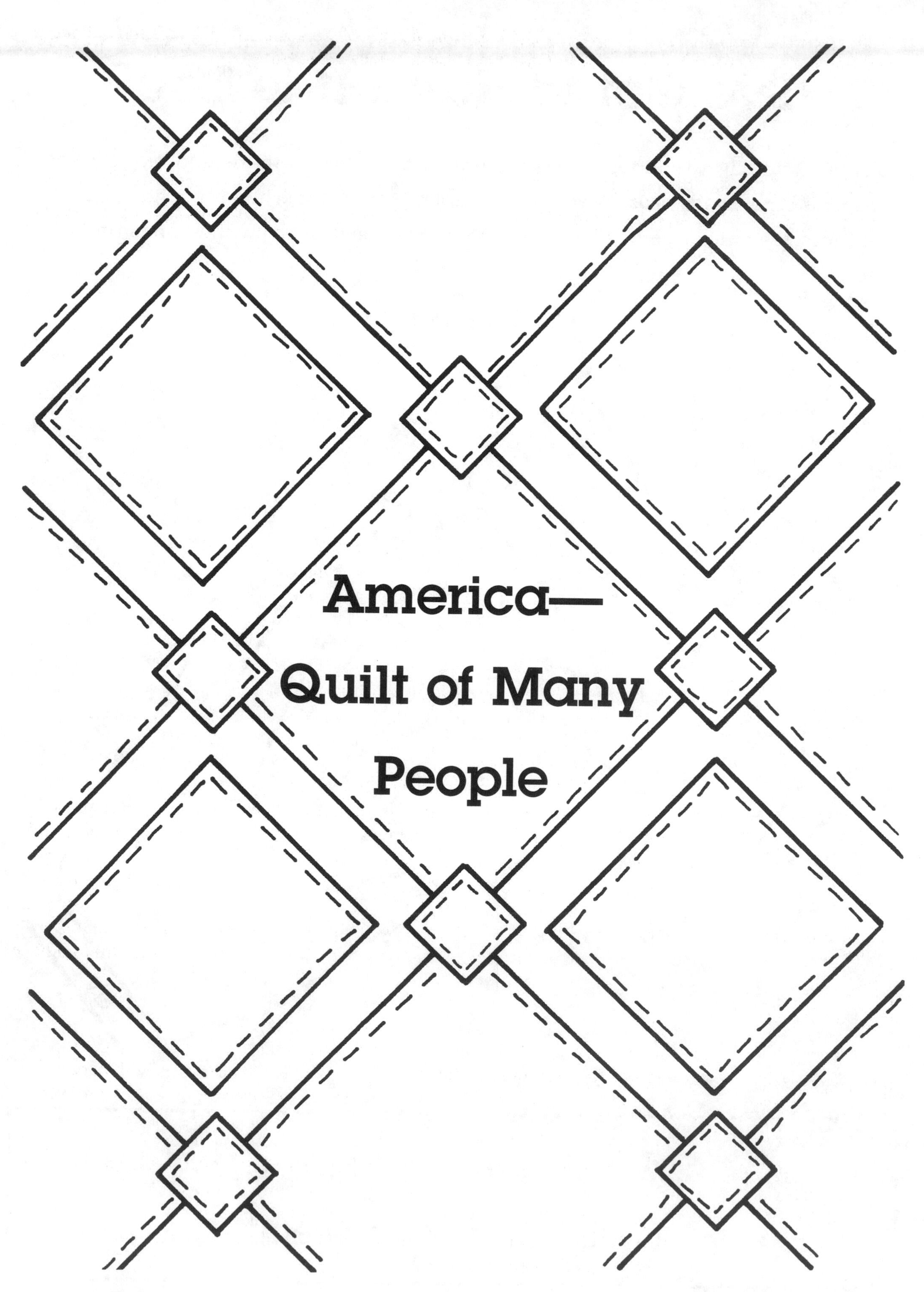
America—
Quilt of Many
People

America—Quilt of Many People

Objectives:

Each child will learn . . .

- why people come to America.
- countries from which people emigrate to America.
- what people bring with them to America.
- how to use different ideas and ways to make America strong.

Discussions:

As a group, the class can discuss . . .

- why many people think America is a good place to live.
- differences in customs, languages, and foods of people new to America.
- the home countries of American immigrants.
- how learning from each other can make a strong country.
- how to become an American citizen.

Activities:

Talk with the children about quilts and how they are made of many pieces sewn together. Tell them that America is like that. Color the quilt (page 172) in a variety of colors.

Use a world map to show the students the countries of the world in relationship to America. Ask them to name their families' homelands for you to point out. (You might wish to ask parents for this information ahead of time since, in many cases, children are unaware of their ancestries.) After your discussion, distribute page 174 and ask the children to color their current home state. For their information, name other states as well, particularly states that neighbor yours.

Choose several immigrant groups that are currently among the greatest numbers coming to America. Explain to the children how these languages differ from American English. Research to find how to say "hello" in those languages, and add the foreign words to the speech bubbles on page 175. Let the children color features onto the figures. As a class, practice saying hello in several languages.

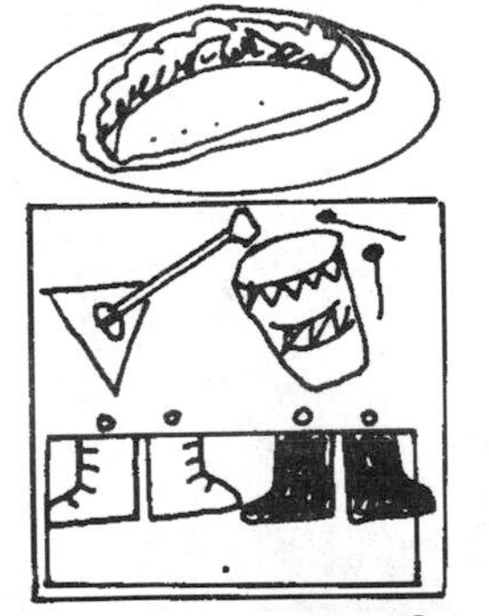

Encourage children to bring magazine pictures from home of foods from other countries. Glue the pictures to the food plates (pages 176) after the children have colored them.

Talk about other people's customs. Help the children to draw musical instruments in the top section of page 177. Also help them to cut out the lower section and to color and cut out the four boots. Attach the boots with paper fasteners at the circles so they are suspended in the opening and can be moved back and forth as though dancing.

Give each child a copy of page 178. Let the child color each of the hands in a different color. Help the children to cut out the hands. As a class, glue everyone's hands in a long chain and hang the chain around the room. Tell the children that this chain represents the different people of America working together to make a strong country.

America

This is America. Find your state and color it. Can you name other states, also?

People in America have come from many other countries.

Languages

Inside the speech bubbles, write words for "hello" in other languages. Color the people.

People bring their languages to America.

Food

Color the plates. Glue pictures of foods from other countries onto the plates.

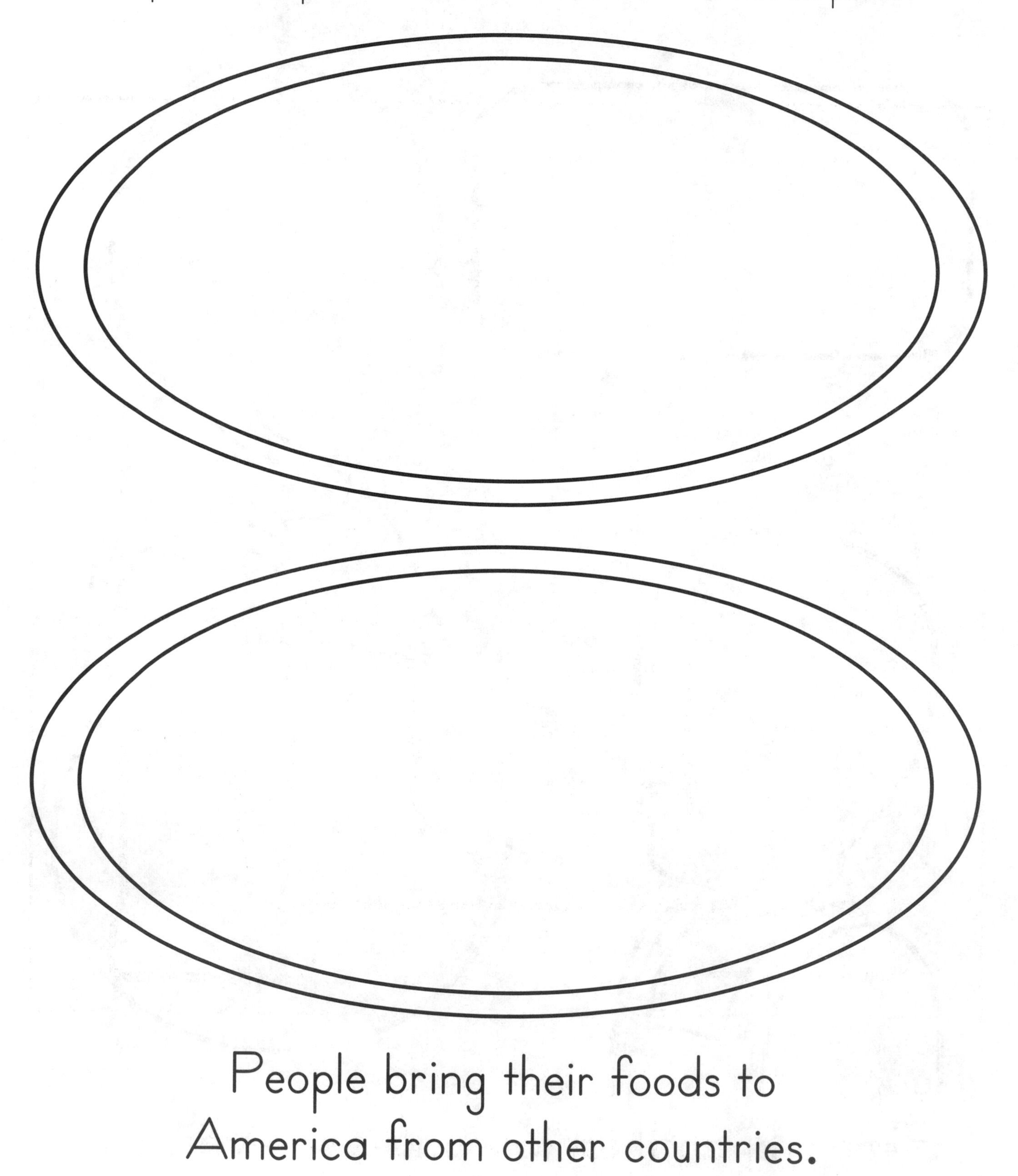

People bring their foods to
America from other countries.

Customs

Draw musical instruments in the top section. Cut out the bottom section. Color and cut out the boots. Attach the boots with paper fasteners at the circles to make the feet dance.

music

dancing

People around the world have different ways of singing and dancing. Every way is fun.

Helping Hands

Color the hands in any colors you like. Cut out the hands, too. They will be glued in a chain with other hands to make a long line of hands working together.

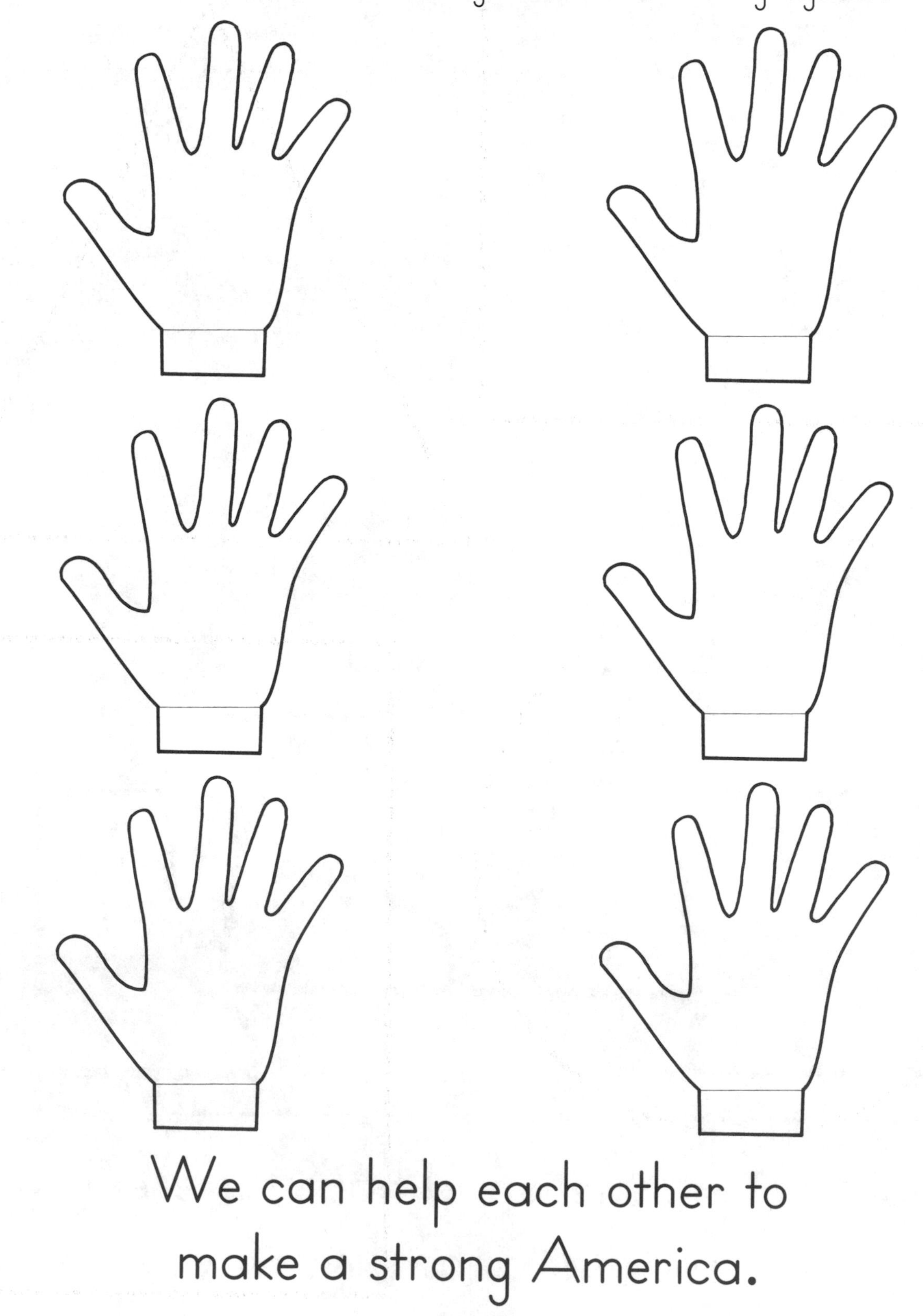

We can help each other to make a strong America.

Shapes

Shapes

Objectives:

Each child will learn . . .

- the shape of a circle, square, rectangle, and triangle.
- names for shapes.
- how shapes are used in our world.

Discussions:

As a group, the class can discuss . . .

- all things have shapes.
- some shapes make things more useful.
- the names for various shapes.
- how to form circles and where they are seen.
- how to form rectangles and where they are seen.
- how to form triangles and where they are seen.
- how to form squares and where they are seen.

Activities:

Using the patterns on page 181, make a black half circle and a large red circle for each child. Also make four small black circles per child. Show the children a model of a completed ladybug. Then instruct them to build one of their own, gluing their pieces to another sheet of paper and adding legs and antennae with crayons. A sentence strip can be glued beneath the ladybug.

Give each child the rectangles and sentence strip from page 182. Draw a train-track line for them across a piece of paper. Let them glue the train car rectangles along the line, drawing in wheels and other details. They can also draw scenery around the train. Glue the sentence strip at the bottom of the page.

Instruct the children to draw a large circle inside each square on page 183. Have the children color all circles the same color and the background of the square another color.

Instruct the children to draw a large triangle inside each square on page 184. Have the children color the design in any way they like.

Provide each child with a copy of page 185. Discuss the shapes and the things that can be made from them. Then let the children draw something from each shape.

Ladybugs

Trace the patterns onto colored paper and cut them out. Assemble the ladybug and glue it to another paper. Draw four spots, legs, and antennae with crayons. Glue the sentence strip beneath the ladybug.

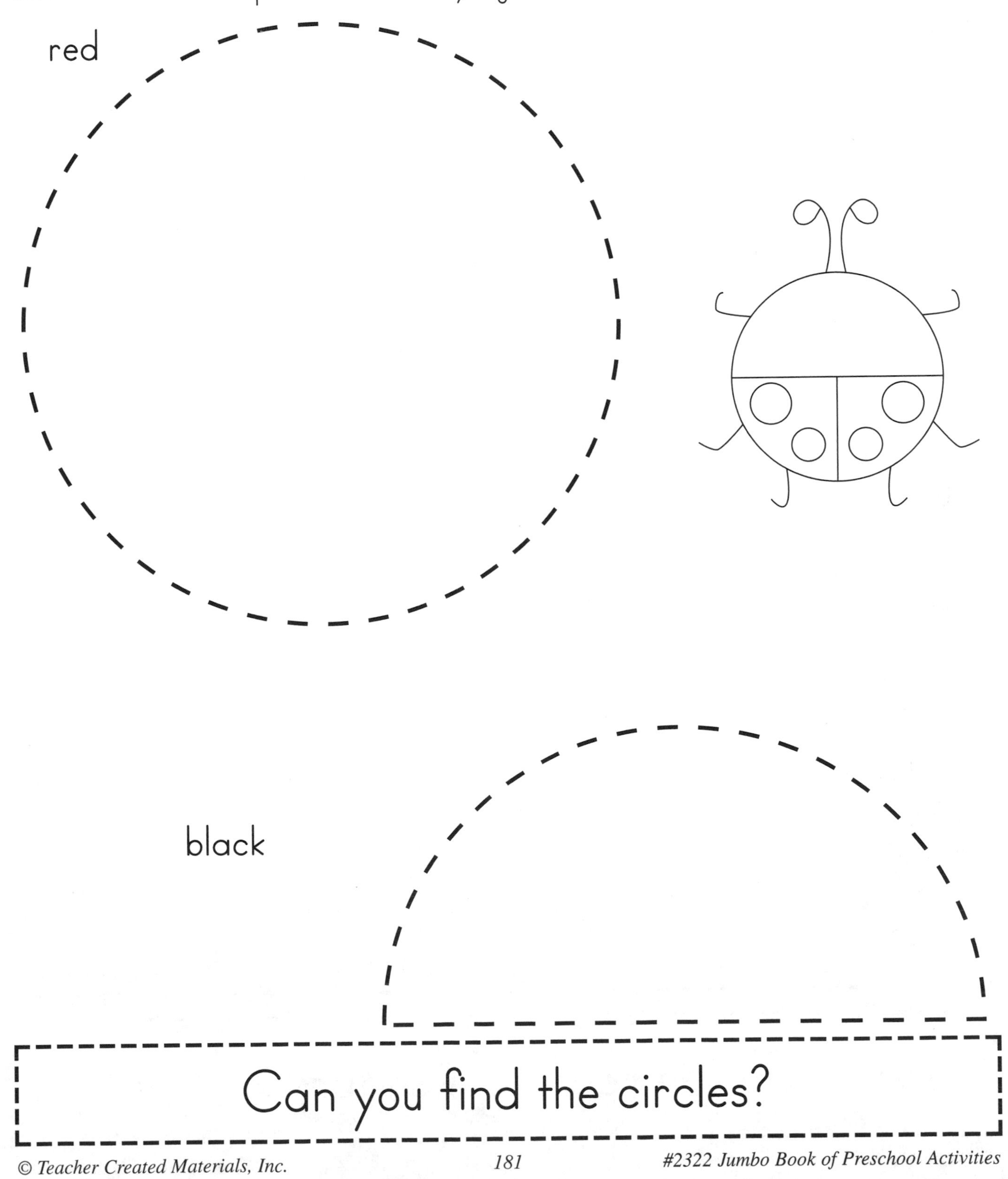

Rectangle Train

Cut rectangles of different colors. On a separate paper, draw a train track. Glue the rectangles along the track to make a train. Color details and scenery. Glue the sentence below the track.

We can see rectangle shapes in trains.

Circles and Squares

Draw a large circle in each square. Color the circles one color. Color the squares around them in a different color.

Circles and squares can make a design.

Triangles and Squares

Draw a large triangle in each square. Color the design.

Triangles and squares can make a design.

What Do You See?

Look at the shapes. Add details to make each shape become something else.

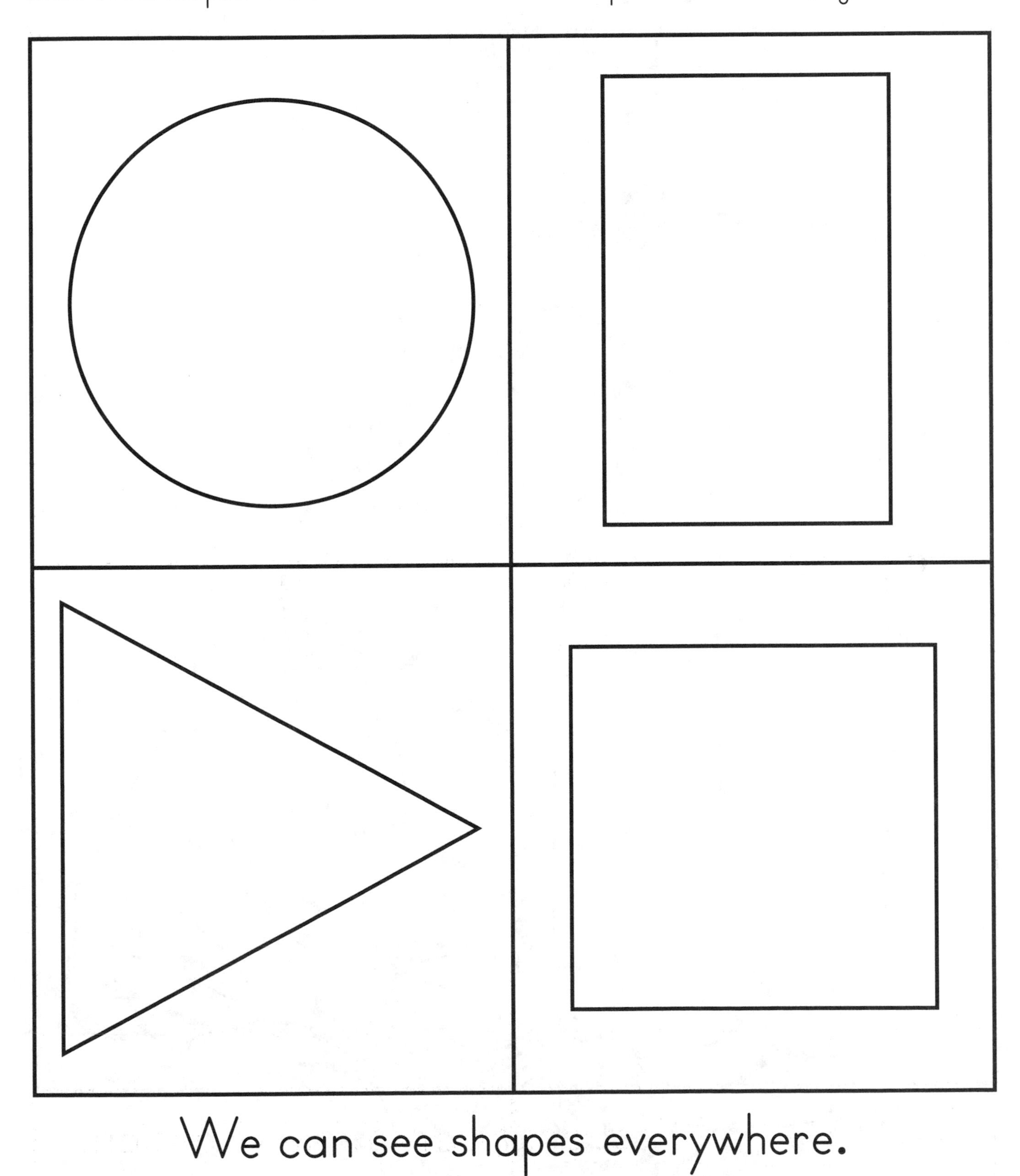

We can see shapes everywhere.

Conservation

Conservation

Objectives:

Each child will learn . . .

- the careful use of water, electricity, gasoline, and paper.
- the meaning of conservation.
- how recycling can help.

Discussions:

As a group, the class can discuss . . .

- how conserving now will help later.
- kinds of paper products and why to use them carefully.
- uses for water and why to use it carefully.
- uses for electricity and how to use it carefully.
- uses for gasoline and how to use it carefully.
- what recycling means and why it is important.
- what can be recycled.

Activities:

Distribute page 188. Let the children color a design for the tissue box. Cut the box at the slit. Insert a tissue through the slit from the back and glue it in place.

Give each child a copy of page 189. Discuss how running errands all at once can conserve time, money, and gasoline. Encourage the children to talk about places their families need to go for errands. Then instruct the children to draw their family members in the van and to color the picture. Let them dictate where they are going in the van. The teacher or aide can write the words in the blank. When the coloring is done, construction paper wheels can be cut and added to the van with paper fasteners.

Have children draw and color a person to stand in front of the sink (page 190). Water can be added with watercolor paints or tissue paper glued inside the sink. Be careful not to spill any!

Use wrapping paper or wallpaper to make a lamp shade the same size as the one pictured (page 191) plus one-half inch (1.25 cm) at the top. Color the lamp shade on the page yellow and the base any color desired. Cut the slit at the top of the lamp shade. Insert the top of the wallpaper shade through the slit and fold it down. Tape it on the reverse to keep it in place. To "turn on" the lamp, lift the shade.

Distribute page 192. Let the children color the recycling container and then glue pieces of newspaper and aluminum foil inside it.

Give each child a copy of page 193, glue, and a variety of "junk mail." Let the children tear bits of paper from the mail and glue it onto the picture to color it in. For example, blue paper can be glued to the sky and green or brown to the ground. It will be all right to use colored bits with print on them as well. The picture effect will still be attractive.

Do Not Waste

Color the tissue box. Cut the slit. Insert a tissue through the slit from behind. Glue it in place.

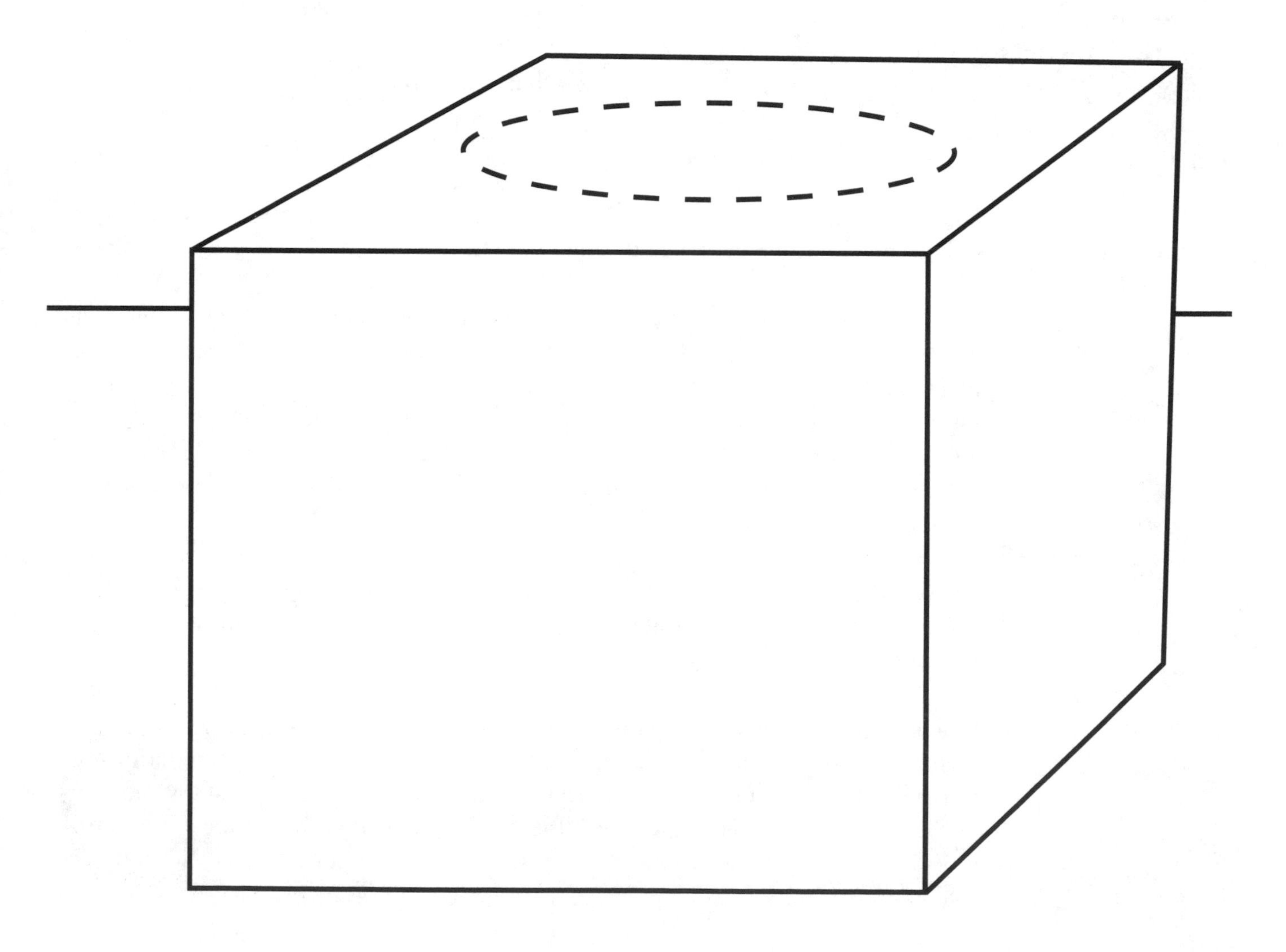

Use one item at a time.

Plan Your Time

Color the van. Draw your family in the van going to do errands. Attach construction paper wheels to the van with paper fasteners. Write the errands your family is doing on the blank.

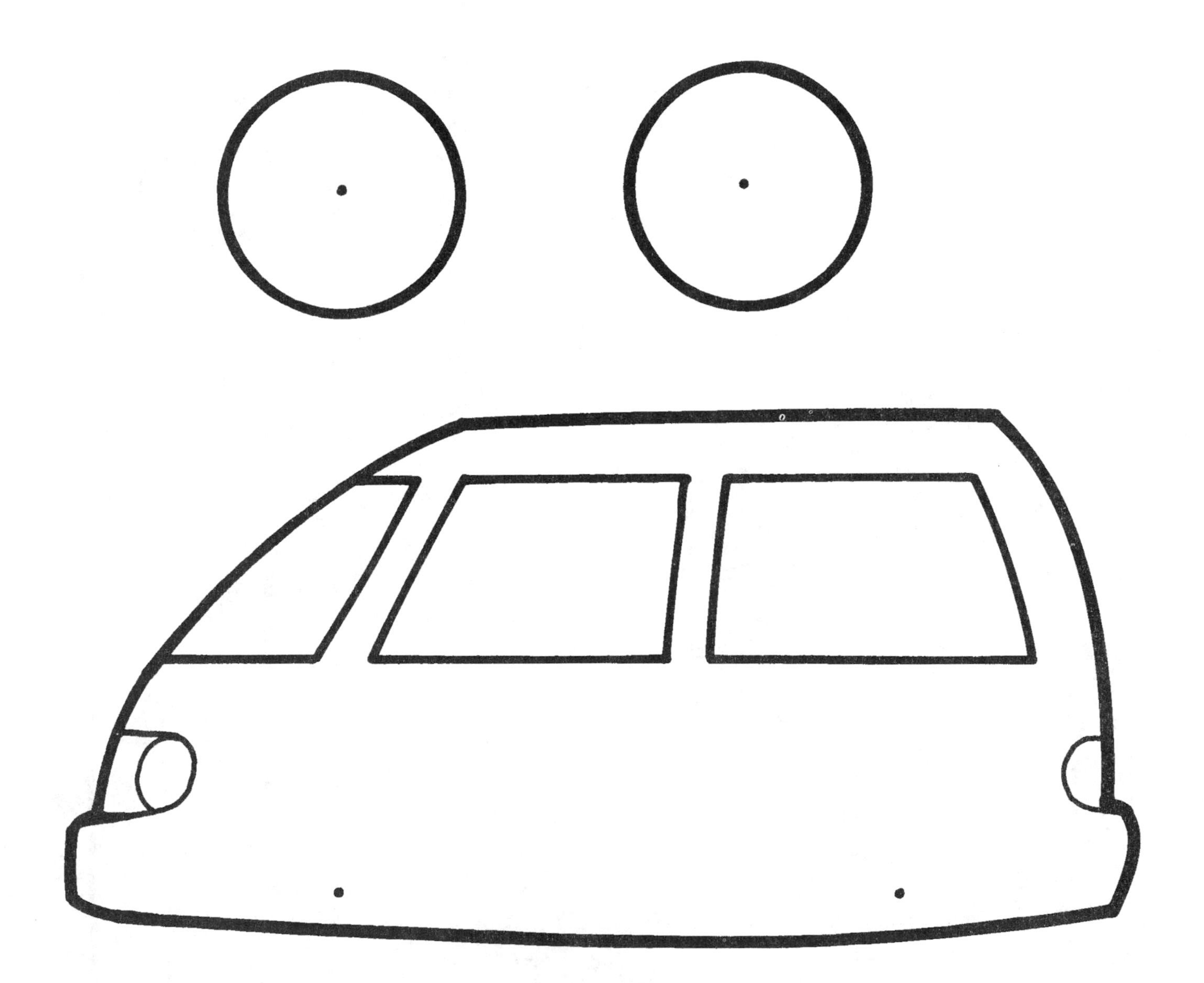

We are doing our errands.
We are going to ______________.

Conserve Water

Color the sink. Draw yourself at the sink. Use watercolor paint to fill the sink with just enough water to wash your face and hands.

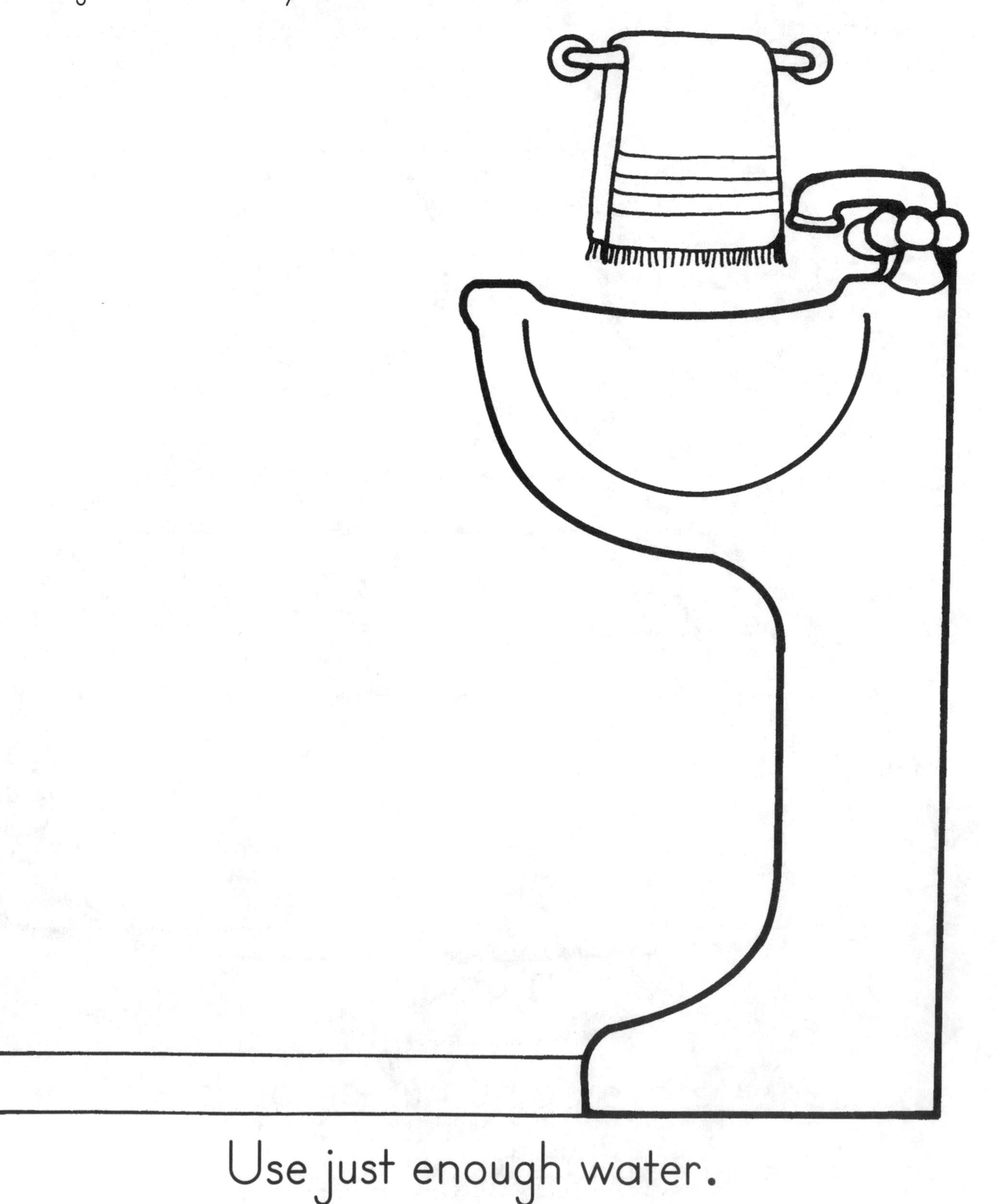

Use just enough water.

Use Electricity Wisely

Color the lamp shade yellow. Color the lamp base any color you like. Make another lamp shade from wrapping paper, cutting it slightly taller than the drawing. Cut the slit at the top of the lamp. Fold the top of the wrapping paper shade into the slit. To "turn on" the lamp, lift the wrapping paper shade.

Turn off the lights when you do not need them.

Recycling

Color the recycle bin. Glue bits of newspaper and aluminum foil inside the bin.

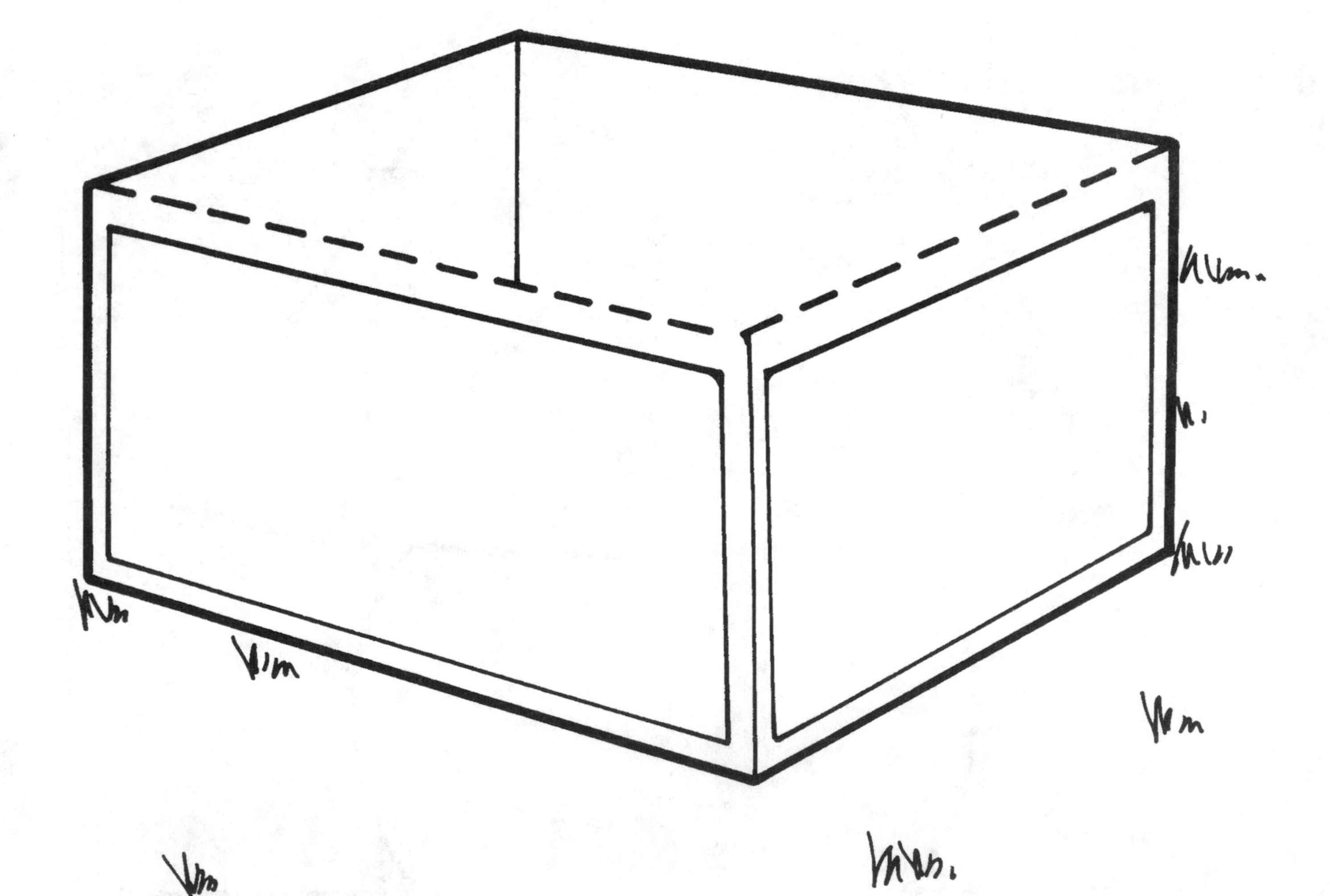

Recycle what you can.

Reuse

Tear bits of junk mail and glue the pieces of paper to the picture. Do not worry about the writing on the mail.

We can find another use for many things.

The Earth, Our Home

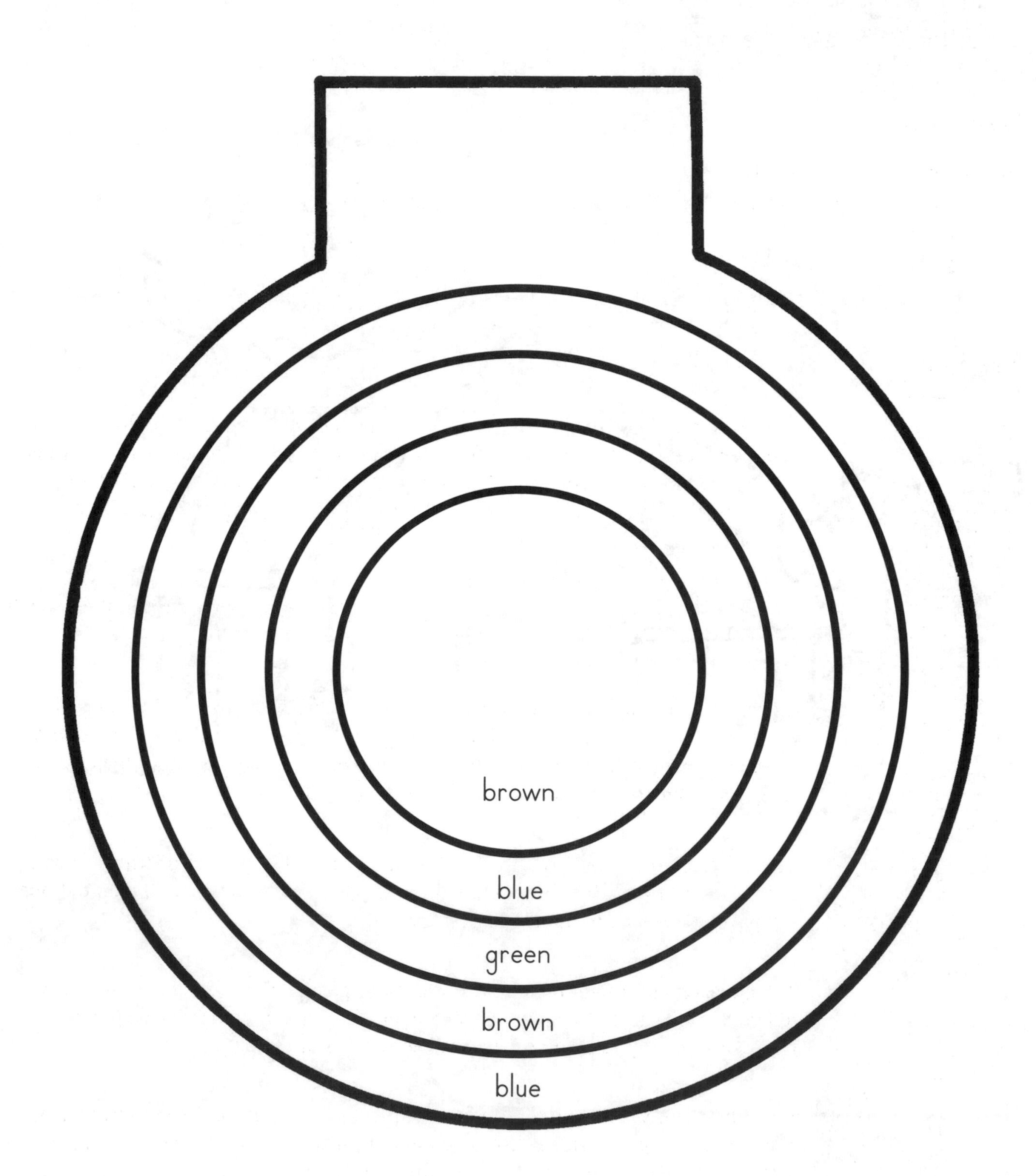

The Earth, Our Home

Objectives:

Each child will learn about . . .

- the earth as a planet.
- kinds of lands.
- kinds of water.
- the air around the earth.

Discussions:

As a class, the group can discuss . . .

- what the earth is (relationship to sun and planets).
- names of continents.
- oceans' names.
- kinds of land.
- other water on the earth.
- gravity.
- names of planets.

Activities:

Distribute page 194 for the booklet cover. Instruct the children to color the rings in browns, blues, and greens (the colors of planet Earth). Cut around the outline of the circle and tab. Glue the title across the center of the circle. All other sheets will be cut out as well and stapled together at the tab to make a book.

Each child is given page 196 and crayons. The child can color in grass, sky, people, and animals. Cut around the circle. Glue the sentence strip to the reverse side of the page.

A circle frame (page 197), two fish patterns, a sentence strip, crayons, and glue are given to each child. The child can color the fish, color water in the circle by lightly coloring with green and blue, and add plants at the bottom of the circle. Fish can be glued in place and the sentence strip glued to the reverse.

Give each child the circle divided five ways (page 198), the word strips, crayons, and paste. With teacher direction, the child can color each area and then cut out and paste the words in their proper places.

Provide each child with the circle frame from page 199, the sentence strip, paste, and crayons. The child can color the water, sky, etc., to complete the picture. The sentence strip should be glued to the reverse of the page.

Each child is given the circle frame with planets (page 200), the sentence strip, paste, and crayons. After a discussion about planets, the child should color the planets and glue the sentence strip to the reverse of the page. For a special effect, add dabs of glue to the outer space scene and sprinkle silver and gold glitter on it. Let dry.

The Land

Color a scene in the circle with animals and people on the green land. Cut out the circle and sentence strip. Glue the sentence strip on the back of the circle.

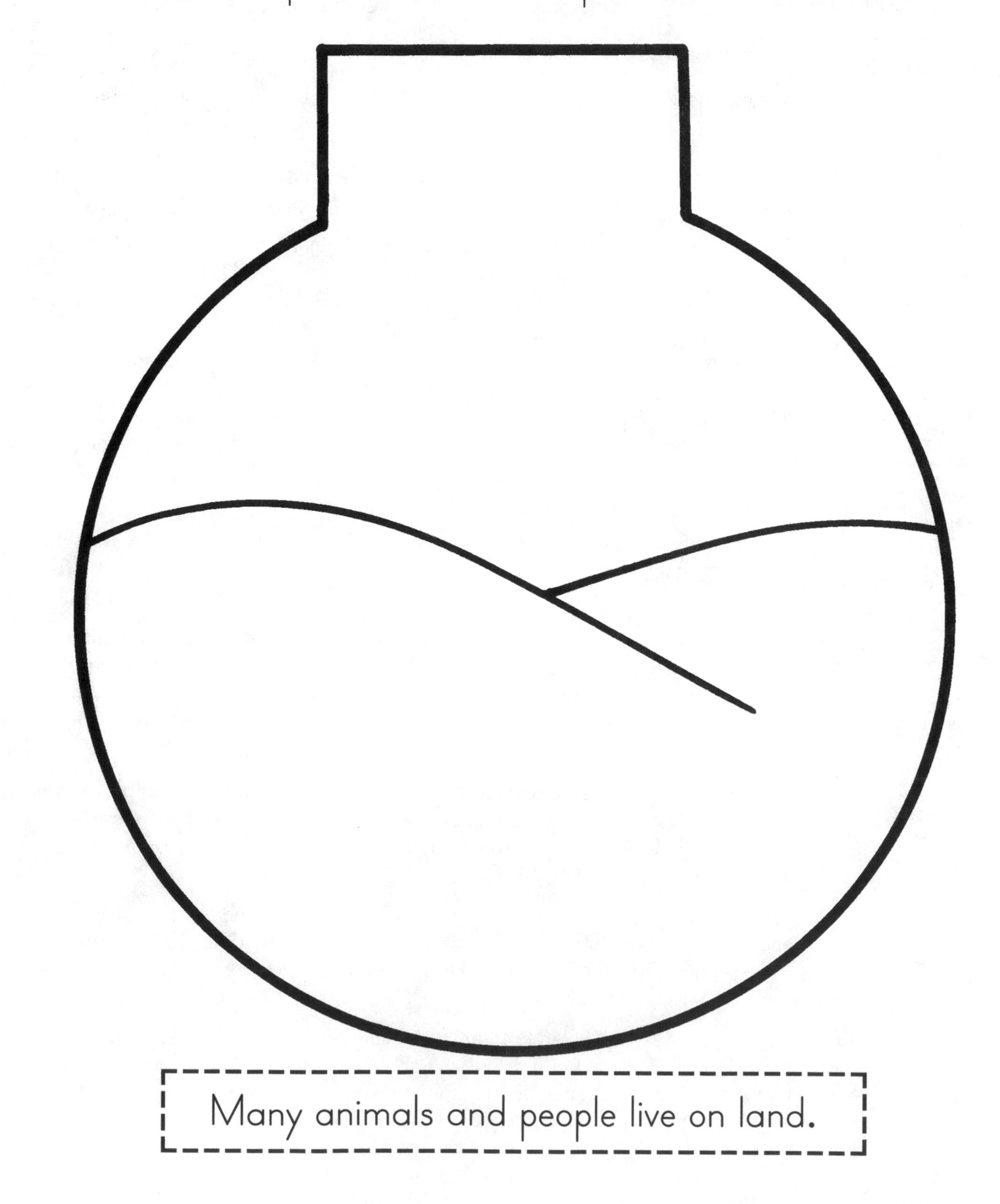

Many animals and people live on land.

The Water

Color the fish. Color the circle blue or green. Glue the fish in the circle. Cut out the circle and sentence strip. Glue the sentence strip behind the circle.

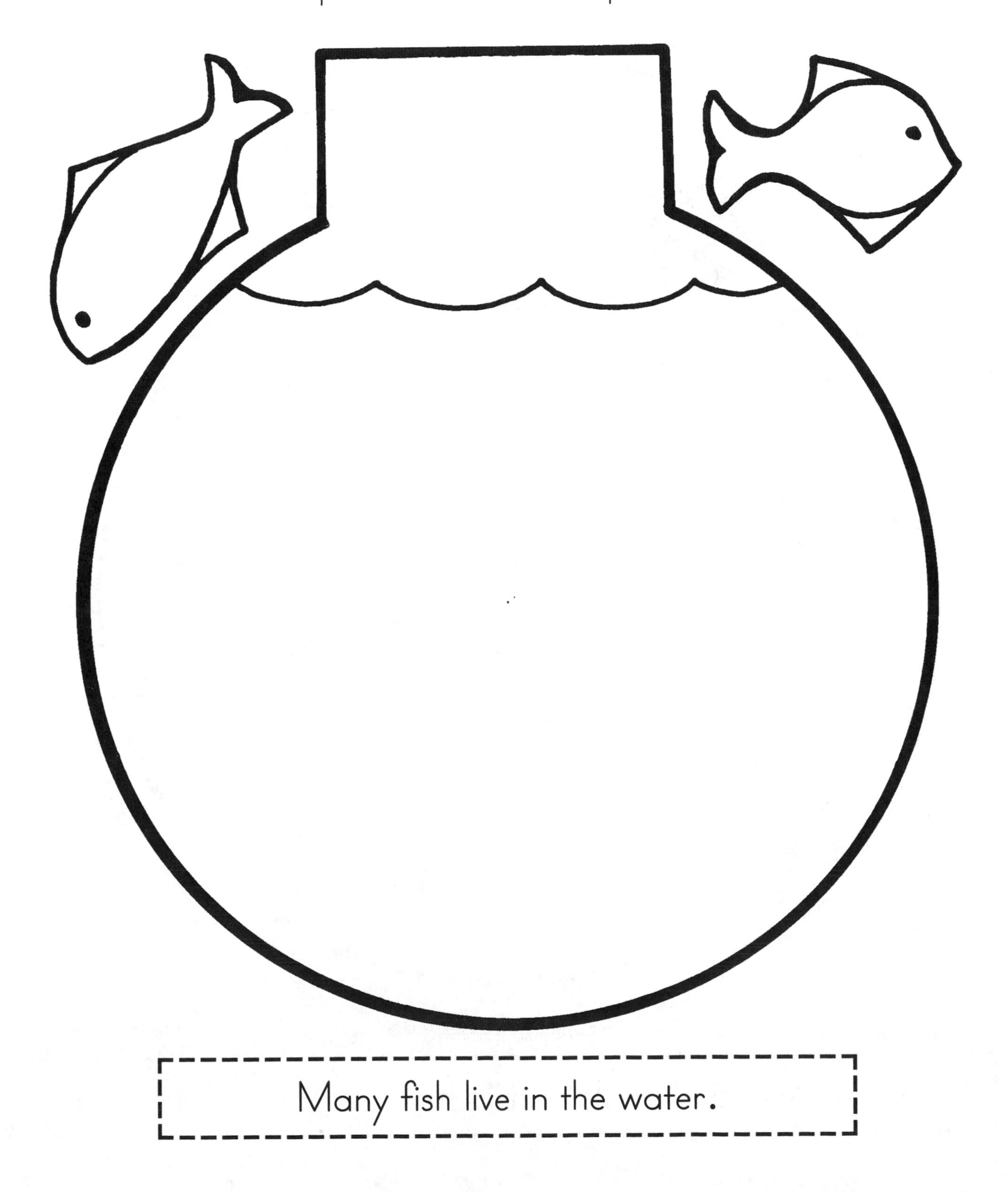

Types of Land

We see many things across the land. Color the pictures of what you see. Cut out the words and glue them in the right places. Cut out the circle.

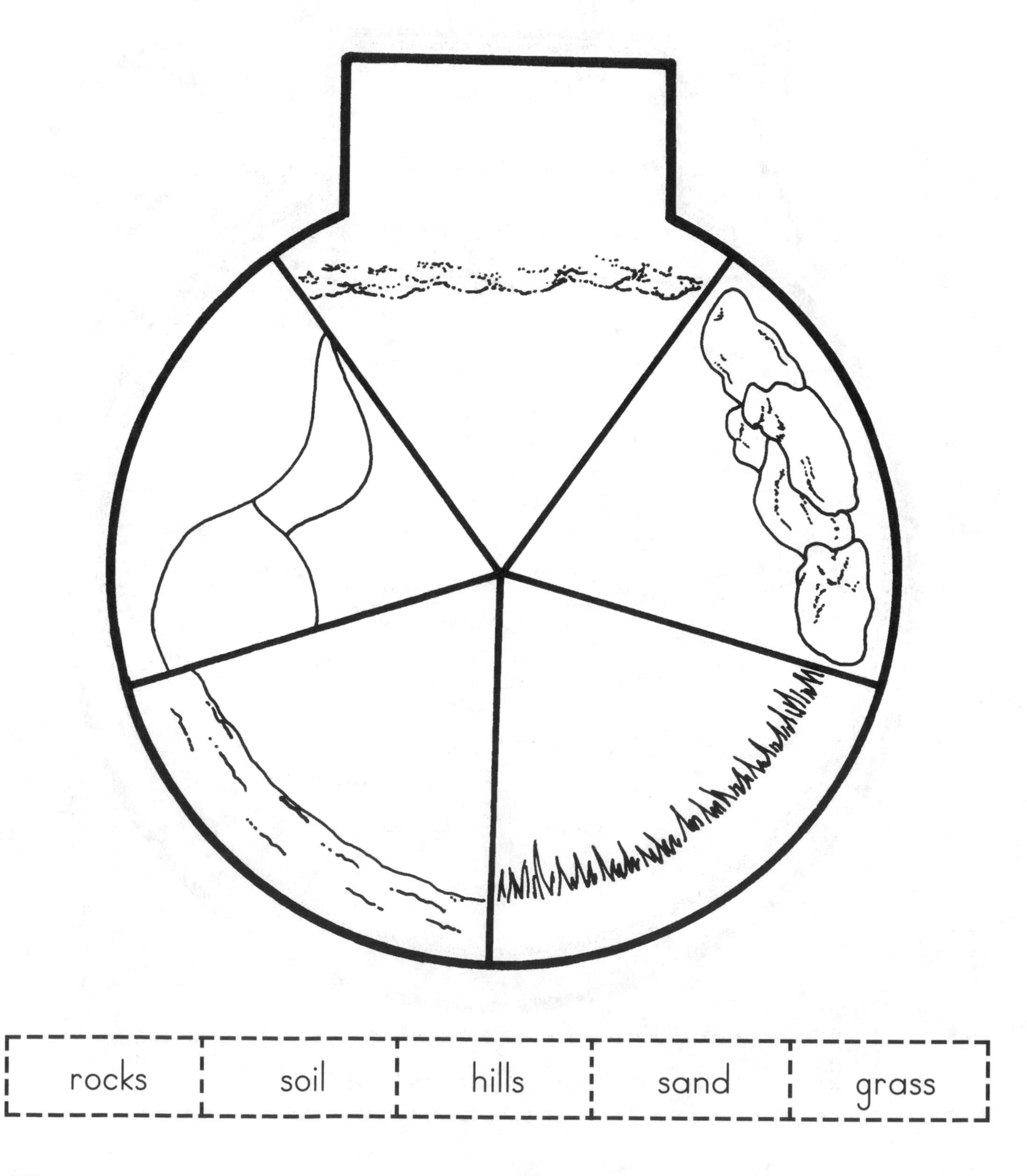

Types of Water

We see many bodies of water on our planet. Color the water in the picture. Say the words. Cut out the circle and sentence strip. Glue the sentence strip behind the circle.

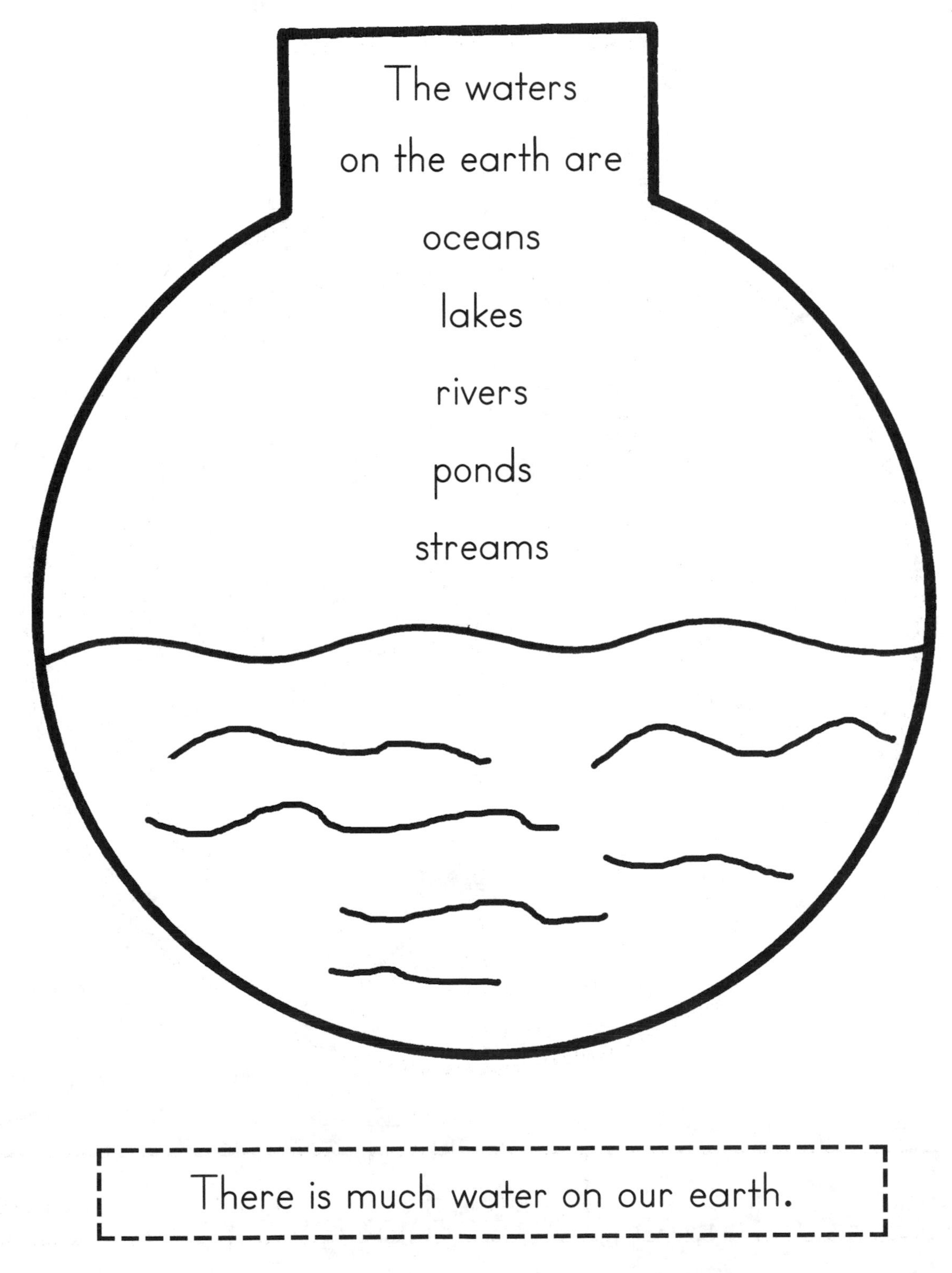

The Planets

Color the solar system. Cut out the circle and sentence strip. Glue the sentence strip behind the circle.

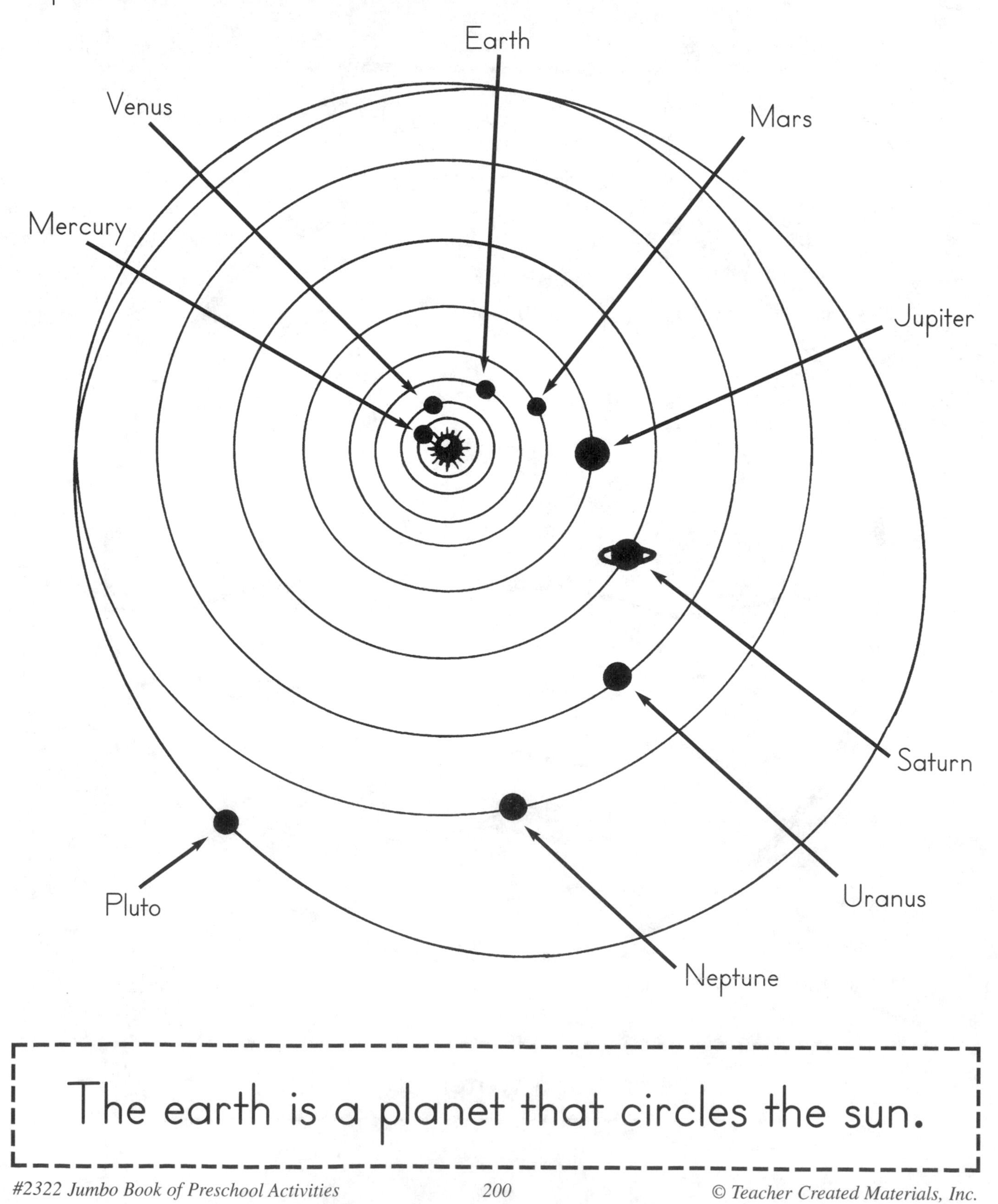

Spring

Spring

Objectives:

Each child will learn about . . .

- the time of spring.
- changes in plants during spring.
- animal activities during spring.
- people activities during spring.
- why spring is a favorite time.

Discussions:

As a group, the class can discuss . . .

- our seasons and how they differ from one another.
- how plants begin to grow.
- animal and bird homes and families.
- outside activities for people during springtime.
- special things we notice in the spring.

Activities:

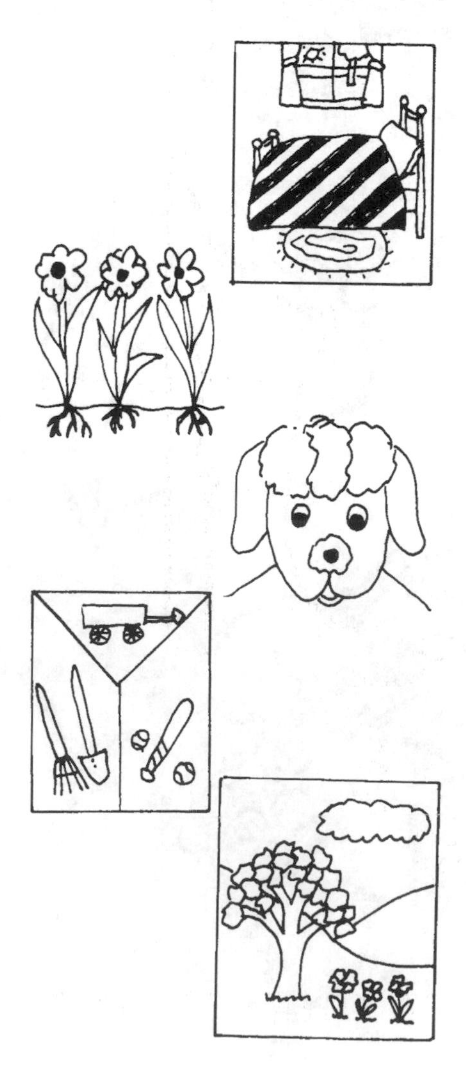

Let the children color the bedroom (page 203), adding any details they would like. Provide them with a piece of fabric to use as a bedcover. Instruct them to "make their beds" by gluing the fabric in place.

Discuss how plants grow. Then, distribute page 204. Tissue-paper flowers with black dot centers can be added to the stems after they are colored. Real seeds can be glued underground.

Instruct the children to color the background and ears for the lamb (page 205). Three cotton balls can be glued to the top of the head for wool. One cotton ball can be spread out with a nickel-size black dot in the middle for the nose. Glue the nose below the eyes.

The children can discuss and draw things that people do outside in the springtime (page 206).

Torn paper can be glued for flowers, leaves, and birds after the picture (page 207) is colored.

Waking Up

It is time to wake up after a long winter sleep! Color the bedroom. Glue a piece of fabric to the bed for a bedcover.

Spring is an awakening after a winter of rest.

Growing Up

Cut flowers from tissue paper. Glue them on top of the stems. Glue seeds under the ground to show how plants grow.

Seeds and plants begin to grow in the spring.

Baby Animals of Spring

Color the lamb's ears. Glue cotton to its head. Stretch out a cotton ball for its wooly snout. Glue a circle of black onto the snout for its nose.

Animals and birds have new babies in the spring.

Outside

What do people do outside in the spring? Draw three things people might use or do outside during the spring months.

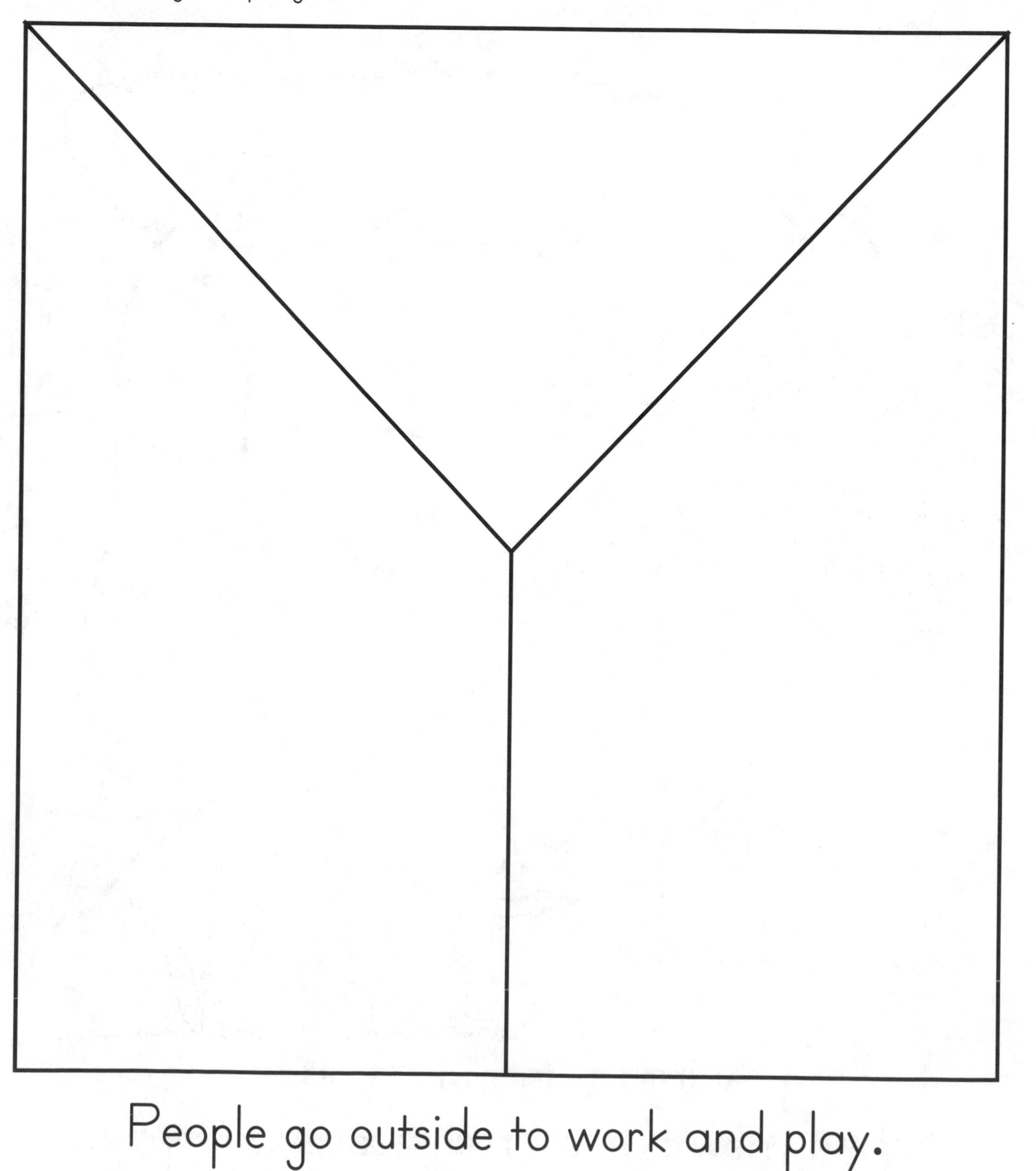

People go outside to work and play.

Beautiful Spring!

Tear bits of colored paper and glue them to make leaves, flowers, and birds. Spring is very bright and colorful!

Spring is lovely! Spring makes us happy.

Butterflies

Butterflies

Objectives:

Each child will learn . . .

- the stages of a butterfly's life.
- how butterflies help us.
- the differences between moths and butterflies.

Discussions:

As a group, the class can discuss . . .

- what butterflies are.
- where we see butterflies.
- how butterflies get food.
- stages of a butterfly's life.
- kinds of butterflies.
- sizes of butterflies.
- how butterflies help us.
- differences between moths and butterflies.

Activities:

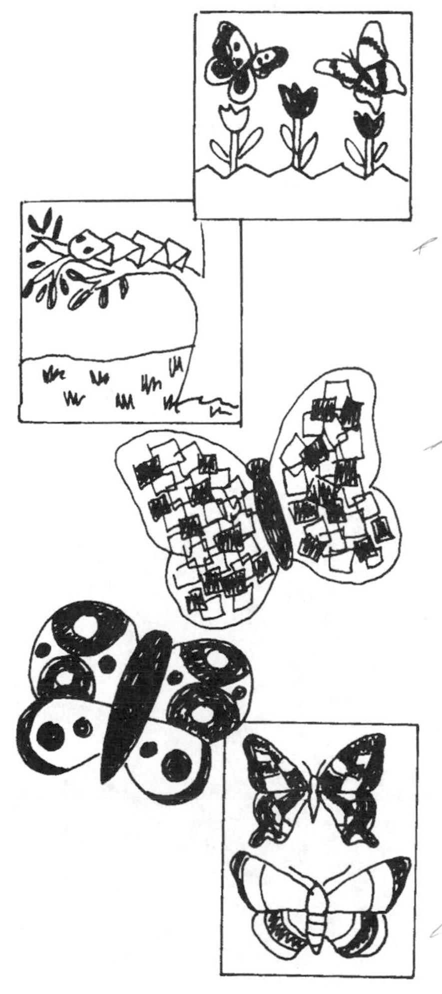

Supply children with page 210, crayons, and scissors (if they can cut). The child can cut the grass across the bottom of the sheet and fold it up, drawing and coloring a row of flowers tucked into the grass.

Each child is given page 211, scissors (if able to cut), and crayons. The child can then cut the caterpillar strip and fold it accordion style. Add eyes. Color to complete the picture. Staple the caterpillar to the branch.

Each child is given a butterfly pattern (page 212), liquid starch, a paintbrush, and small pieces of colored tissue paper. The child uses the paintbrush to apply starch to the butterfly, placing many pieces of tissue paper on the wings and then putting another coat of starch to seal it in. Let dry completely.

Each child should have a folded 12" x 9" (30 cm x 22.5 cm) paper, crayons, and scissors (if able to cut). The child will need help drawing a butterfly outline on the paper, cutting it, and opening and decorating it. The butterfly body (page 213) can be stapled in the center of the wings.

Page 214 depicts a moth and a butterfly. Let the children color the pictures. Discuss the differences the children see between the two.

Butterflies Among the Flowers

Cut the jagged edge. Fold at the line. Color the grass green. Draw flowers sticking up from the grass. Color the butterflies, too, to show them sipping nectar from the flowers.

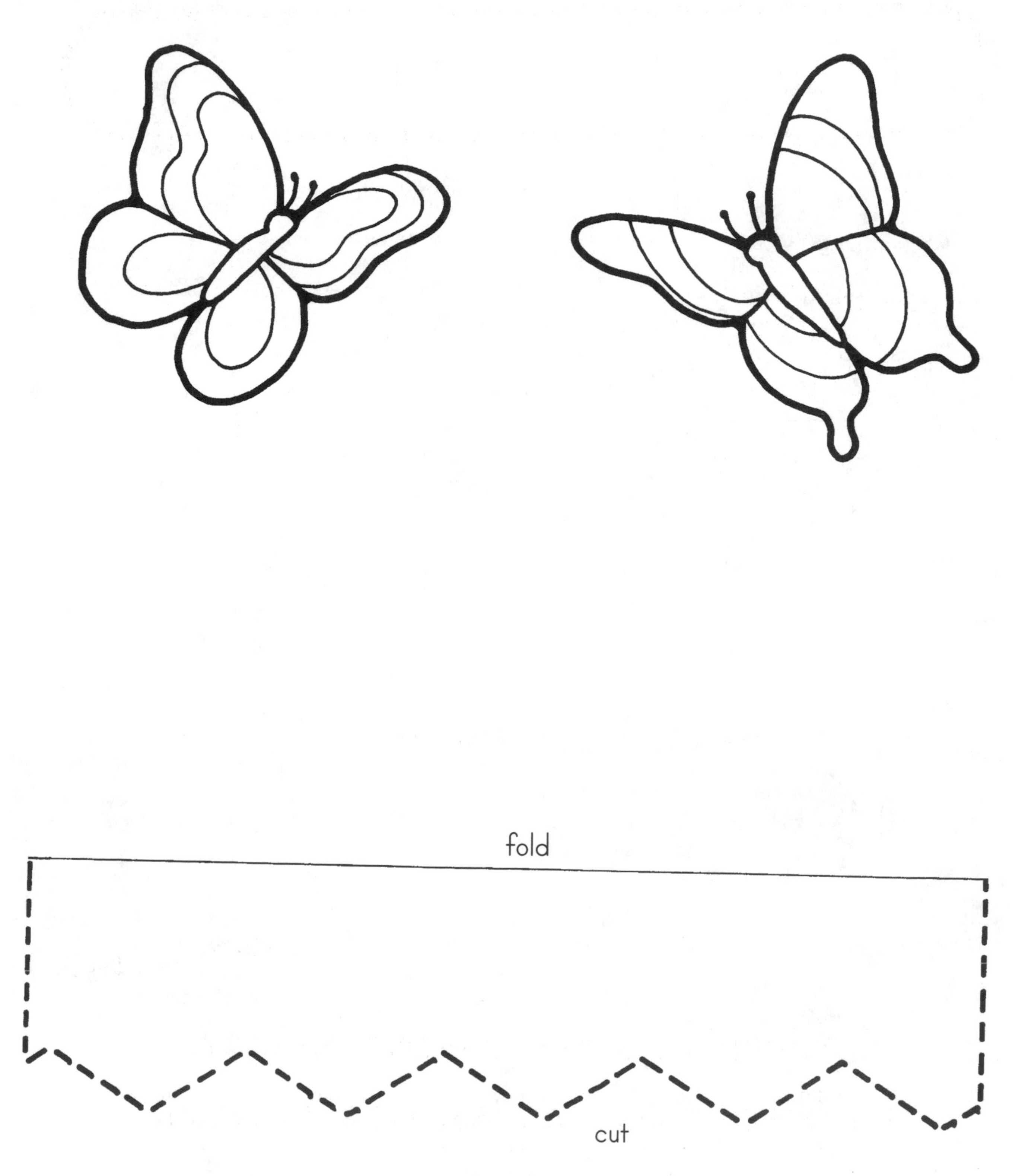

Caterpillars

Color and cut out the caterpillar strip. Fold it like an accordion. Draw eyes on the caterpillar. Color the picture. Glue the caterpillar to the tree branch.

Caterpillars are always hungry.
They eat fruit, leaves, and flowers.

Beautiful Butterflies

Cut out the butterfly. Use liquid starch to "paint" bits of colored tissue onto the butterfly's wings.

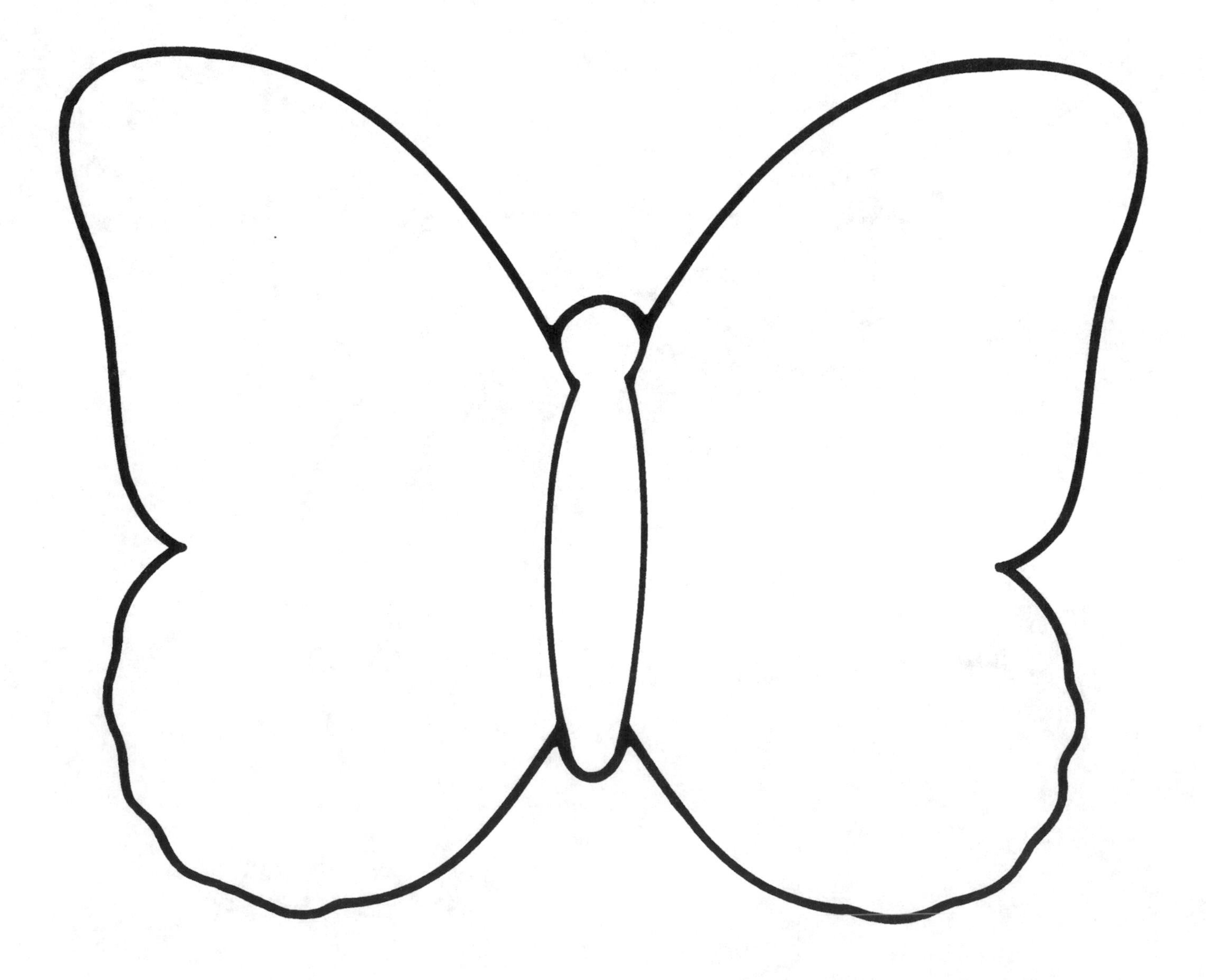

Making a Butterfly

Fold a sheet of 9" x 12" (22.5 cm x 30 cm) paper in half. Draw an outline of half a butterfly. Cut out the butterfly and decorate it with crayons. Color and cut out the butterfly body (below). Glue it to the wings you made.

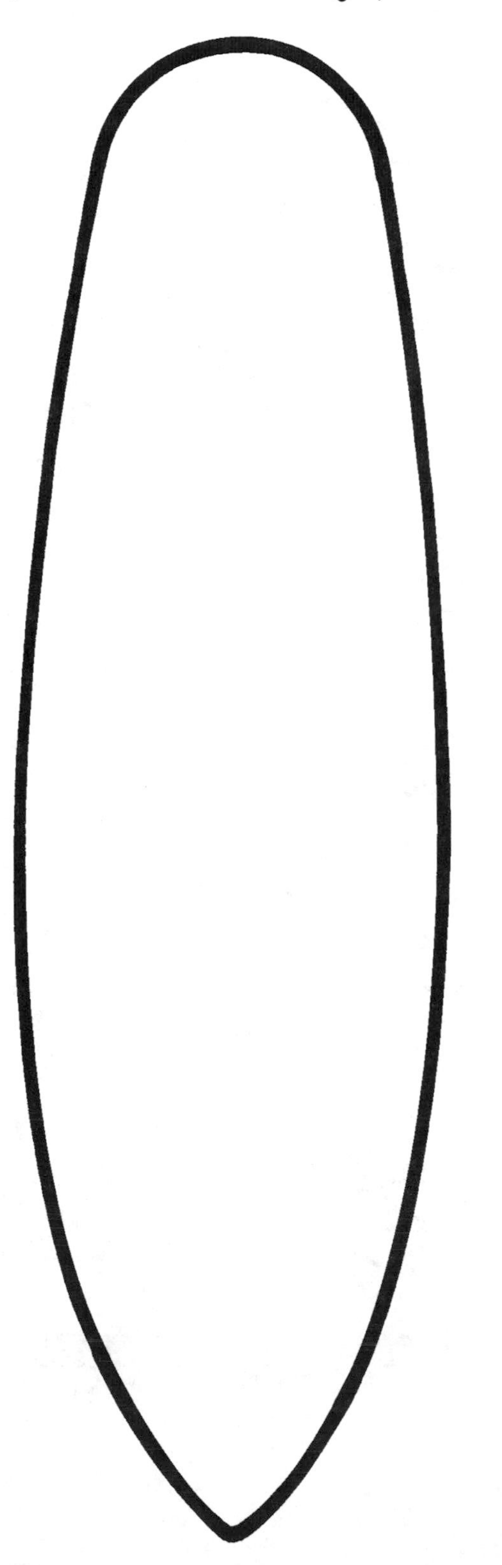

body

Moths and Butterflies

Look at the pictures. Compare the butterfly and the moth.

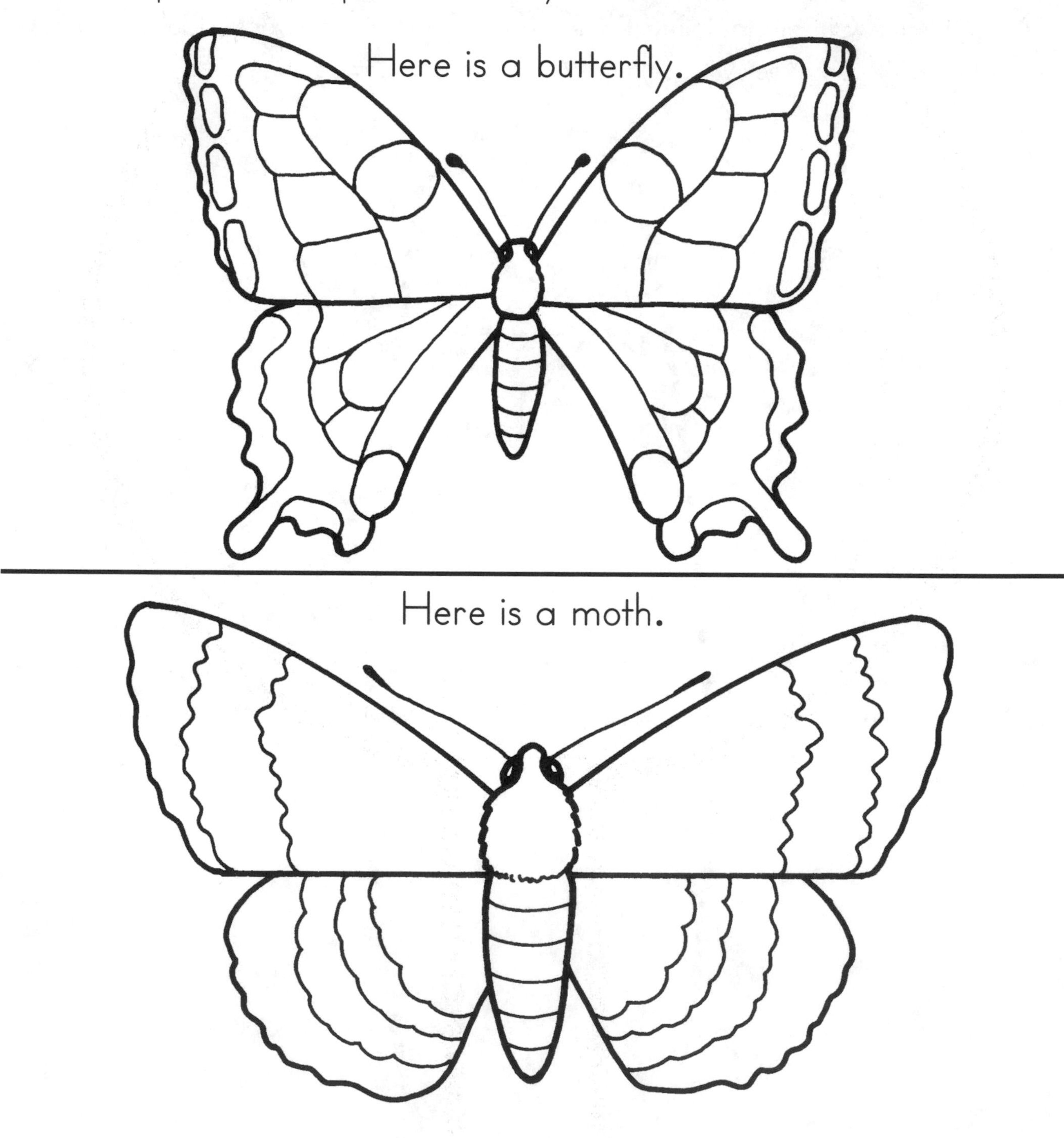

What differences do you see?

Insects

Insects

Objectives:

Each child will learn . . .

- how insects are alike and different.
- about common insects.

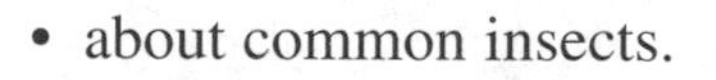

- about helpful and harmful insects.

Discussions:

As a group, the class can discuss . . .

- insect types and where they live.
- similarities among insects.
- differences in insects.
- how insects help.
- how insects harm.

Activities:

Let the children draw a bug under the magnifying glass (page 215). Remind them that the bug should be large!

Provide each child with page 217 and crayons. Read the words aloud and instruct the children to follow along. Color each section as you read it.

Talk about ways that insects differ from one another. Instruct the children to color the sections on page 218 and then cut the strips from the bottom of the page and paste them in place around the shape to complete the activity.

Guide the children as they draw and color a ladybug (page 219) in the circle.

Discuss with the children how some insects are pests and that others can cause damage. For example, moths might eat holes in our wool sweaters. Give each child a strip of wool to use for a scarf in the picture on page 220 after they have added extras, including small holes in the sweater, and colored the picture.

Encourage the children to color the left and right sides of the butterfly wings (page 221) symmetrically (the same).

What Insects Have

Insects have . . .

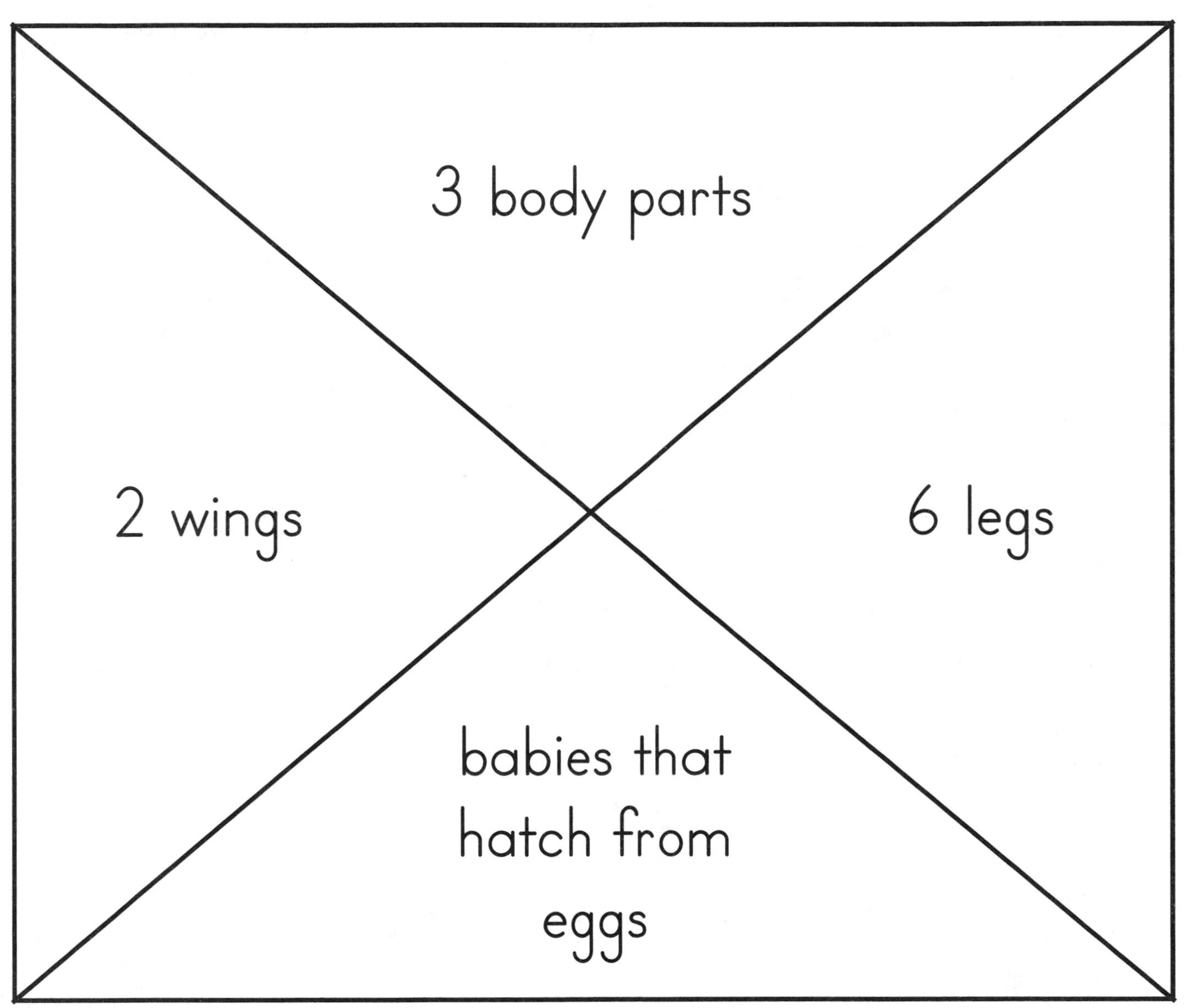

There are many kinds of insects.

They live in many places.

Draw a very small insect here.

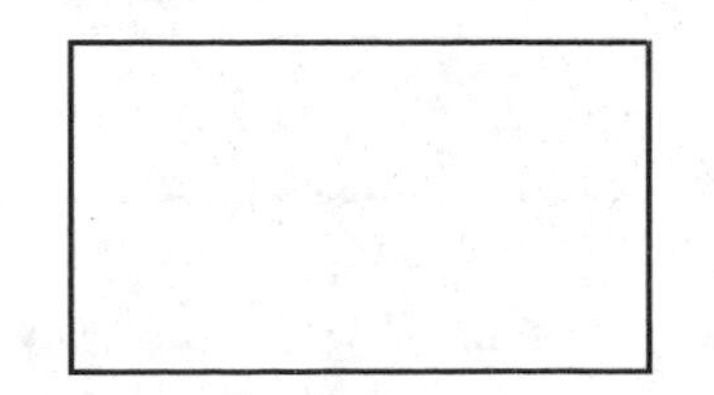

How Are Insects Different?

Insects are different from one another in many ways. Color each section below in a different color. Cut out the words and glue one to each space to show the differences.

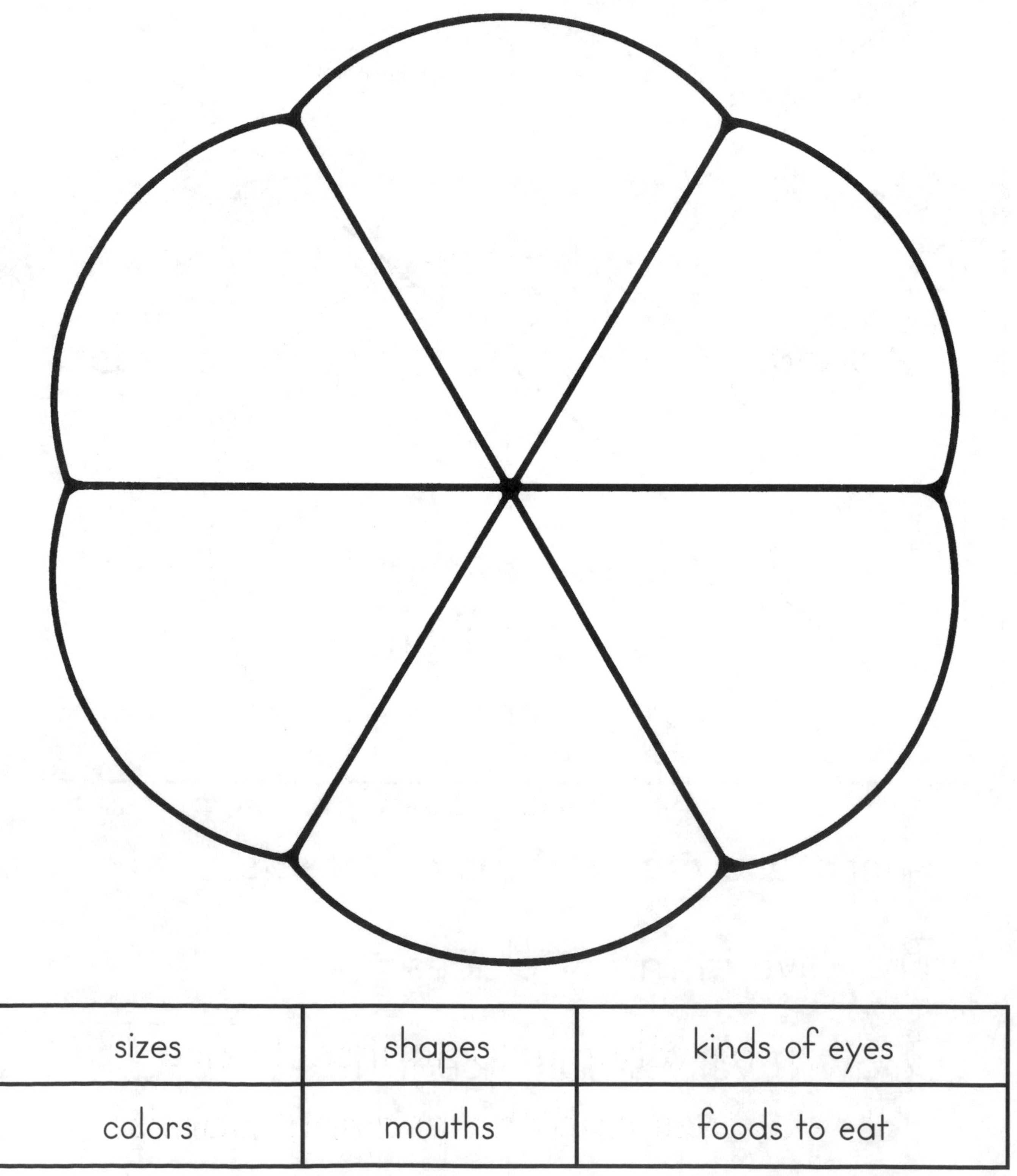

sizes	shapes	kinds of eyes
colors	mouths	foods to eat

Helping Bugs

Some insects help us. Draw a ladybug, using the circle for its body. Ladybugs are helping bugs.

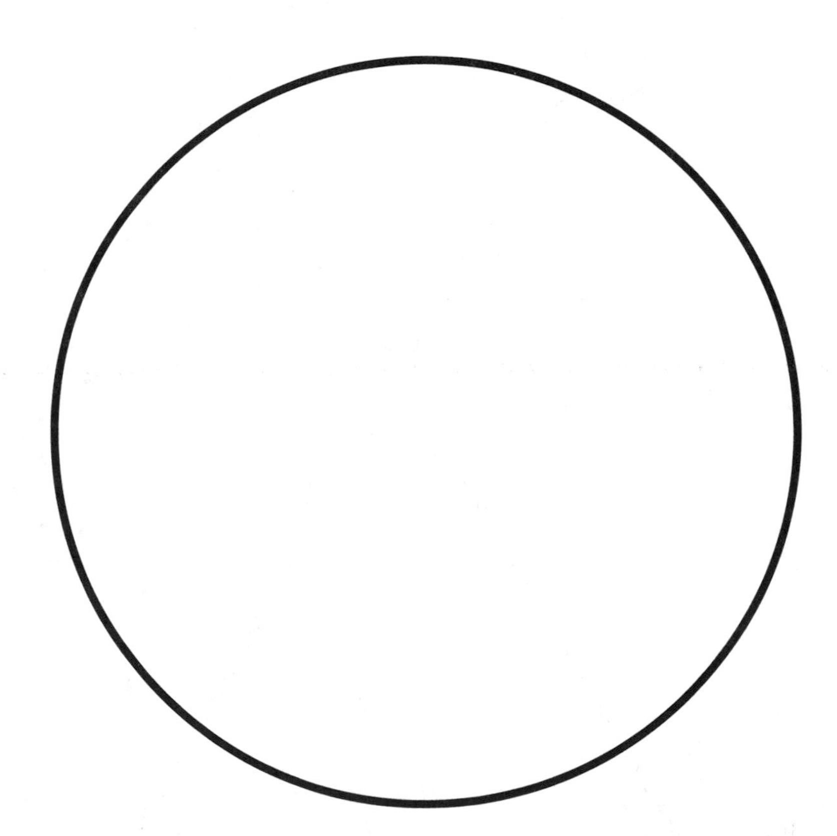

Some other helping insects are honeybees and the praying mantis.

Harmful Bugs

Some insects are harmful. For example, moths can eat holes in our sweaters. Color the person. Draw holes in the person's sweater.

Some other harmful insects are grasshoppers, fleas, lice, cabbage worms, and boll weevils.

Insects All Around Us

Many insects live near us. Some insects we often see are ants, moths, flies, ladybugs, wasps, crickets, mosquitoes, and fireflies. We also see many butterflies. Color each side of this butterfly's wings to match the other side.

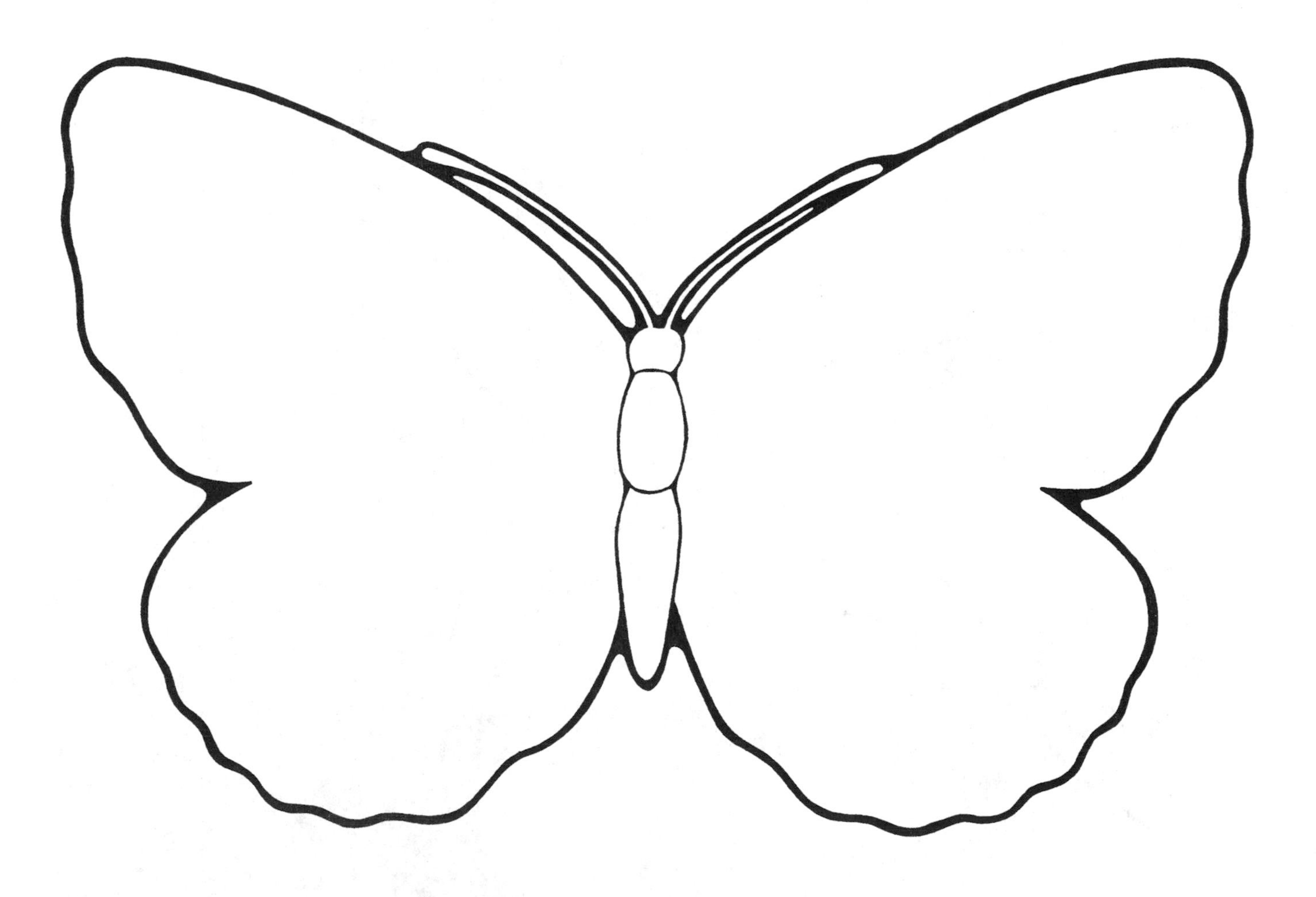

Birds

Birds

Objectives:

Each child will learn . . .

- how birds are alike.
- how birds are different.
- why birds are different.
- kinds of birds: perching, climbing, scratching, night-flying, swimming, wading, running.

Discussions:

As a group, the class can discuss . . .

- how birds are alike.
- how birds are different.
- why birds are different.
- different kinds of birds.

Activities:

Each child is given the bird patterns from page 224 to trace and cut from an appropriate color of paper. (If this is too difficult for the children, the teacher may certainly do this ahead of time.) Help the child to fold the wings and to staple them to the bird. Attach a cut orange beak and use a white hole reinforcement for the eye. The bird can be used for decoration.

Provide each child with prepared brown or black "telephone pole" (page 225) to fold and staple. Help the child to draw a woodpecker head (draw around thumb and add a beak). Color and cut out the woodpecker and glue it into the opening in the pole. Glue the bird and pole to another sheet of paper and glue the sentence strip below it.

Provide each child with page 226, brown paper, glue, and crayons. Let the child color the picture. Then, help the child to tear small bits of brown paper and glue it to the owl's breast to make it appear covered with feathers.

Provide the child with a copy of page 227. Instruct the children to color the duck and water. Help them to glue real feathers to the duck's tail.

Each child is given a copy of page 228, crayons, colored paper, scissors (if able to cut), and glue. Instruct them to color the picture as is. Then help them to cut eggs and leaves from the paper, gluing them to the nest and branch. If desired, also provide the children with bits of straw and string to glue onto the nest to give it texture.

Colorful Birds

Cut out the patterns. Trace the bird and wing onto colored paper and cut them out. Trace the beak onto orange paper and cut it out. Glue the pieces together onto another sheet of paper. Attach a hole reinforcement for the bird's eye. Glue the sentence strip below the bird.

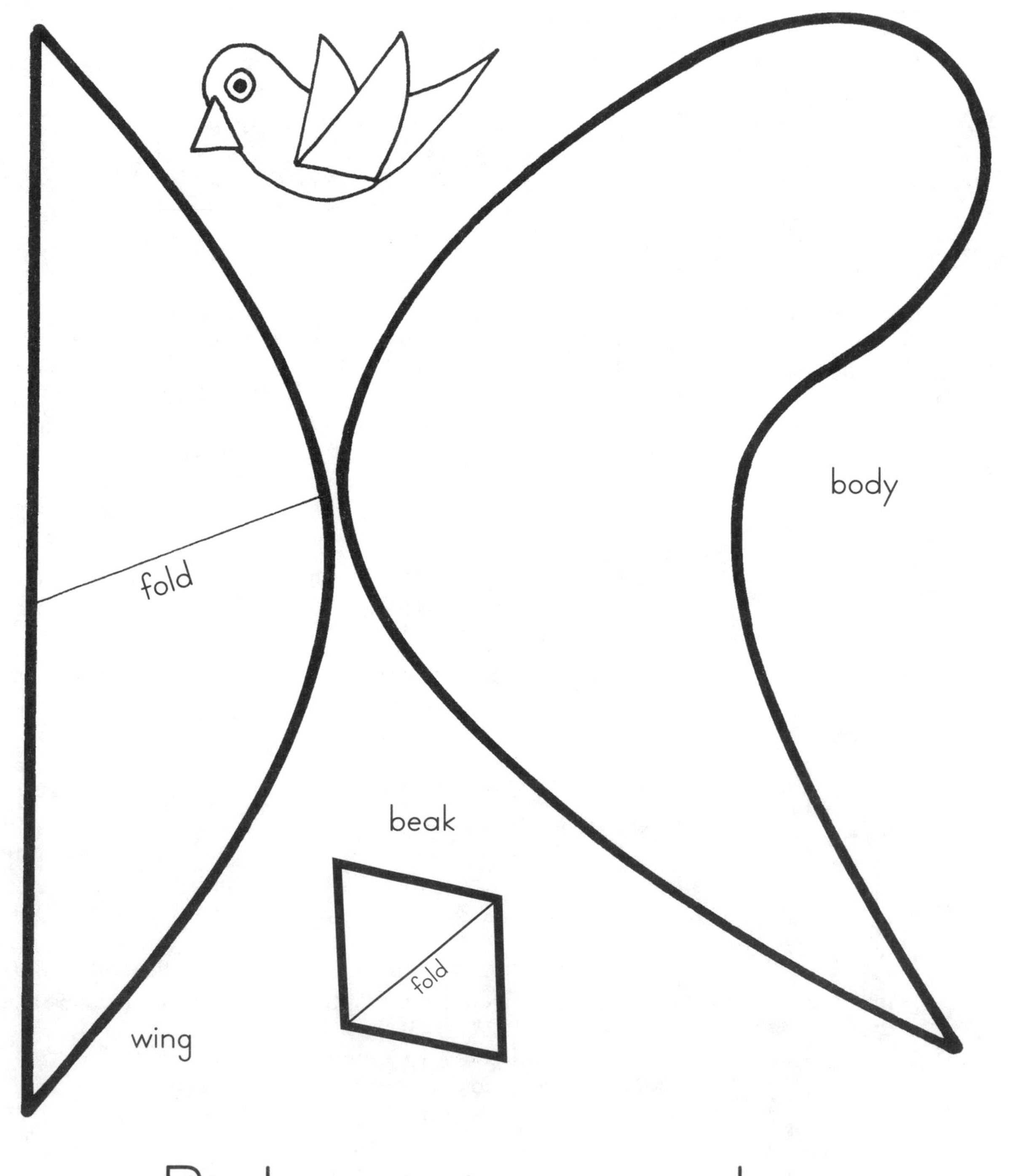

Birds come in many colors.

Woodpecker

Draw a woodpecker head on a separate sheet of paper. To make the head, trace around your thumb and add a beak. Trace the telephone pole pattern onto brown paper. Cut it out, also cutting the hole. Glue the woodpecker head through the hole. Fold the pole back where shown. Glue the pole and bird to another paper and glue the poem strip below it.

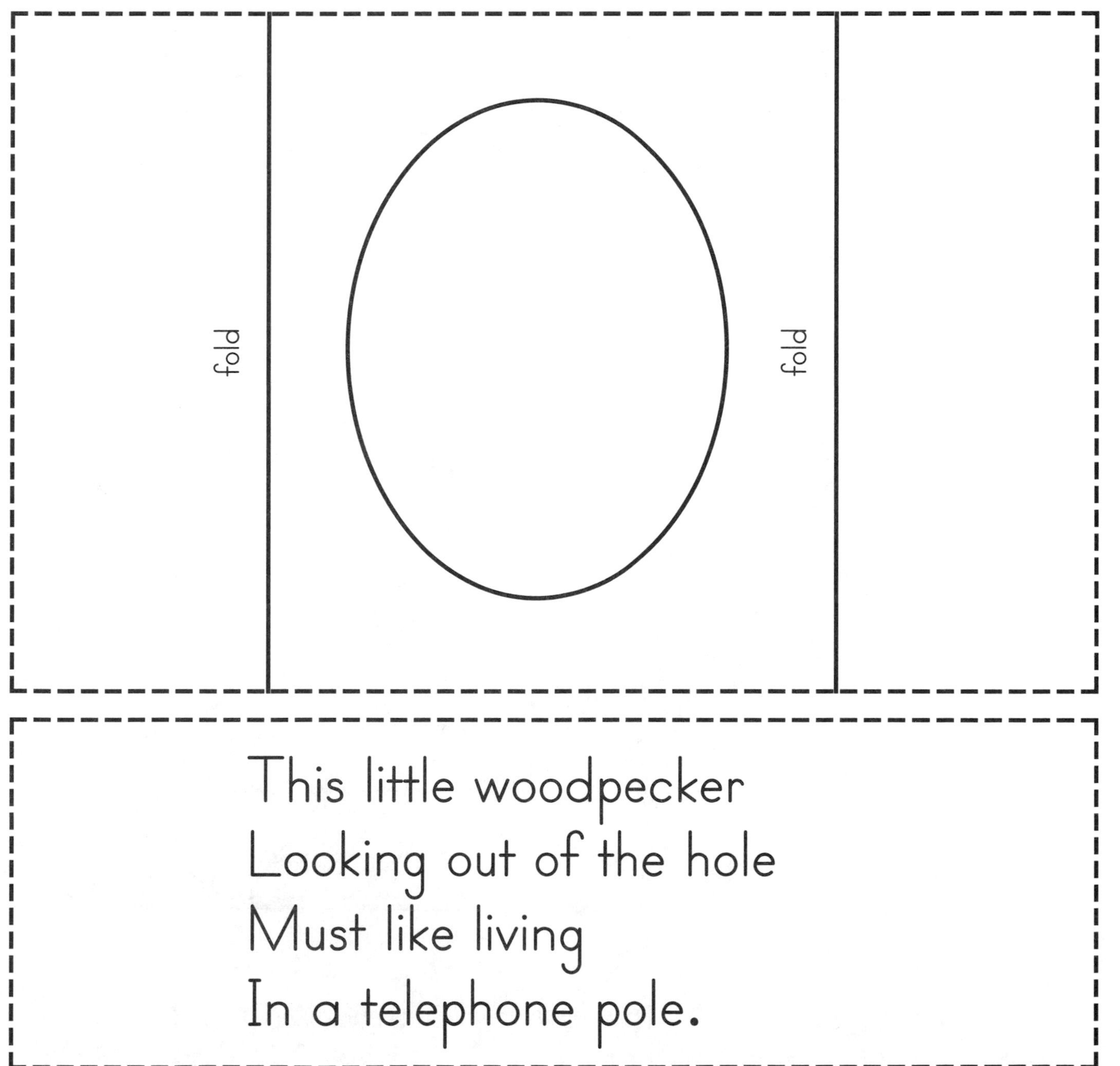

This little woodpecker
Looking out of the hole
Must like living
In a telephone pole.

Owls

Color the owl. Tear bits of brown paper and glue it to the owl's breast.

Owls have good eyes to see at night.

Ducks

Color the picture. Glue feathers to the duck's tail.

Ducks have webbed feet for swimming.

Eggs in a Nest

Color the picture. Cut eggs from colored paper and glue them into the nest. Cut leaves from green paper and glue them on the branches.

Birds make many kinds of nests. They lay their eggs in the nests to keep them safe.

Water

Water

Objectives:

Each child will learn . . .

- the source of water.
- the uses for water.
- how water is life-giving.
- how water helps and harms.

Discussions:

As a group, the class can discuss . . .

- the source of water.
- water's life-giving quality.
- how we use water.
- what lives in water.
- how water helps us.
- how water can harm.

Activities:

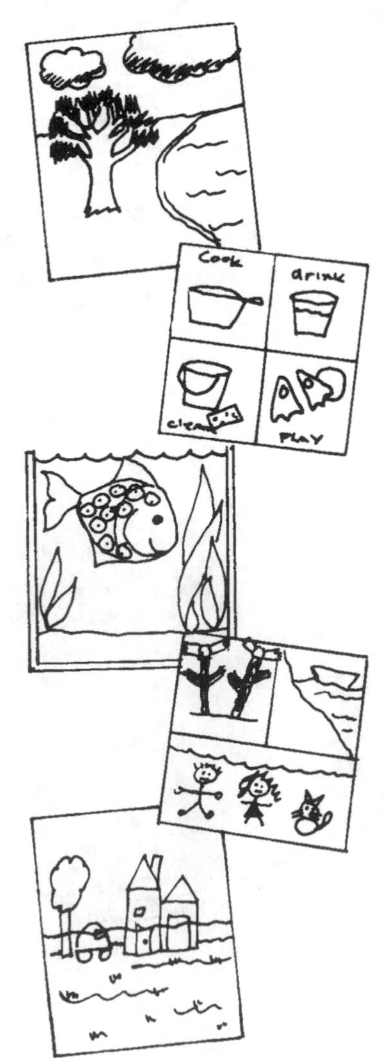

Show the children how to use a combination of blue, purple, and green to color the water on both the cover sheet (page 229) and page 231. On page 231, some black can be added at the bottom of the rain clouds. Fat yarn pieces or cut bits of felt can be glued to the tree to make the leaves.

Provide each child with a copy of page 232. Discuss with the children some uses for water. Instruct them to color a use in each box. A small piece of sponge can be glued to the picture in the cleaning box to provide a tactile experience for the children.

Distribute page 233, crayons, glue, and sequins. Instruct the children to color the picture. When finished, dab glue on the fish and place sequins on the glue to make the fish's scales sparkle.

Provide the children with page 234, crayons, green yarn, and glue. Help the children to understand what needs to be in each space on the work sheet (growing plants in the first space, water filled to the boat's level in the second space, and people and animals swimming in the water in the bottom space). Yarn can be glued to make growing green plants in the first space. You might even cut a slit in the bottom of the section and let the children pull the yarn through the slit to make the plant grow before their eyes.

Discuss with the children the dangers of flooding and drowning. Tell them about water safety. Then let them draw a picture on page 235, showing water that has flooded someone's home.

Water from Rain

Use blue, purple, and green crayons to color the water. Color raindrops, too. Add black crayon to the bottom of the rain clouds. Glue bits of yarn or felt to the tree's branches to make leaves.

Water comes from rain.

Uses for Water

Think of things we use water for. Read the words in the spaces. Draw a picture in each space to show how we use water.

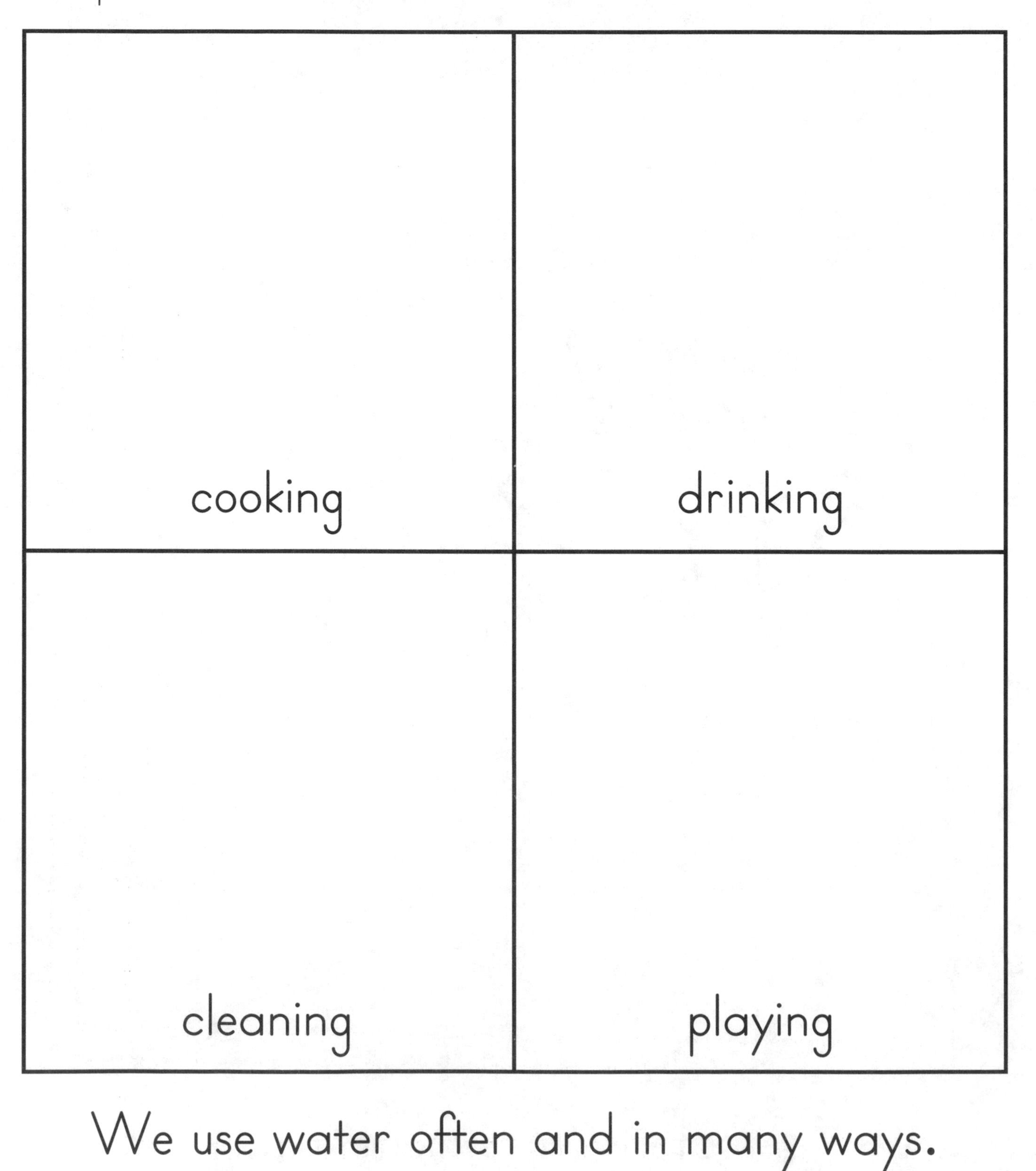

We use water often and in many ways.

Water Homes

Color the picture. Glue sequins onto the fish to make it sparkle.

Water is a home for some animals.

Water Helps

Color growing plants in the first space. Color water up to the bottom of the boat in the second space. Color people and animals swimming in the water in the bottom space.

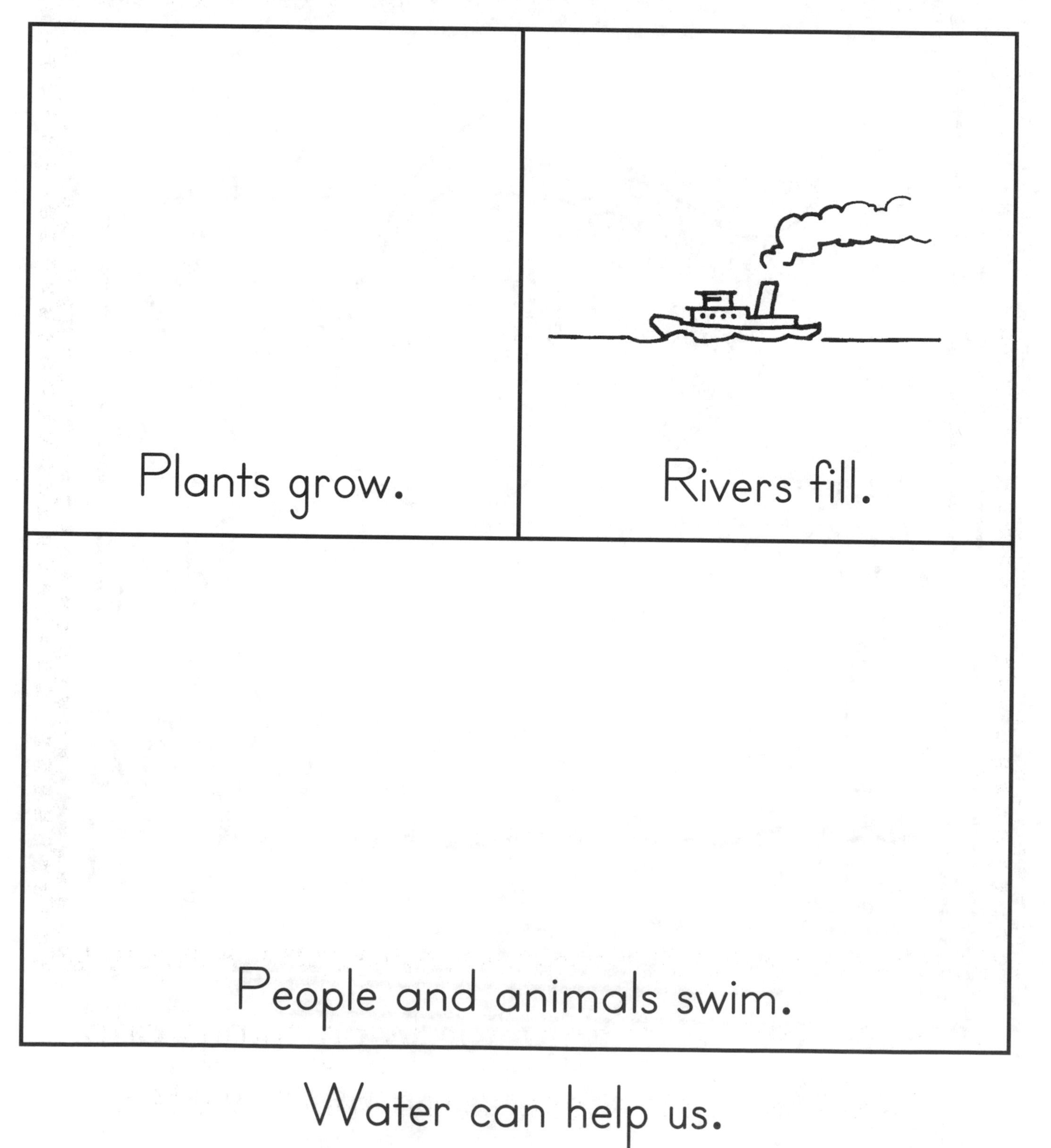

Water can help us.

Water Can Harm

Sometimes too much water can cause problems. Color a flood scene in the space below.

There can be danger for living things and property when there is too much water.

Money

Money

Objectives:

Each child will learn . . .

- why we have money.
- about different kinds of money.
- how we use money.

Discussions:

As a group, the class can discuss . . .

- what money is.
- why we have money.
- forms of money long ago.
- kinds of money.
- coins and bills and their symbols.
- how we use money.
- where and when we use money.
- how we save money.
- why we save money.
- how family members can make (earn) money.
- why it is important to use money wisely.

Activities:

Distribute page 238. Help the children to fill in the blanks and to color corresponding pictures.

Give each child a folded "store" pattern (page 239) and crayons. After a class discussion about stores, the child can choose a type of store and decorate the outside of the building. Then the goods sold can be drawn inside the store behind the flaps. Help the child to write the name of the store or have the child dictate it to you. Glue the store and sentence strip to another paper.

The children are given a small milk carton (clean and dry) with the top cut off. Also provide them with the pattern from page 240 (with a hole cut in the center as shown), paste, and crayons. With direction, each child can carefully paste the pattern over the top and sides of the carton. Designs and decorations can be added to the sides to form a bank.

Give each child a copy of page 241, crayons, and a variety of coins. With the available coins, show the child how to make a rubbing in the top section of the paper. (Place the coin under the paper and rub a crayon over the area of the coin so that an impression appears.) If the children are able to count and write numbers, instruct them to complete the bottom of the page.

A Little and a Lot

Fill in the blanks. Draw the pictures that go along with the words.

This costs a little money. It is ____________________.	This costs a lot of money. It is ____________________.
What can I buy with $1.00?	What can I buy with $100.00?

Store

Think of a type of store. Cut out the pattern and fold it where shown. On the outside flaps, draw the outside of the store. Open the flaps to draw the inside of the store. Write the name of the store on the blank. Glue the store and sentence strip to another paper.

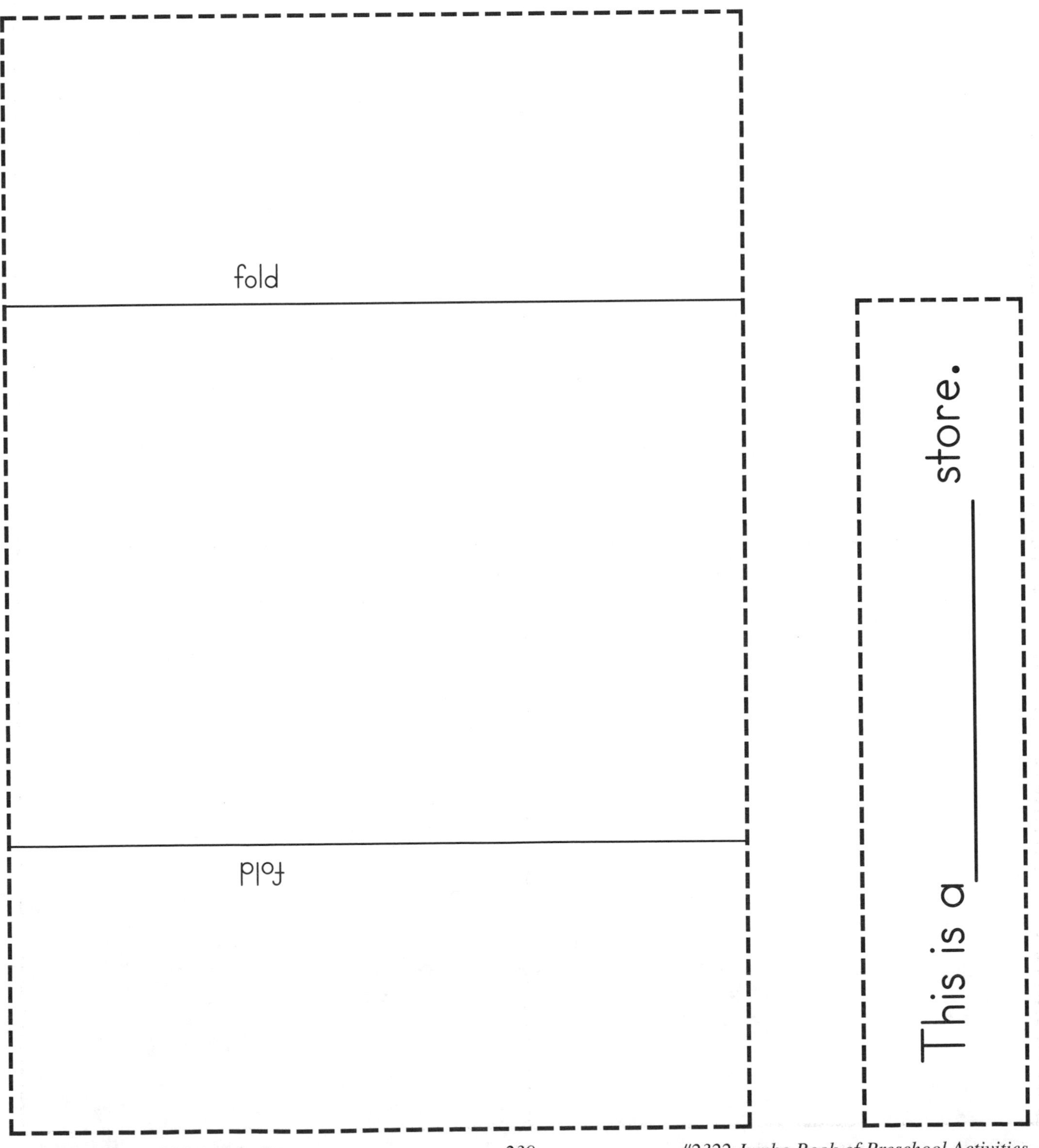

Bank

Cut out the pattern and the hole in the middle. Glue the pattern over a milk carton with the top cut off. Color the bank.

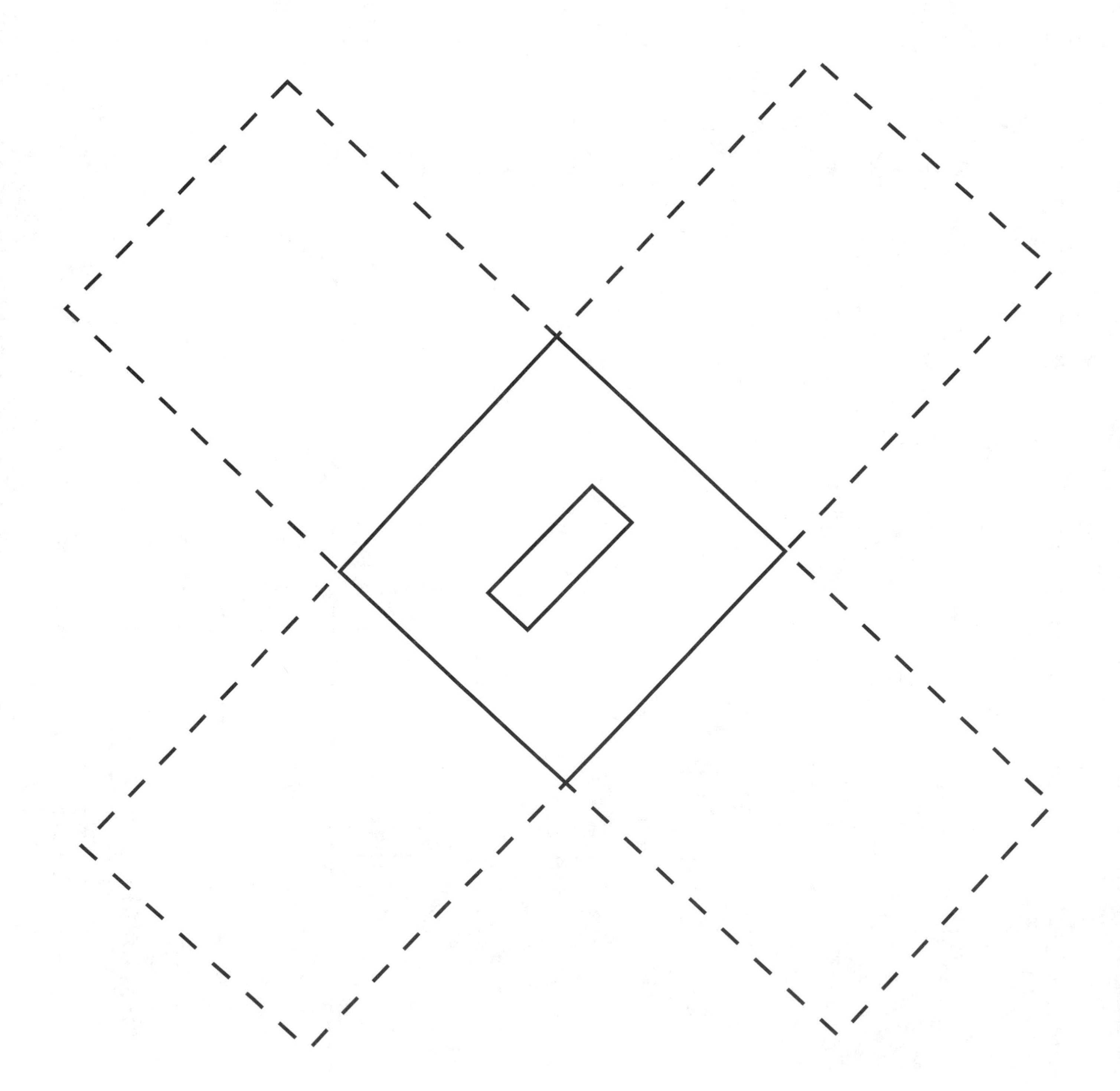

Money Rubbings

Place some coins under the top section of this paper. Rub the paper where the coins are with crayon. Then write the numbers in the blanks below.

rubbings

Here are _______ coins.

Here are _______ coins.

Here are _______ coins.

Working Hands

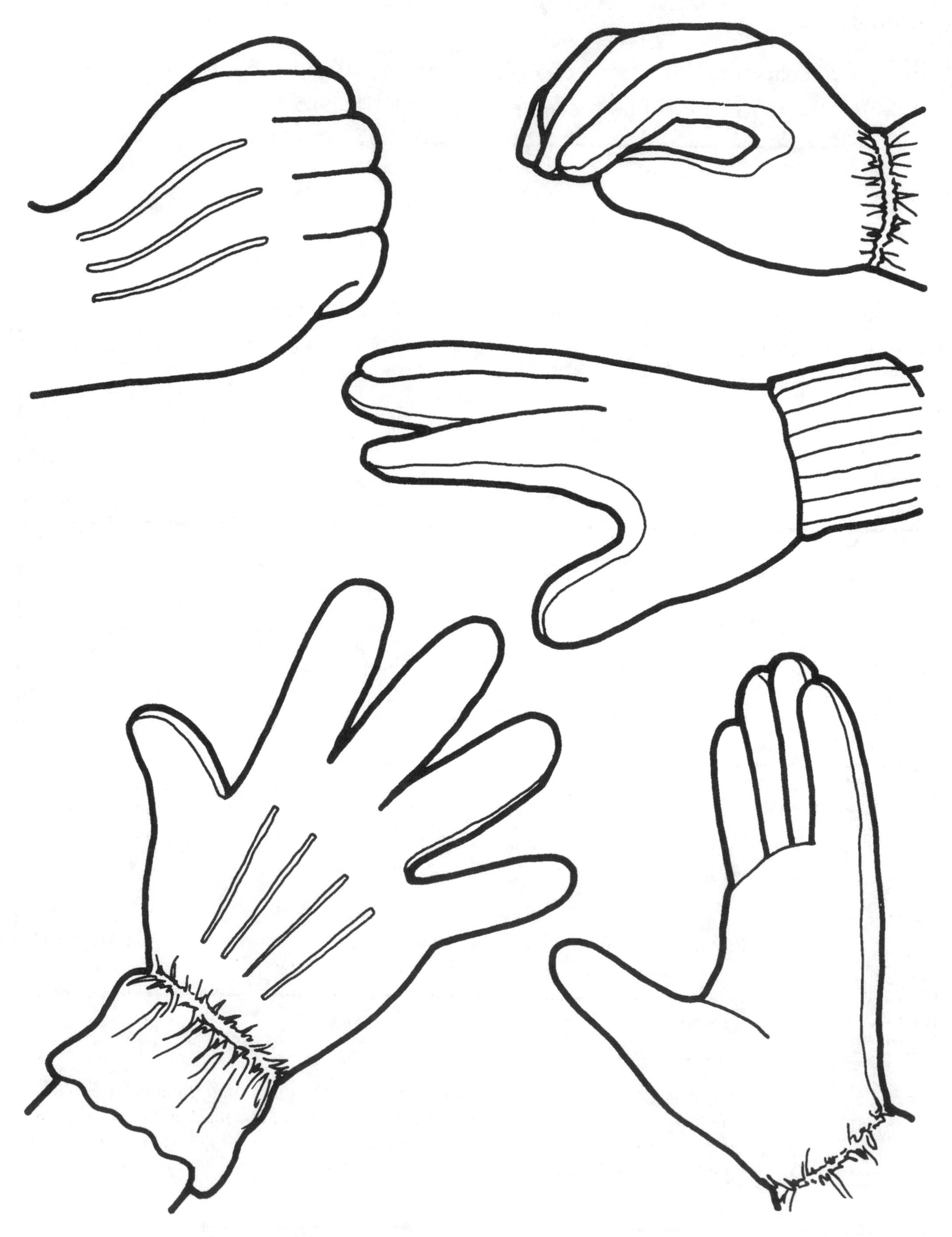

Working Hands

Objectives:

Each child will learn . . .

- about people-to-people jobs.
- about people-to-nature jobs.
- about people-to-things jobs.
- reasons for jobs.
- who does which jobs.

Discussions:

As a group, the class can discuss . . .

- reasons for jobs (careers).
- who can do jobs.
- people-to-people jobs.
- people-to-nature jobs.
- people-to-things jobs.
- jobs parents have.
- jobs children would like to do when they grow up.

Activities:

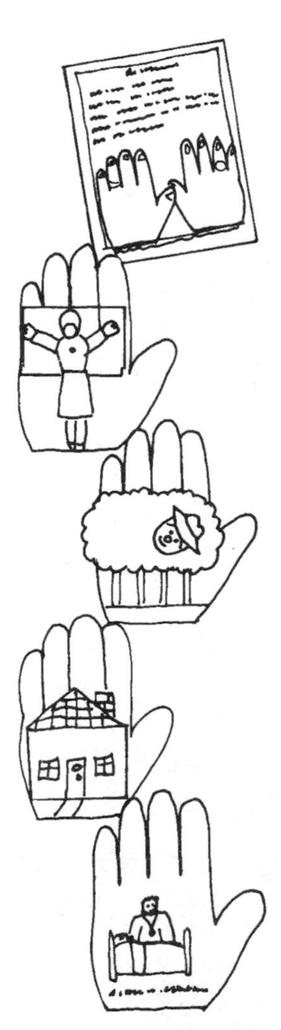

Each child is given a story sheet (page 244). The child can follow as the teacher reads the words. Then discuss what the words mean. The child can decorate the sheet by adding details to the hands and coloring a border.

Provide each child with a copy of page 245 and the teacher and arm patterns (page 303). The child can color the hand, chalkboard, and teacher/arms. Attach the teacher figure to the arms with a paper fastener. Glue the teacher to the hand, keeping the arms free to "write" on the chalkboard.

Provide each child with a copy of page 246 and the tree leaves and ranger head patterns from page 303. The hand, tree trunks, leaves, and head can be colored. Glue the leaves to the trunks. Attach the ranger's head at the nose with a paper fastener as if he is peeking out of the leaves in the trees.

Provide each child with a copy of page 247 and the house pattern from page 302. Instruct the children to color the hand and to glue the house pattern onto it. With direction, the child can use the basic pattern to "build a house" by adding a door, windows, etc.

Give each child a copy of page 248. Discuss with them their dreams for future careers. Help them to write the career in the blank. (The teacher can do this for them, if necessary.) Instruct the children to draw and color themselves at the job they have chosen inside the helping hand pattern.

Good Workers

Read the words. Color the picture.

There are many kinds of work.
Work of all kinds is important.
Children learn to be good workers when they are young so they will be good workers when they are grown.

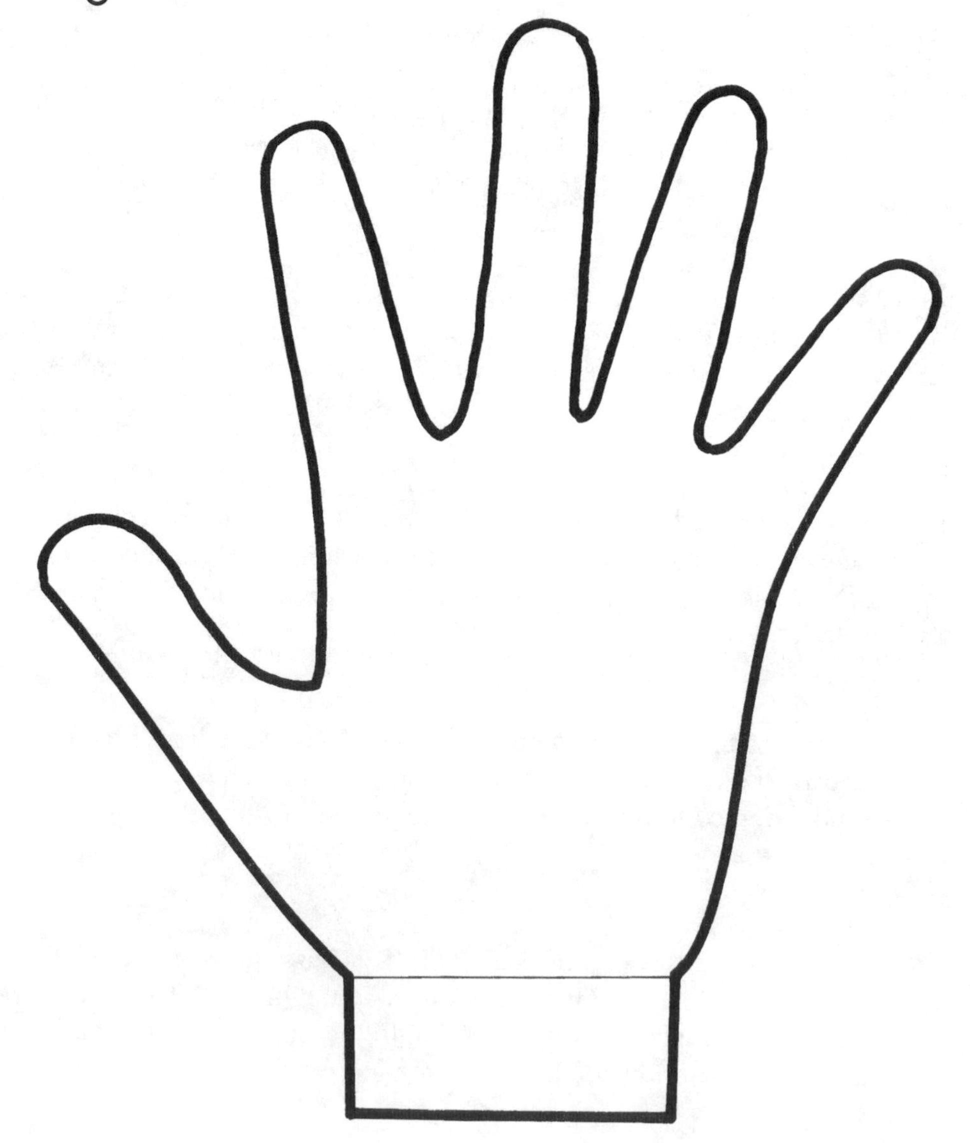

Teachers

Color the hand and chalkboard. Color the teacher and arms (page 303). Attach the arms to the teacher with a paper fastener. Glue the teacher onto the hand.

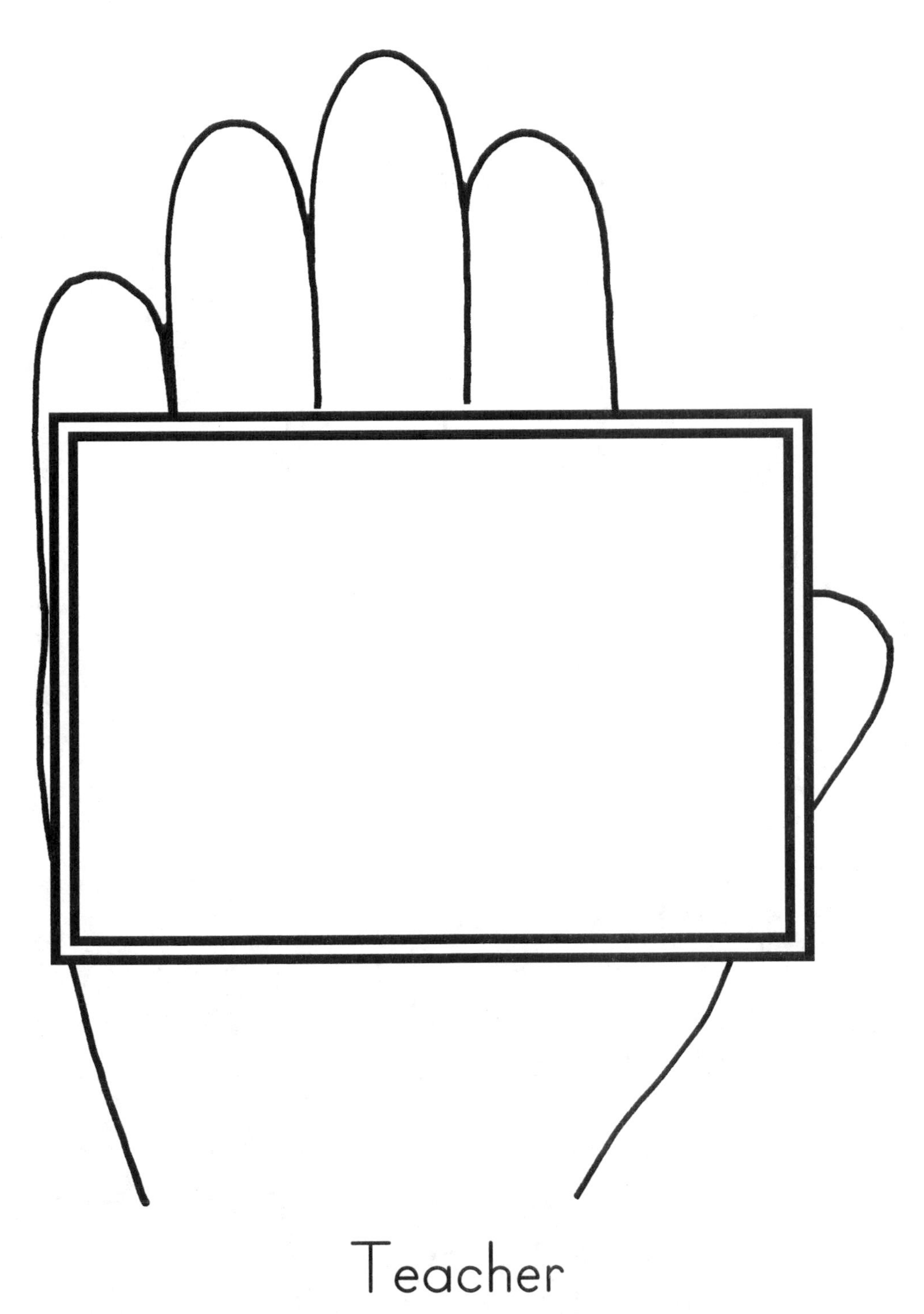

Teacher

Forest Rangers

Color the hand and tree trunks. Color the tree leaves and forest ranger (page 303). Glue the leaves to the trunks. Attach the ranger's head in the leaves, using a paper fastener to make the ranger's nose.

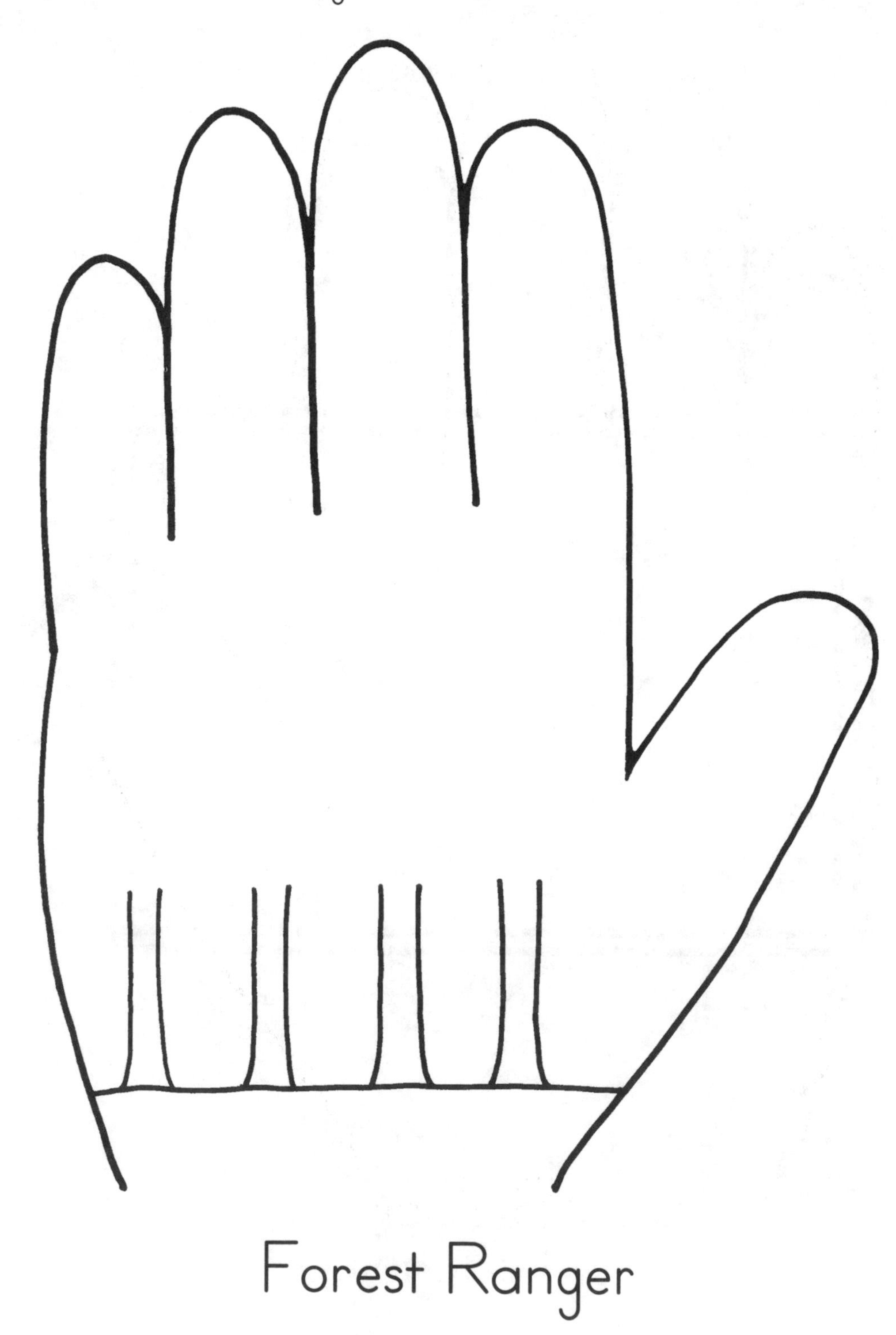

Forest Ranger

Builders

Color the hand. Glue the house frame (page 302) to the hand. "Build" a house by adding a door, windows, and more.

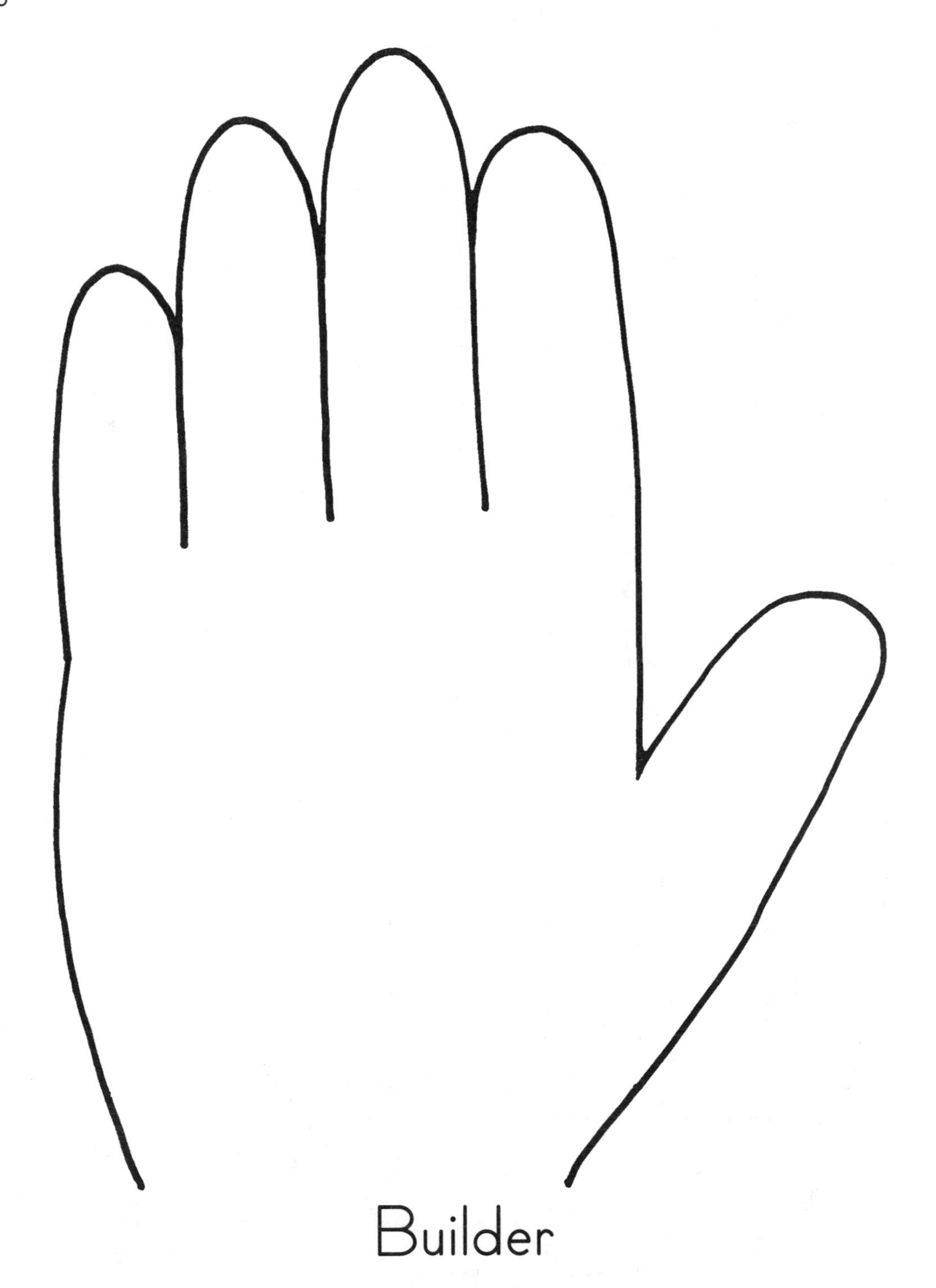

Builder

When I Grow Up

In the blank, write what you would like to be when you grow up. Inside the hand, draw yourself doing that job.

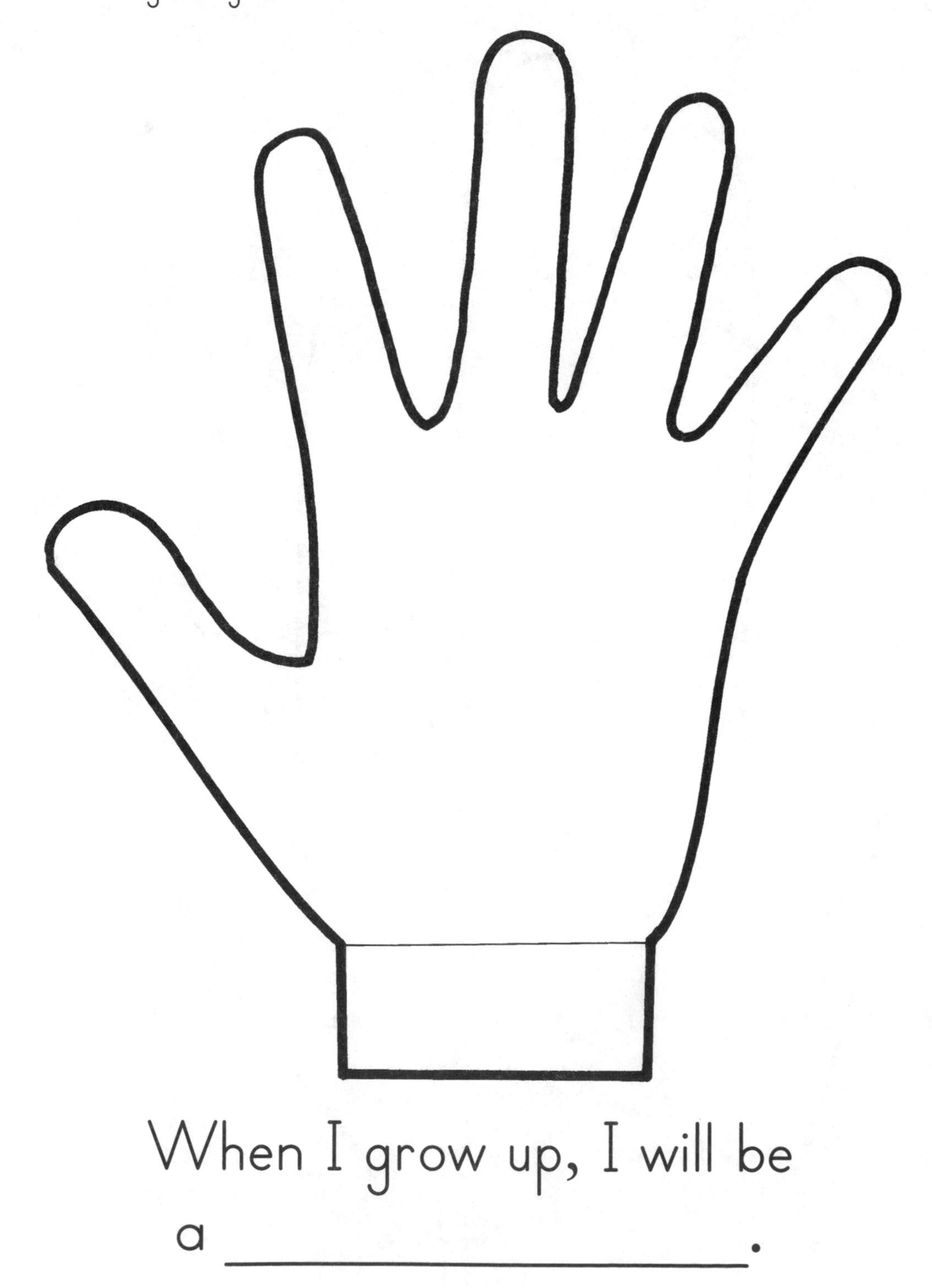

When I grow up, I will be

a _______________________.

Farms

Farms

Objectives:

Each child will learn . . .

- what a farm is.
- why we need farms.
- who works on farms.
- about different kinds of farms.

Discussions:

As a group, the class can discuss . . .

- what a farm is.
- where farms are located.
- why they are important.
- crop farms (what is grown there and why).
- poultry farms (what is raised there and why).
- cattle farms (what is raised there and why).
- dairy farms (what is raised there and why).

Activities:

If desired, Cut open the barn doors on page 249. Glue the barn to another sheet of paper. Let the children color animals inside the barn behind the doors.

Each child is given a farm scene (page 251). After discussion, the child can color the picture according to the directions at the bottom of the page.

Give each child a crop farm sheet (page 252). The child can draw fruits and vegetables in the barn, ready for shipment. Alternatively, let them cut out bits of colored paper to make the fruits and vegetables and glue them on the shelves in the barn.

Provide the children with the poultry farm sheet (page 253) and the hen pattern (page 302). Instruct the children to color the barn, basket, and hen. Attach the hen to its legs with a paper fastener so the hen can move.

Each child is given the cattle farm sheet (page 254). The child can color the picture. Corn kernels may be glued to the sheet as food for the cow.

Supply the children with the dairy farm sheet (page 255) and the cow head/tail pattern (page 302). Instruct the children to color the picture. Then help each child to cut on the dotted line (an adult will probably need to do this) and to add the cow pattern in the slot with a paper fastener.

On the Farm

Read the directions. Color the picture.

Crop Farms

Color the picture. Add fruits and vegetables on the shelves in the barn.

Crop farmers raise many kinds of fruits and vegetables for us to eat.

Poultry Farms

Color the barn and basket. Color the hen (page 302). Attach the hen to its legs with a paper fastener.

Poultry farmers raise many chickens that lay eggs.

Cattle Farms

Color the picture. Glue kernels of corn for the cow to eat.

Cattle farmers (ranchers) raise many animals that we use for meat.

Dairy Farms

Color the cow body and barn. Color the cow head and tail pattern (page 302). Cut the top of the cow at the dotted line. Attach the cow head and tail at the slit with a paper fastener.

Dairy farmers raise cows for milk and milk products.

Transportation

Transportation

Objectives:

Each child will learn about . . .

- transportation on land.
- transportation on water.
- transportation in the air.
- some history of transportation.
- why different kinds of transportation are needed.

Discussions:

As a group, the class can discuss . . .

- the history of ways to travel.
- why better ways were necessary.
- why such a variety of ways are needed.
- a list of ways to travel on land.
- trains and how they are used.
- boats and how they are used.
- planes and how they are used.

Activities:

Supply children with page 258 and crayons. Each child can draw a way to travel, using the wheels on the page.

Provide each child with the four patterns from page 259. Instruct the children to color the boat, sail, sky, and water. Cut the water at the slit. Glue a drinking straw behind the sail and boat to make the mast. The straw should extend below the boat. Insert the straw through the slit in the water to make the boat "sail."

Give each child the garage pattern (page 260). Instruct the child to color the garage. Cut the sides of the garage door and fold it up. Glue the garage (except for the door) to another sheet of paper. Tell the children to color the things that are inside the garage. They can also color a driveway, trees, etc., around the garage. Glue the sentence strip below the garage.

Give each child the train pattern (page 261). Fold the pattern. Let the child color both sides. Show the children how to stand their trains. Push them along a table and make train noises.

Let the children color page 262. Fold the page to make a little book. Read the pages with the children.

Wheels

What moves on wheels? Draw something on these wheels to make a picture of something that moves in this way.

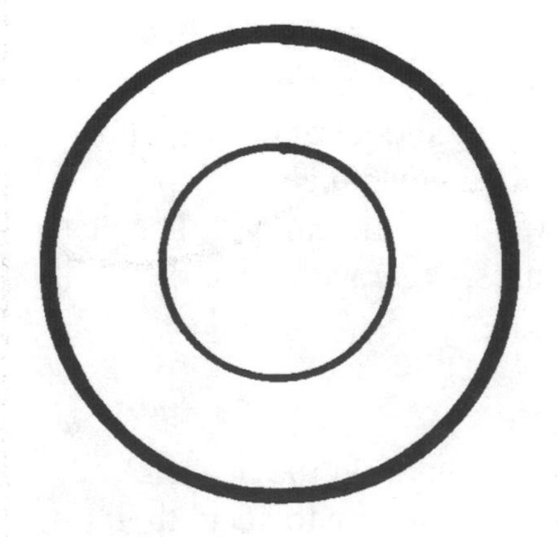

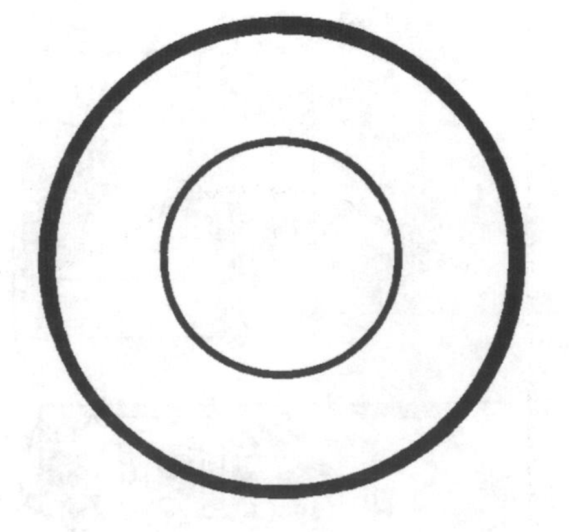

Sailboat

Color and cut out the sail and boat. Color the water and sky. Cut the slit in the water. Glue a straw behind the sail and boat to make the mast. Be sure that the straw sticks out below the boat. Insert the straw through the slit to make the boat sail on the water.

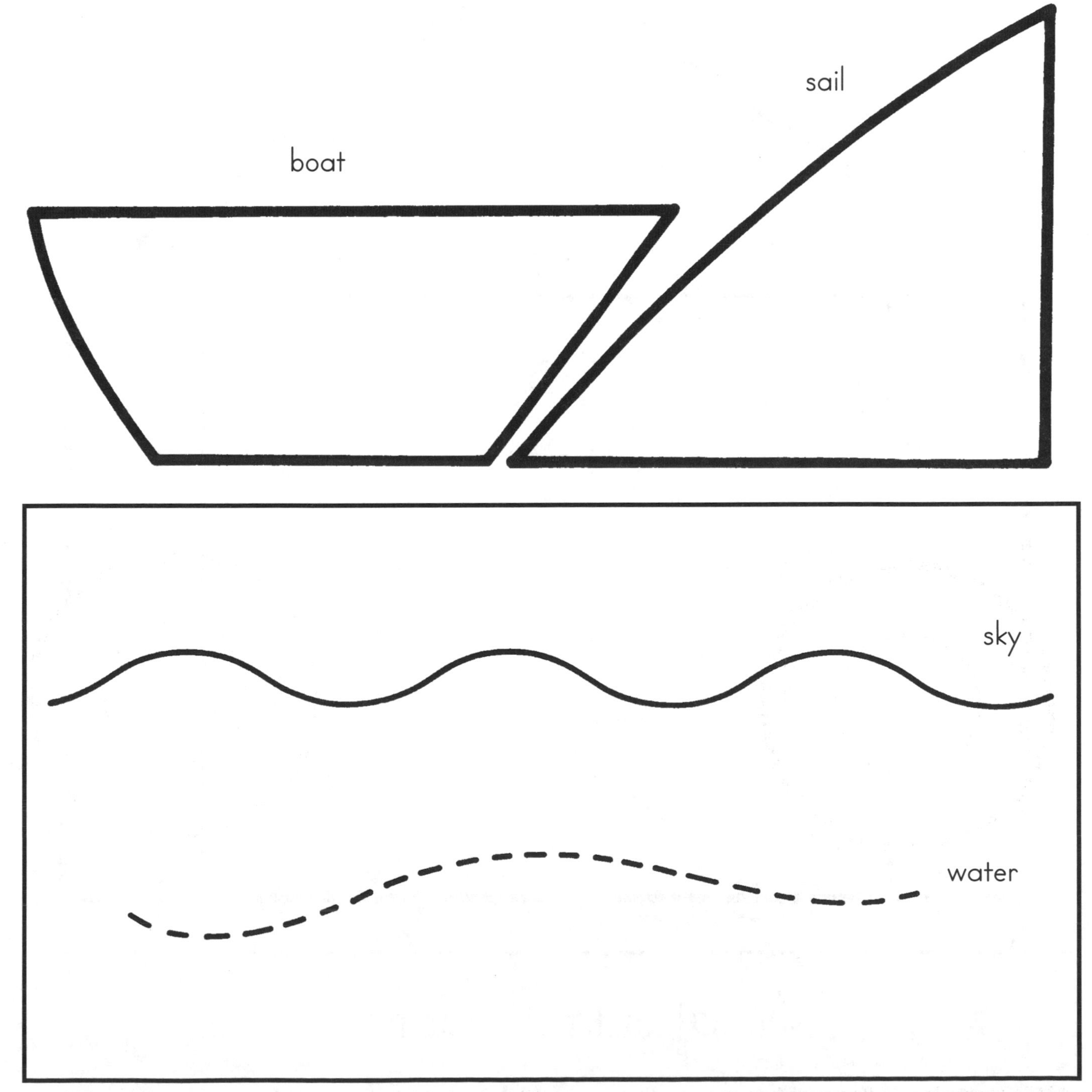

In the Garage

Color and cut out the garage. Cut open the garage door at the sides and fold it up. Glue the garage (except for the door) to another paper. Lift the garage door and draw what is inside the garage. Draw a driveway and other details around the garage, too. Glue the sentence strip below the garage.

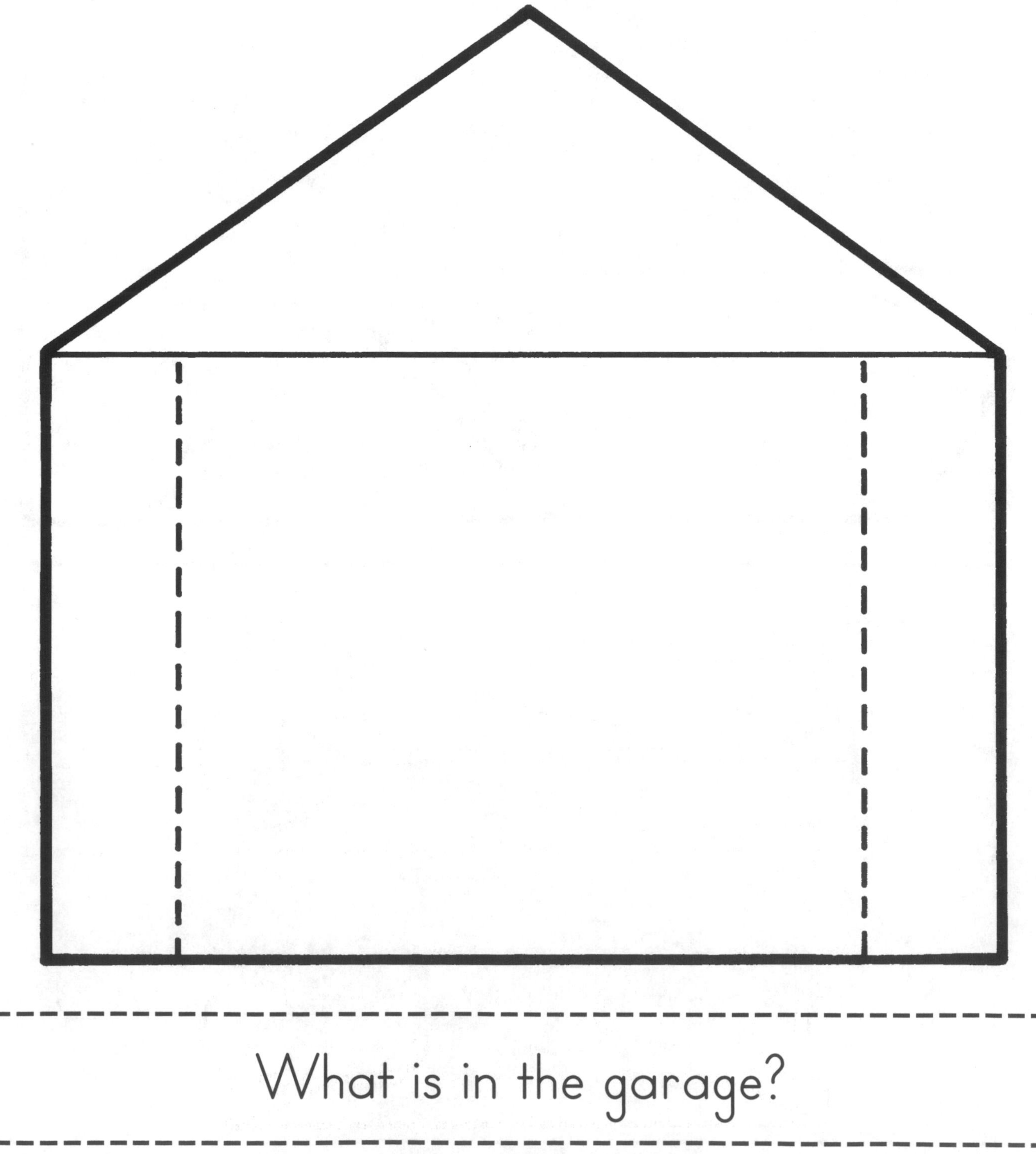

Train

Color both sides of the train and cut it out. Fold the train to make it stand.

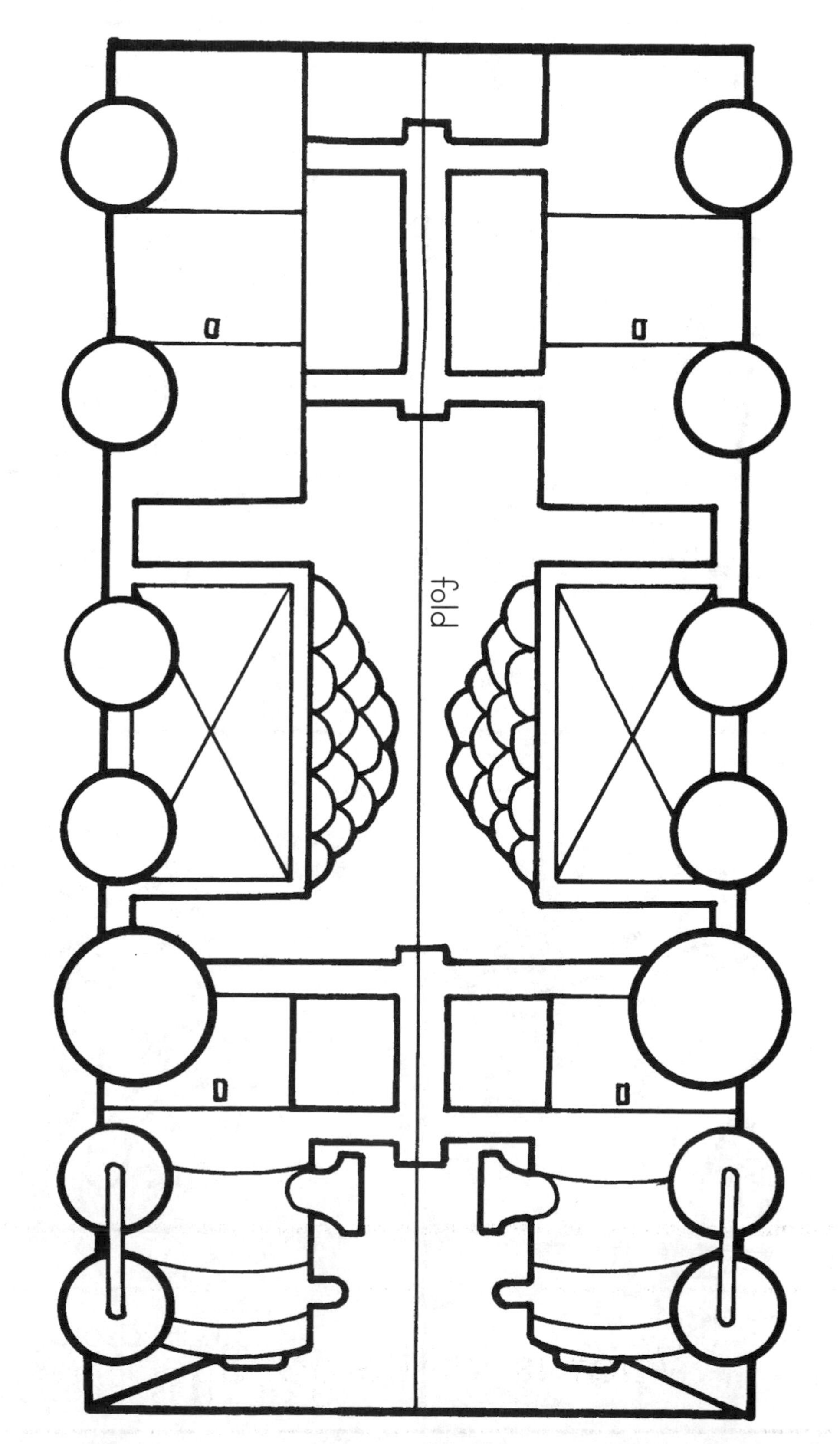

Airplane

Color the airplanes. Fold the page to make a little book.

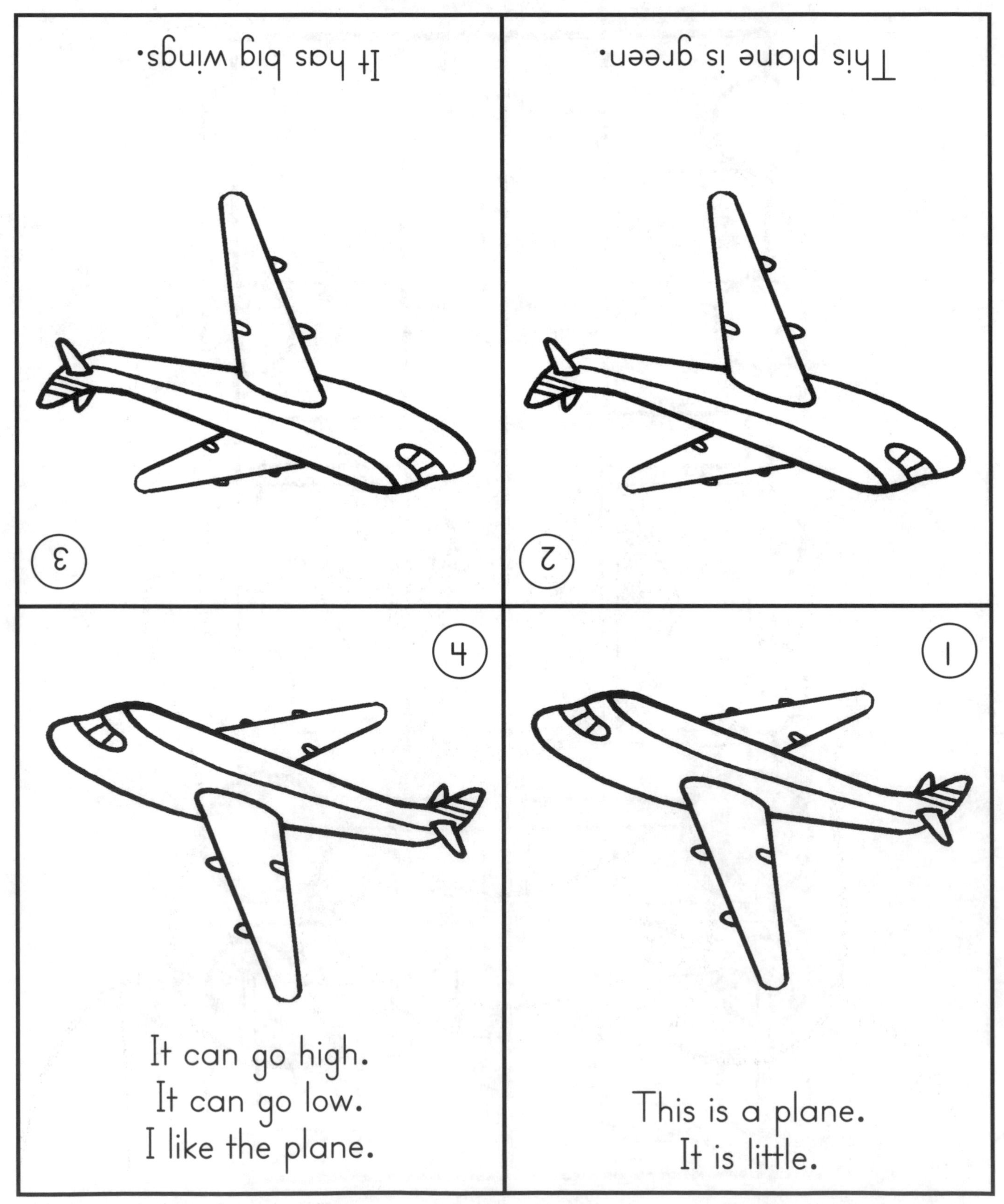

Vacation Time

Vacation Time

Objectives:

Each child will learn . . .

- the meaning of vacation.
- why vacations are important.
- things to do outside.
- activities for indoors.
- about trips away from home.
- ways to help grown ups.

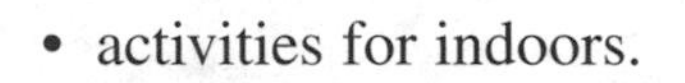

Discussions:

As a group, the class can discuss . . .

- what vacation means and why vacations are important.
- why we need a variety of activities.
- safety for all activities.
- why some time alone is good.
- how helping at home gives everyone more time for fun.

Activities:

Distribute page 265 to the children. Discuss the different kinds of vacations. As you say each word on the sheet, let the children color in the section on their papers, using a different color for each one.

Give each child a copy of page 266. Instruct them to draw at least two activities they can do outside during summer days.

Give each child a copy of page 267. Instruct them to draw at least two activities they can do inside to relax.

Give the children page 268. Instruct them to draw their families inside the car. Read the words to them. Ask them to color the word that names the family trip they would like to take.

Ask each child to draw something he or she can do to help his/her parents at home. Write the word for the child on the blank. Let the children share their work by acting out the task for the class.

Vacation Words

Read the words. Color the sections.

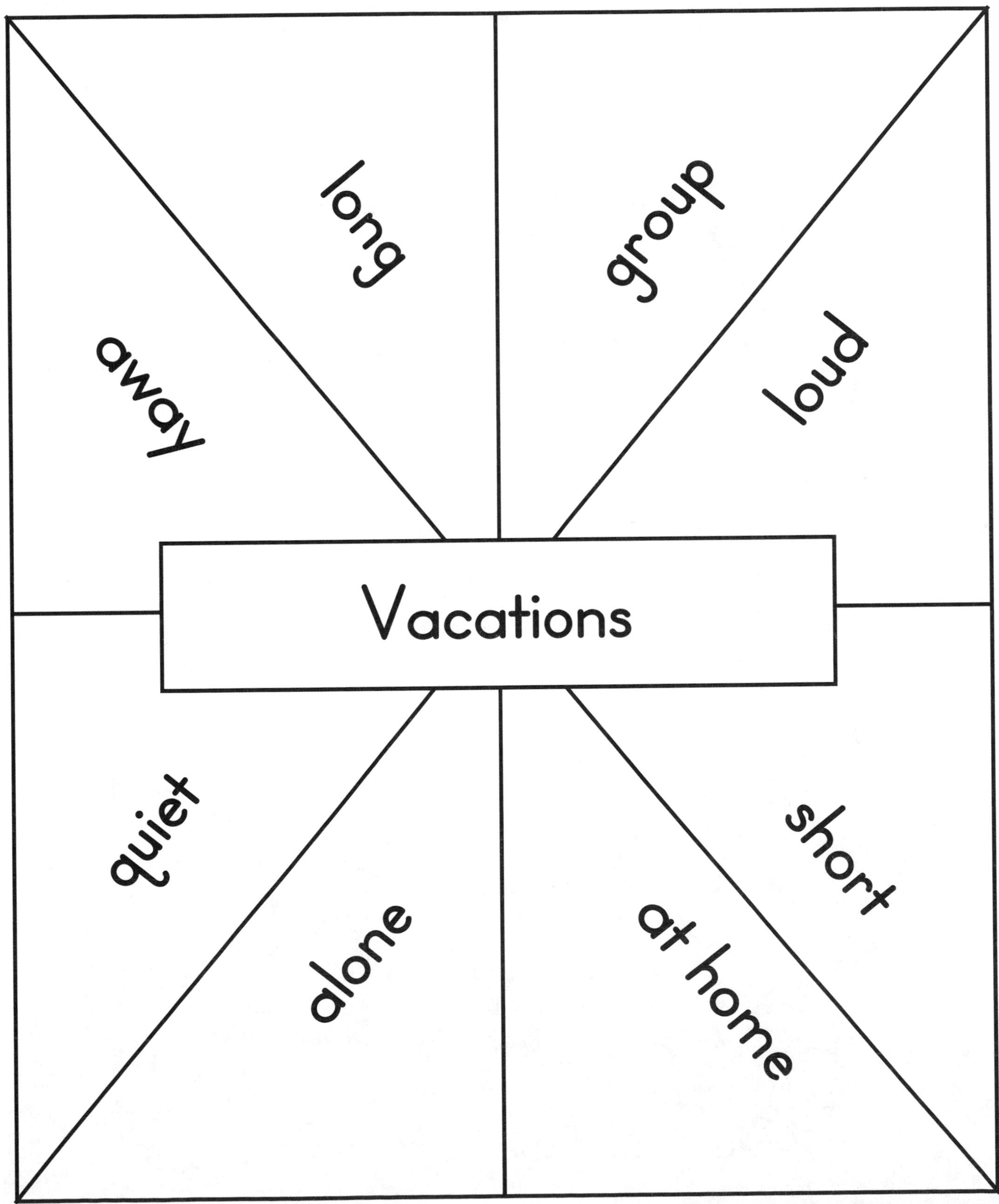

Outside Fun

Inside the sun, draw two or more things you can do outside during your summer days.

Outdoor time can be fun.

Relaxing Indoors

Inside the house, draw two or more things you can do inside to relax.

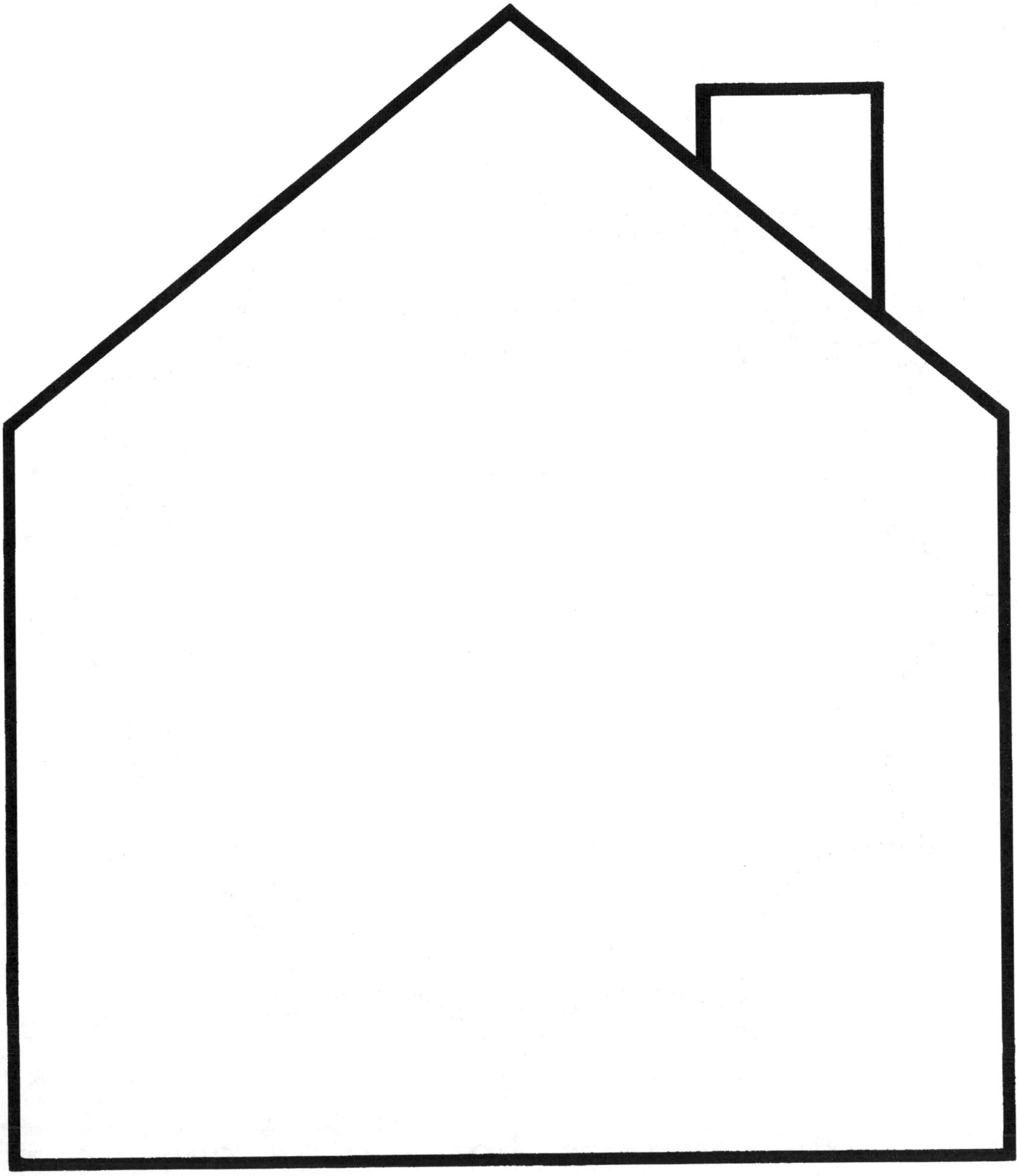

Indoor time helps us to slow down.

Family Trips

Draw your family inside the car. Color the word that names the family trip you would most like to take.

zoo	swimming
park	visiting
library	fishing

Trips give us a change of scenery and a time to enjoy being together.

Helping at Home

Draw something you can do at home to help your parents so they will have more time to play with you!

I can help at home by

____.

Alphabet Activities

When learning about any letter of the alphabet, the activities on the following pages will help. Follow the directions below for the letter you want.

A (page 272): Color the leaf. Tear red, green, or yellow paper and glue it to the apple.

B (page 273): Cut the water line and fold it up. Color the picture.

C (page 274): Draw in the face. Color the picture. Cut out three or four curls (page 298) and paste them around the head.

D (page 275): Color the doll top half and cut on the dotted line. Cut out and color the desired bottom half (page 298). Attach the body with a paper fastener.

E (page 276): Trace and cut out the circles and the right triangle (page 299). Paste them in the correct places to form a train engine.

F (page 277): Color the fish. Draw plants and sand in the aquarium and color the water light blue. Cut the slits above and below the aquarium. Attach wax paper through the slits and tape it in place on the back. This will be the aquarium "glass."

G (page 278): Color and cut out the clown. Glue the clown to a long sheet of paper, leaving space between the top and bottom halves. Draw long lines to connect the top and bottom halves. Fold the sheet down on the lines. Open and close the clown to make him grow.

H (page 279): Color the page to make the capital H a house.

I (page 280): Color the picture. Cut out and attach a spoon (page 299) and a napkin. (Use a piece of an actual napkin.)

J (page 281): Cut out the box at the dotted lines. Fold it up. Color the box. Cut out and color the "jack's" head (page 299). Accordion-fold a strip of paper (page 299) and glue it behind the head. Glue the other end of the strip inside the box. Close the lid. When you open it, the jack will jump out.

K (page 282): Color the picture. Add a yarn tail.

L (page 283): Color the lollipop stick and the lollipop (page 300). Wrap the lollipop in plastic wrap. Draw a hand holding the stick. Glue the lollipop to the stick.

M (page 284): Color the mouse. Add a yarn tail.

Alphabet Activities *(cont.)*

N (page 285): Draw a funny nose on the face. Draw and color the other features, too.

O (page 286): Trace the patterns from page 300 onto orange and brown paper. Cut them out. Color the owl and cut the slit at its bottom. Glue the brown triangle to the owl's head. Glue the orange triangle to its face for a beak. Fold the feet and insert them through the slit. Attach the feet with a brass fastener so they move.

P (page 287): Cut and color the pattern as in the directions for letter J (page 281). Draw a present inside the package.

Q (page 288): Color the quilt in beautiful colors. (If desired, delete the quilt lines when duplicating the page and let the children draw their own patterns or glue fabric squares to the page to make their quilts.)

R (page 289): Color the rooster and cut the slit at its bottom. Color and cut out the feet (page 300). Secure the feet through the slit with paper fasteners (so the rooster can run).

S (page 290): Color the table setting. Tear strips of green tissue paper and glue them to the plate to make a salad. Add orange strips for carrots, green paper circles for cucumbers, tan paper squares for croutons, etc. Alternatively, the patterns on page 301 can be used to make the salad.

T (page 291): Color and cut out the truck (page 300). Color the scene on page 291. Cut the slit. Glue the truck to a craft stick. Insert the stick through the slit. Move the truck along the road.

U (page 292): Color the picture. Splash blue paint from a paintbrush onto the picture to make rain.

V (page 293): Color the picture. Glue dry alphabet noodles or cereal in the bowl.

W (page 294): Cut out the window frame. Draw what you see inside the window. Cover the window with clear plastic wrap and tape it on the reverse.

X (page 295): Color the picture. Color the x-ray machine black or silver. Glue toothpicks horizontally across the x-ray machine to make the person's ribs.

Y (page 296): Draw and color a yard inside the fences.

Z (page 297): Cut out the pattern, removing the center sections so only the bars remain. Cut out and color the animal pattern (page 301). Glue the animal to another sheet of paper and glue the cage on top of it. Add yarn to make the animal's tail.

A is for apple.

Color the picture. Tear bits of colored paper and glue them to the apple.

B is for boat.

Cut the water line. Fold up the water. Color the picture.

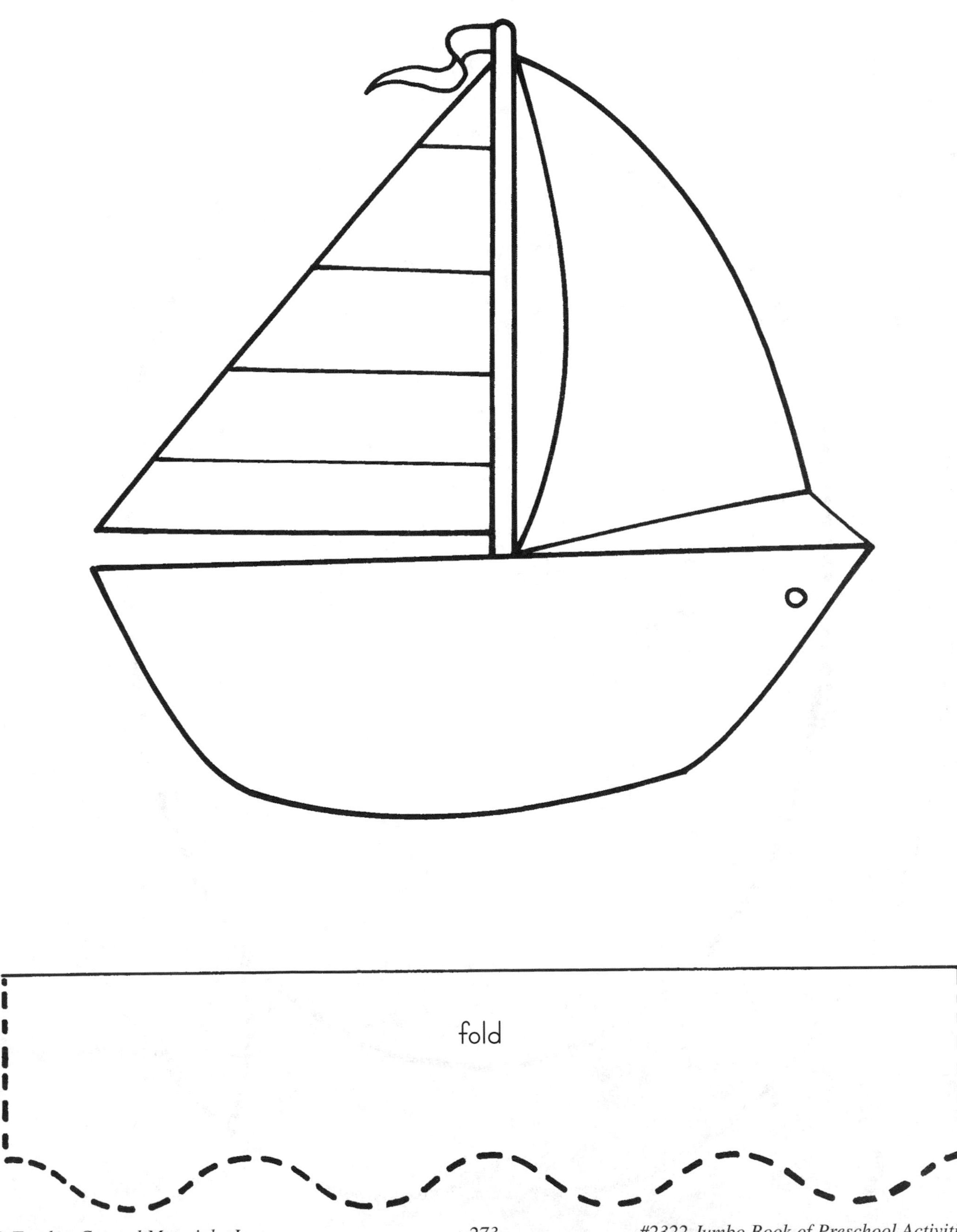

C is for curls.

Color the face. Cut out several curls (page 298). Glue the curls around the head.

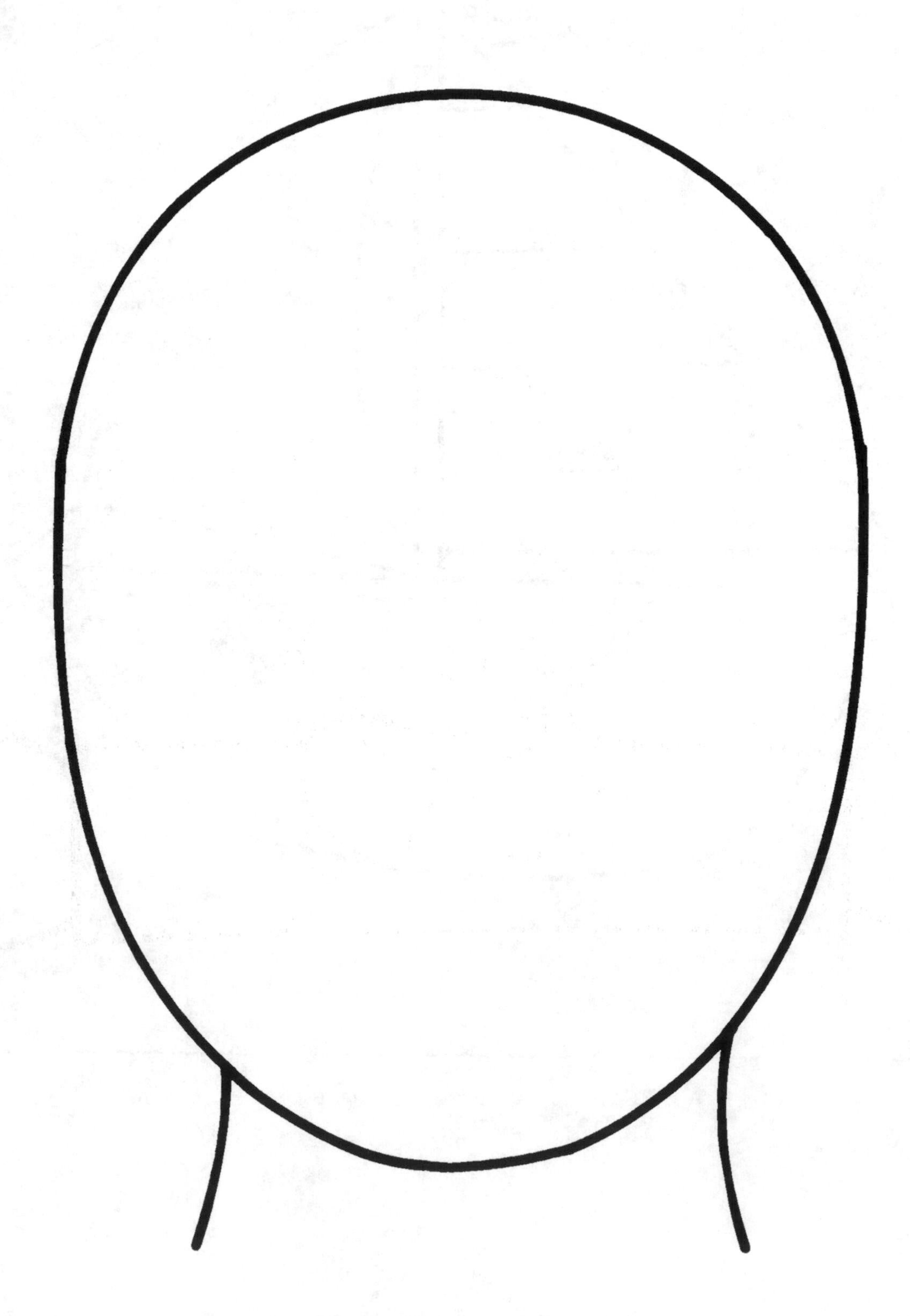

D is for doll.

Color the doll. Cut the slit. Color and cut out the doll's bottom half (page 298). Attach it through the slit with a paper fastener.

E is for engine.

Trace the patterns (page 299) onto colored paper and cut them out. Glue them in place on the engine.

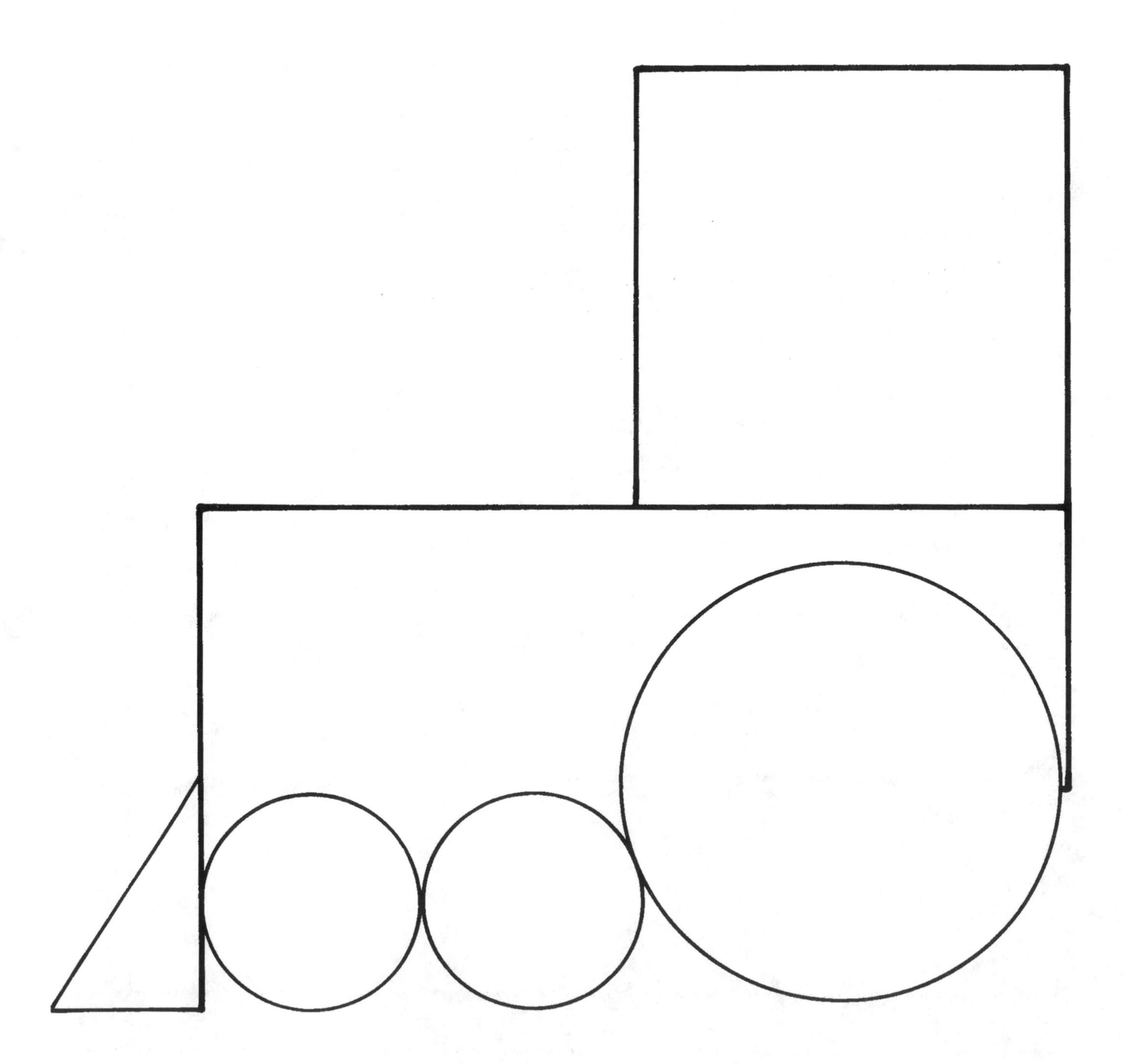

F is for fish.

Color the fish and the water. Add plants and sand. Cut the slits at the top and bottom of the aquarium. Cut a piece of wax paper and push it through the slits at both ends. Tape it in place from behind.

G is for growing.

Color the clown. Cut out the halves and glue them far apart on another sheet of paper. Draw lines to connect the two halves. Fold the body down at the lines. Open and close the body to make the clown grow.

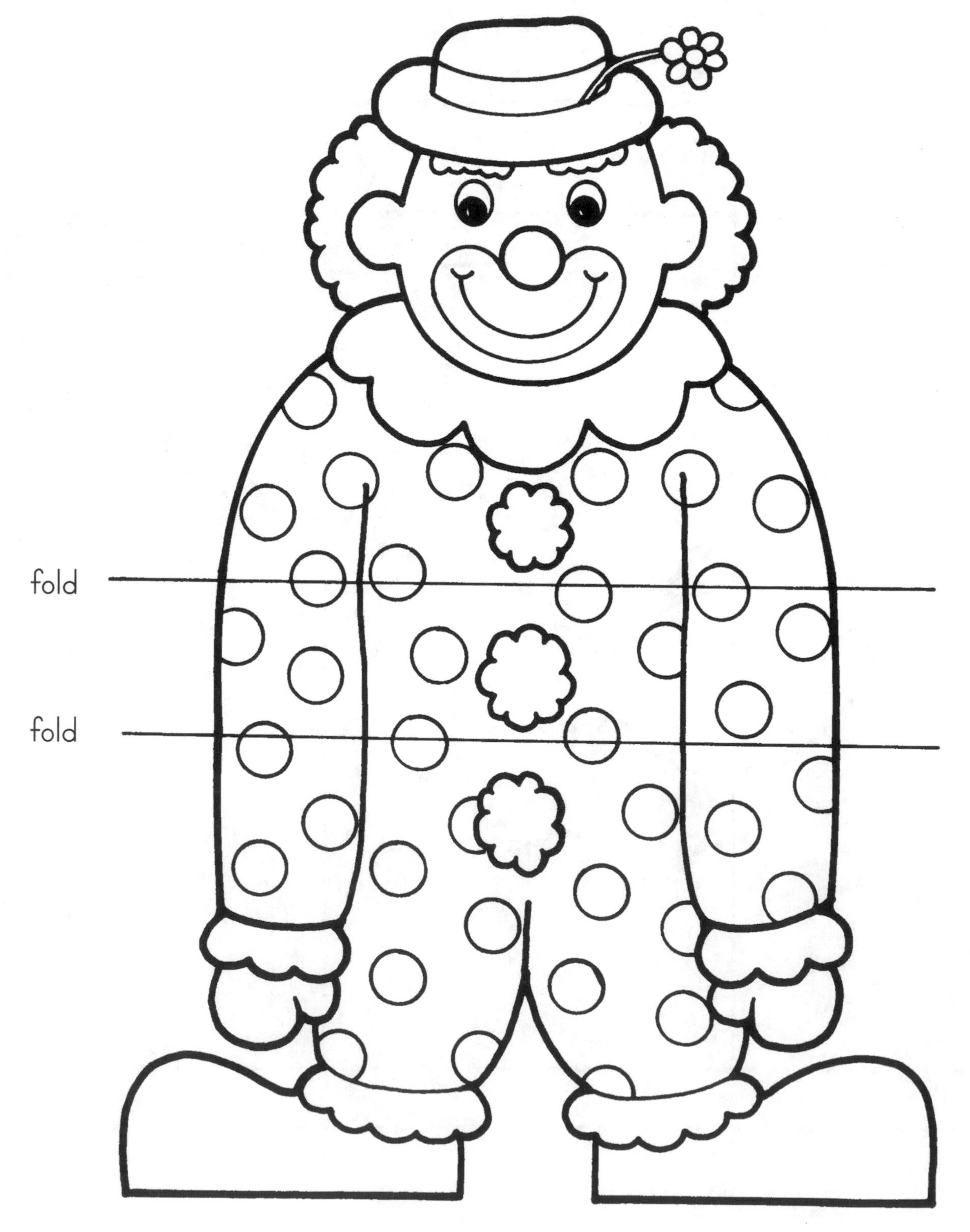

H is for house.

Color the H to make it a house.

I is for ice cream.

Color the ice cream. Color and cut out the spoon (page 299) and glue it to the picture. Cut a triangle of napkin and glue it to the picture, too.

J is for jack-in-the-box.

Cut on the dotted lines. Fold up the box. Color the box. Color and cut out the jack head and jumping strip (page 299). Accordion-fold the strip. Glue it behind the head and glue the other end inside the box. Close the box. When you open it, the jack will jump.

fold

K is for kite.

Color the kite. Glue a tail of yarn or ribbon to it.

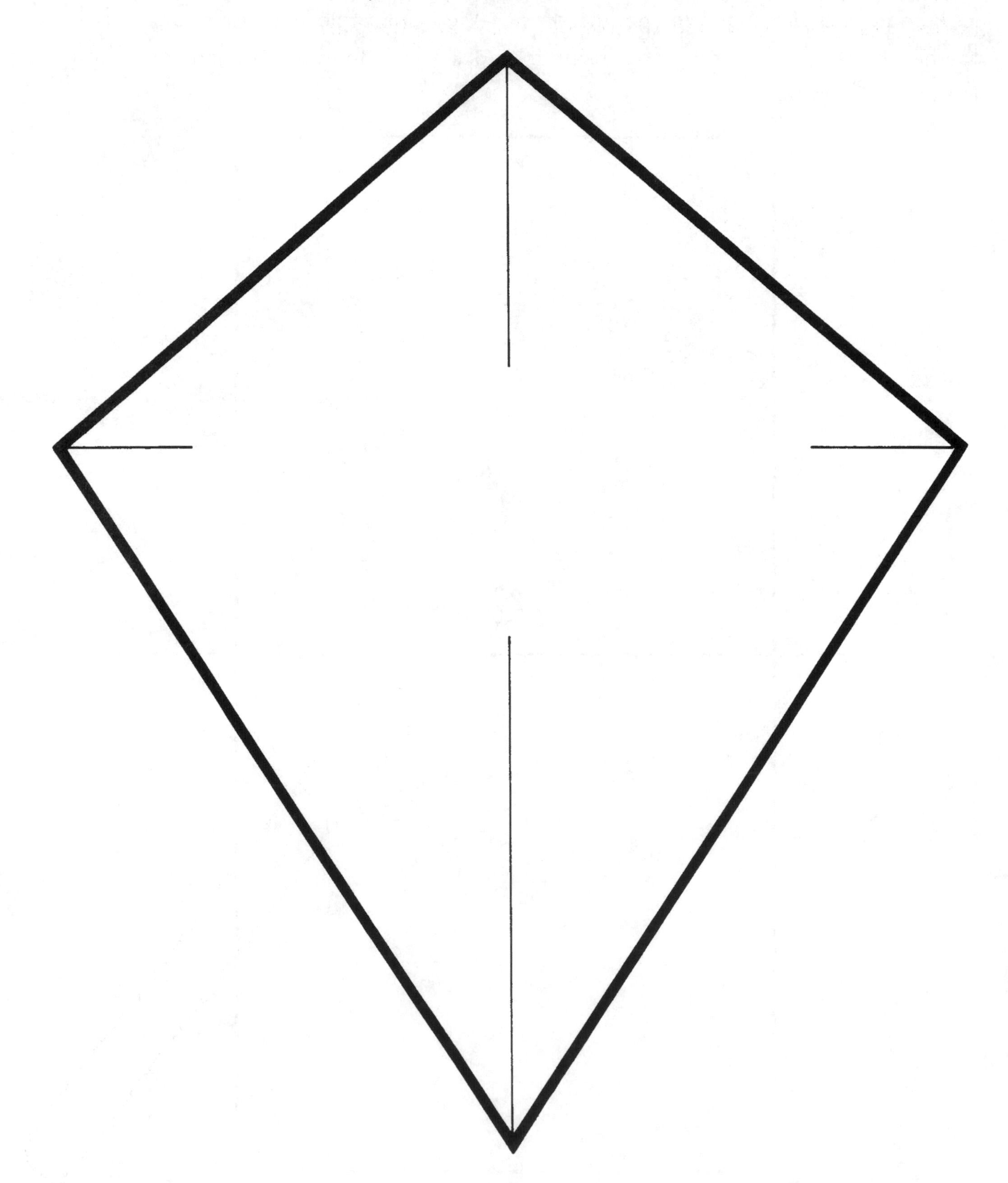

L is for lollipop.

Color the lollipop (page 300) and the stick. Color a hand holding the stick. Wrap plastic wrap around the lollipop. Glue it to the stick.

M is for mouse.

Color the picture. Glue a yarn tail to the mouse.

N is for nose.

Color the face. Draw a funny nose and other features.

O is for owl.

Trace the patterns from page 300 onto orange and brown paper. Cut them out. Color the owl and cut the slit at its bottom. Glue the brown triangle to the owl's head. Glue the orange triangle to its face for a beak. Fold the feet and insert them through the slit. Attach the feet with a brass fastener so they can move.

P is for present.

Cut on the dotted lines. Fold up the box. Color the box. Color a present inside the package.

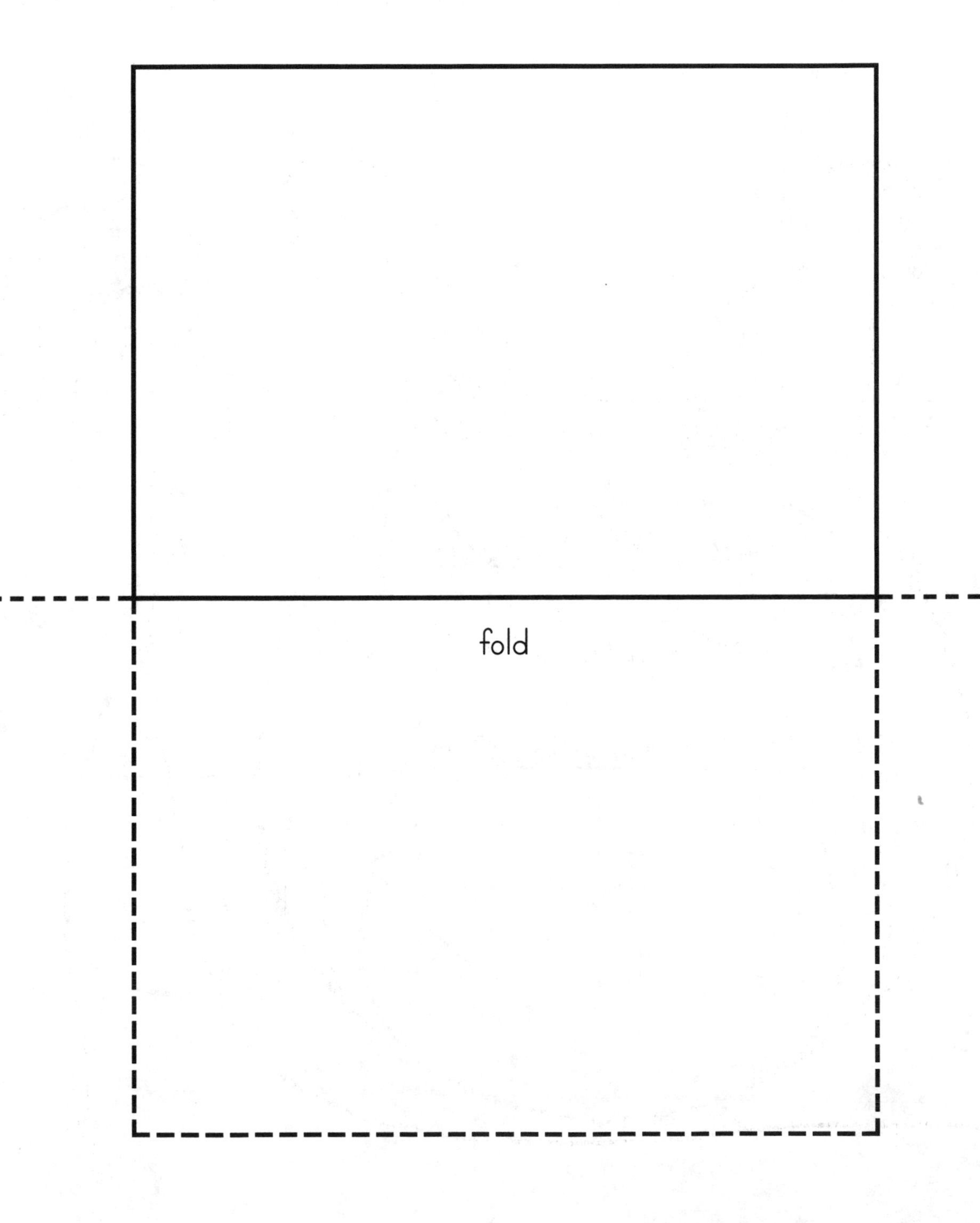

Q is for quilt.

Color the quilt in beautiful colors.

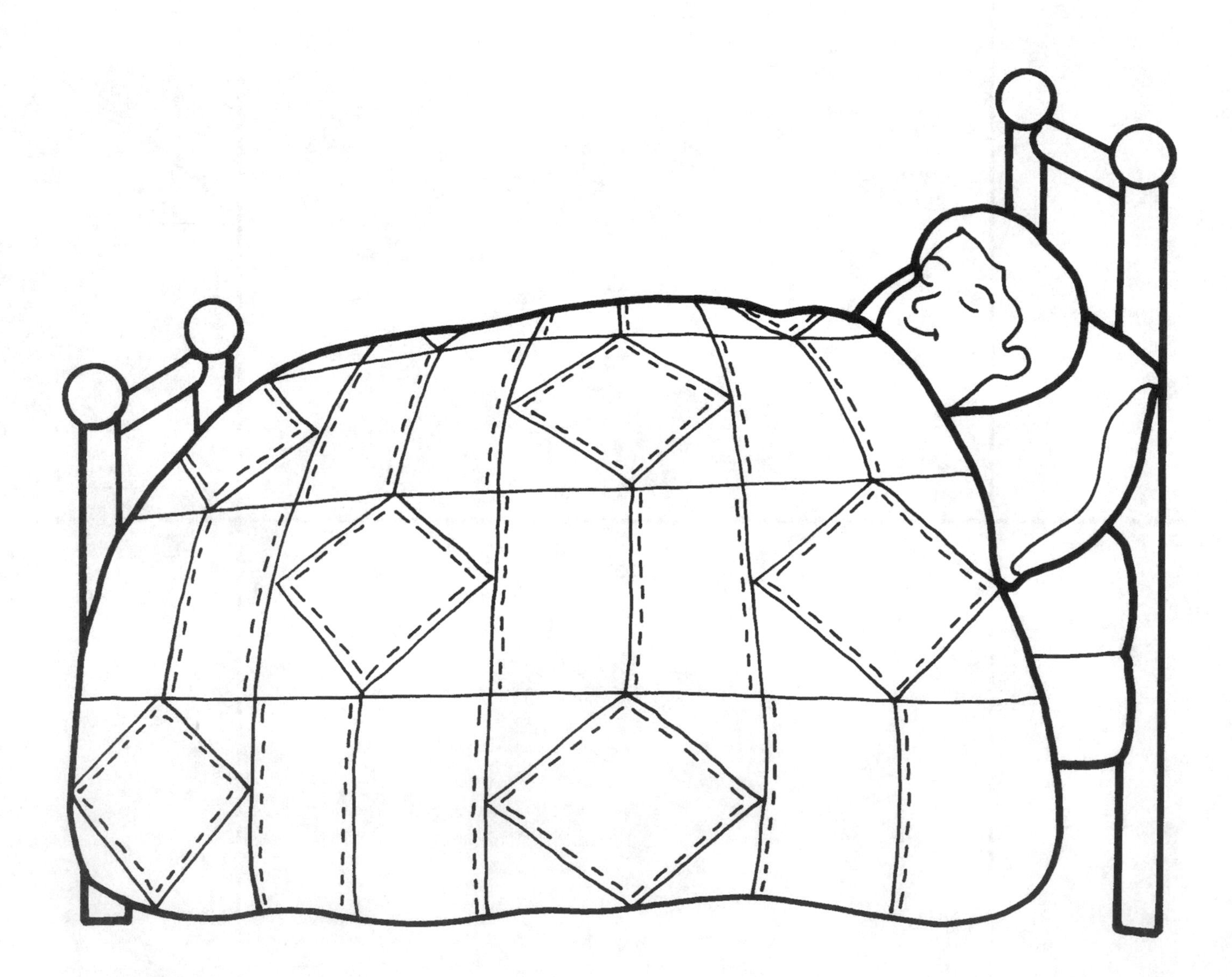

R is for rooster.

Color the rooster. Cut the slit. Color and cut out the rooster's feet (page 300). Attach the feet through the slit with paper fasteners.

S is for salad.

Color the table setting. Tear green tissue paper and glue it to the plate to make some lettuce. Cut other papers to make carrots, croutons, cucumbers, and more.

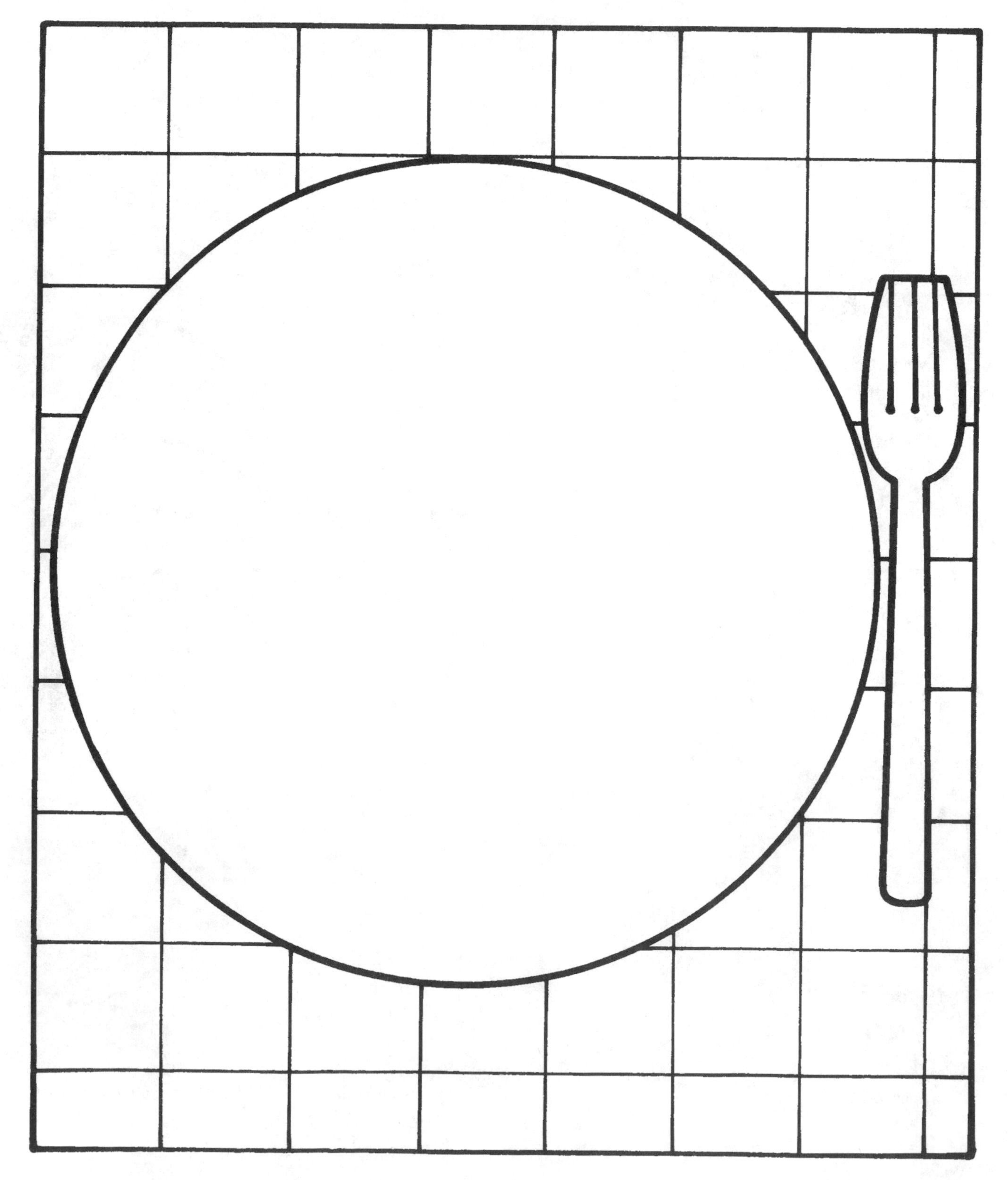

T is for truck.

Color the scene. Cut the slit in the road. Color and cut out the truck (page 300). Glue the truck to a craft stick. Insert the stick through the slit to make the truck move.

U is for umbrella.

Color the picture. Splash blue paint onto the picture to make rain.

V is for vegetable soup.

Color the picture. Glue alphabet cereal or noodles into the bowl to make the soup.

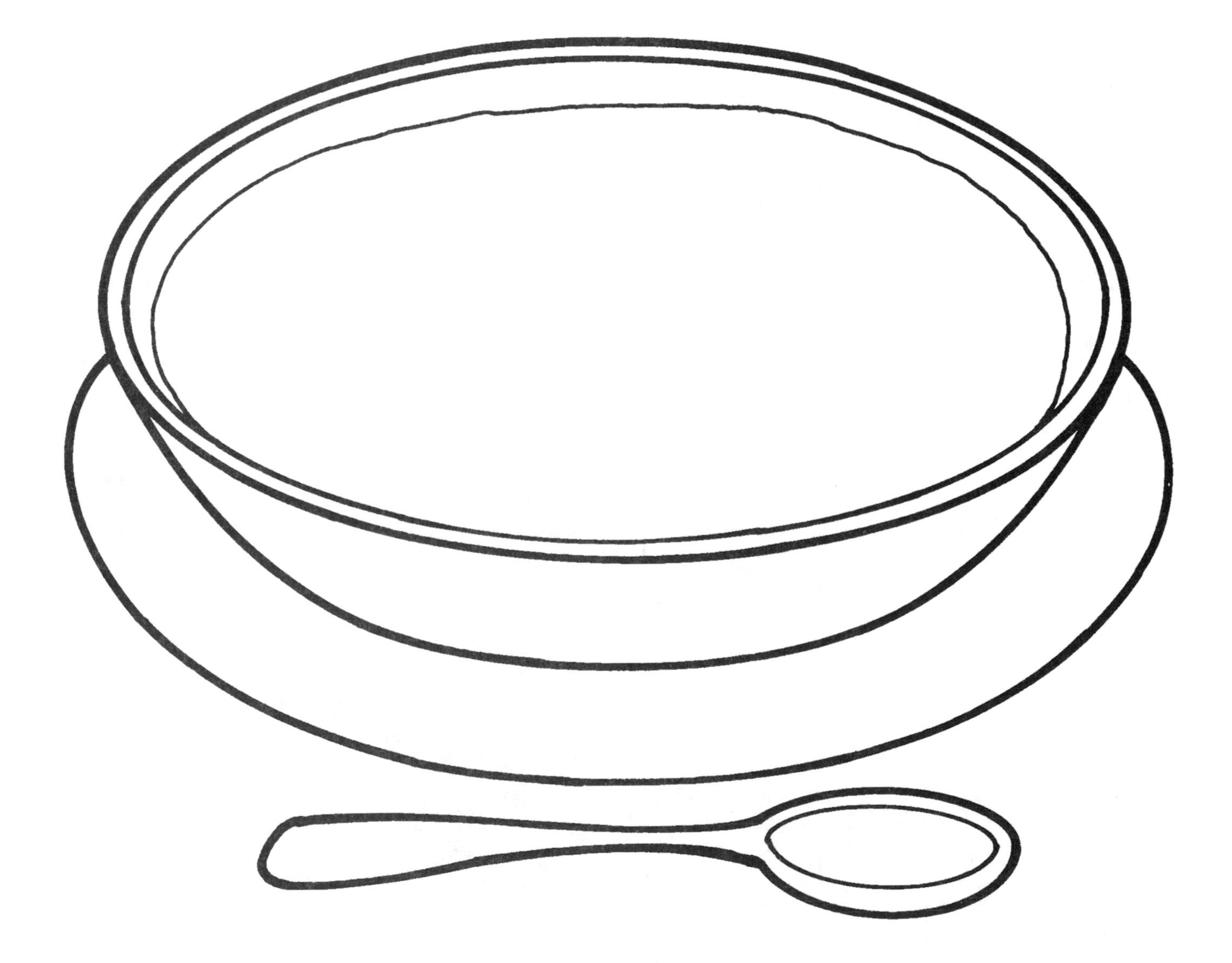

W is for window.

Cut out the window frame. Draw what you see inside the window. Cover the window with plastic wrap and tape it behind to make the glass.

X is for x-ray.

Color the person. Color the x–ray machine black or silver. Glue toothpicks down the x–ray to make the person's ribs.

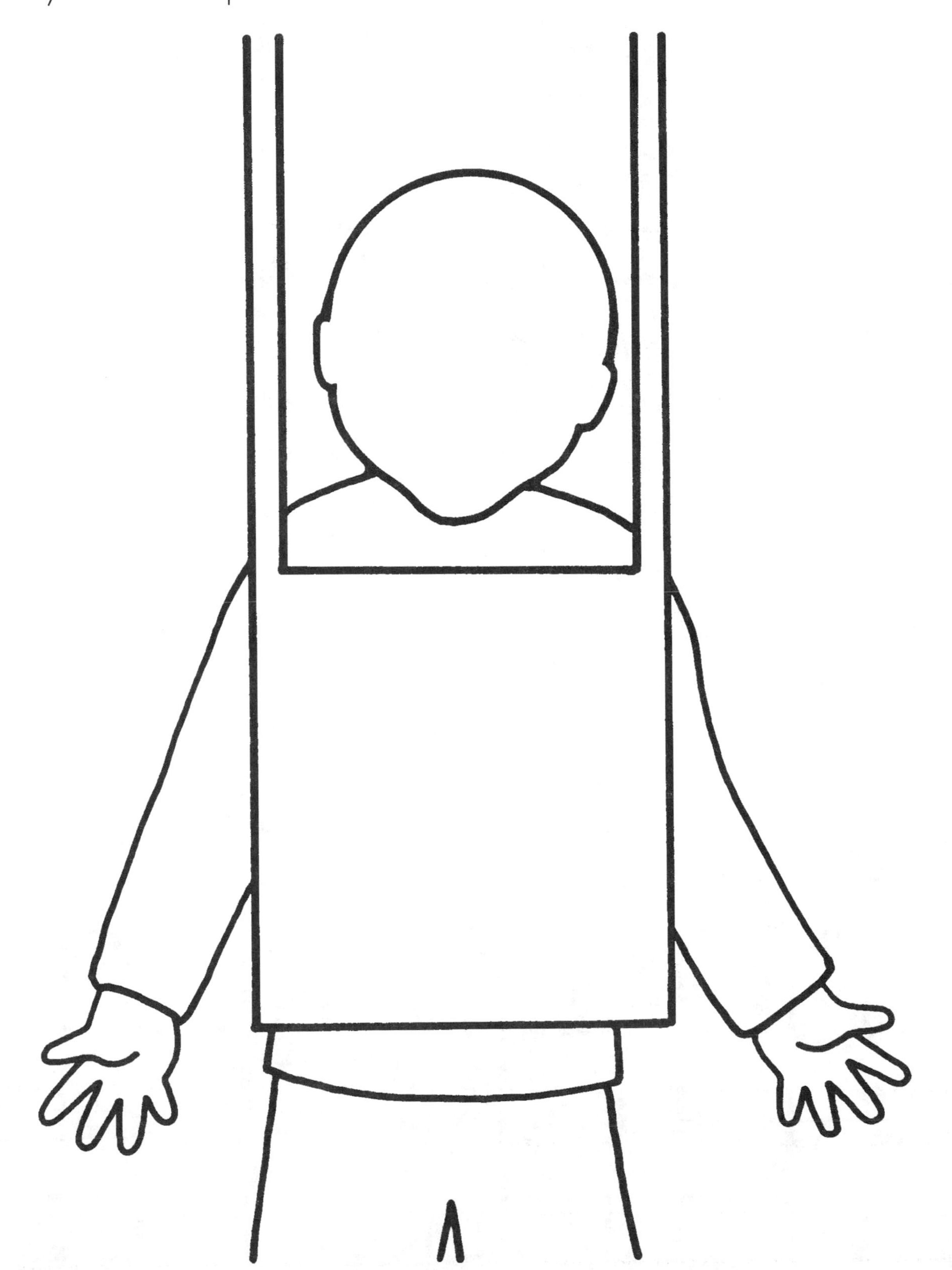

Y is for yard.

Draw a yard inside the fences.

Z is for zoo.

Cut out the cage so only the bars remain. Color and cut out the animal pattern (page 301). Glue the animal to another sheet of paper. Glue the cage on top of the animal. Glue bits of yarn to the animal to make a tail.

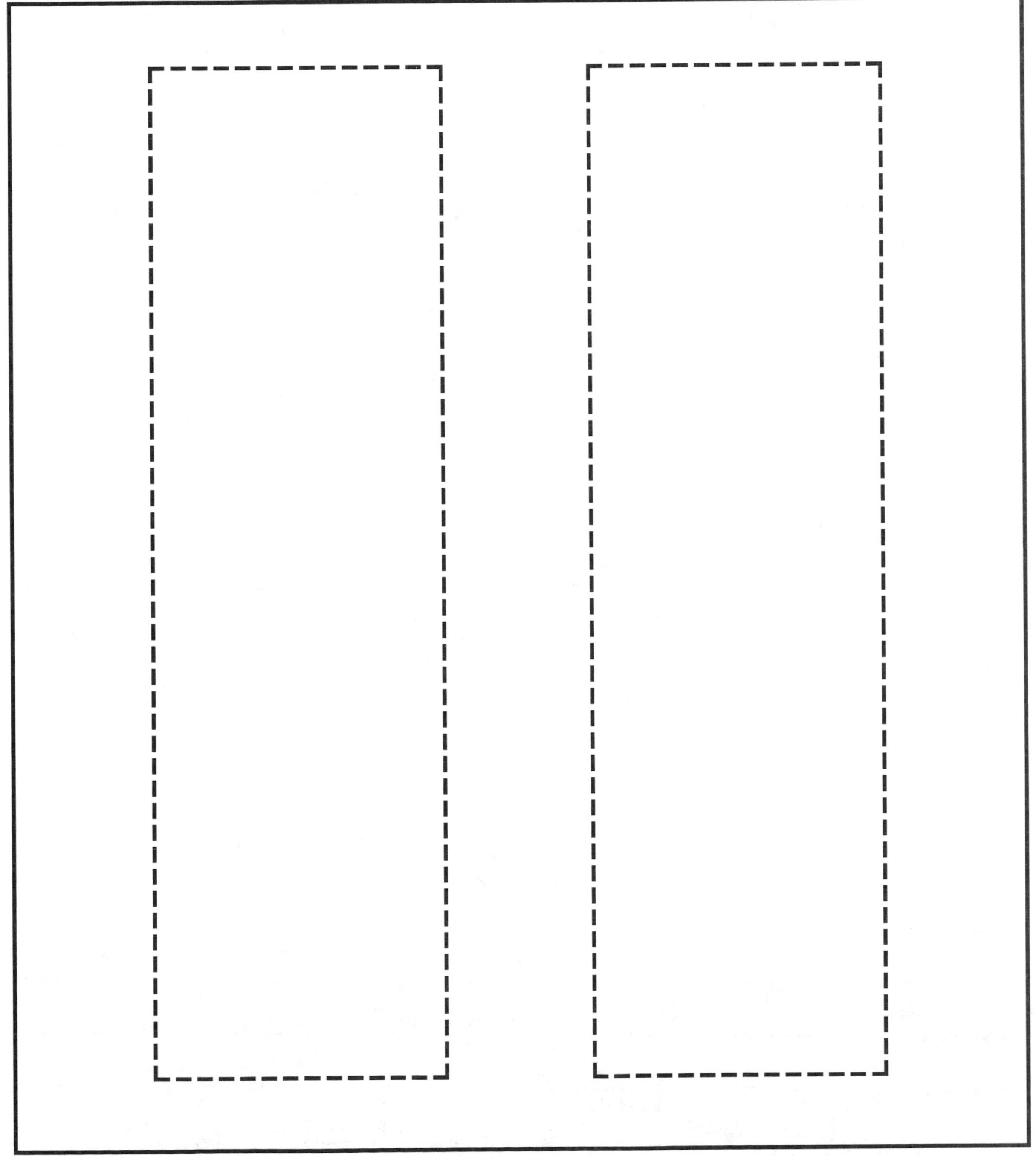

Additional Patterns

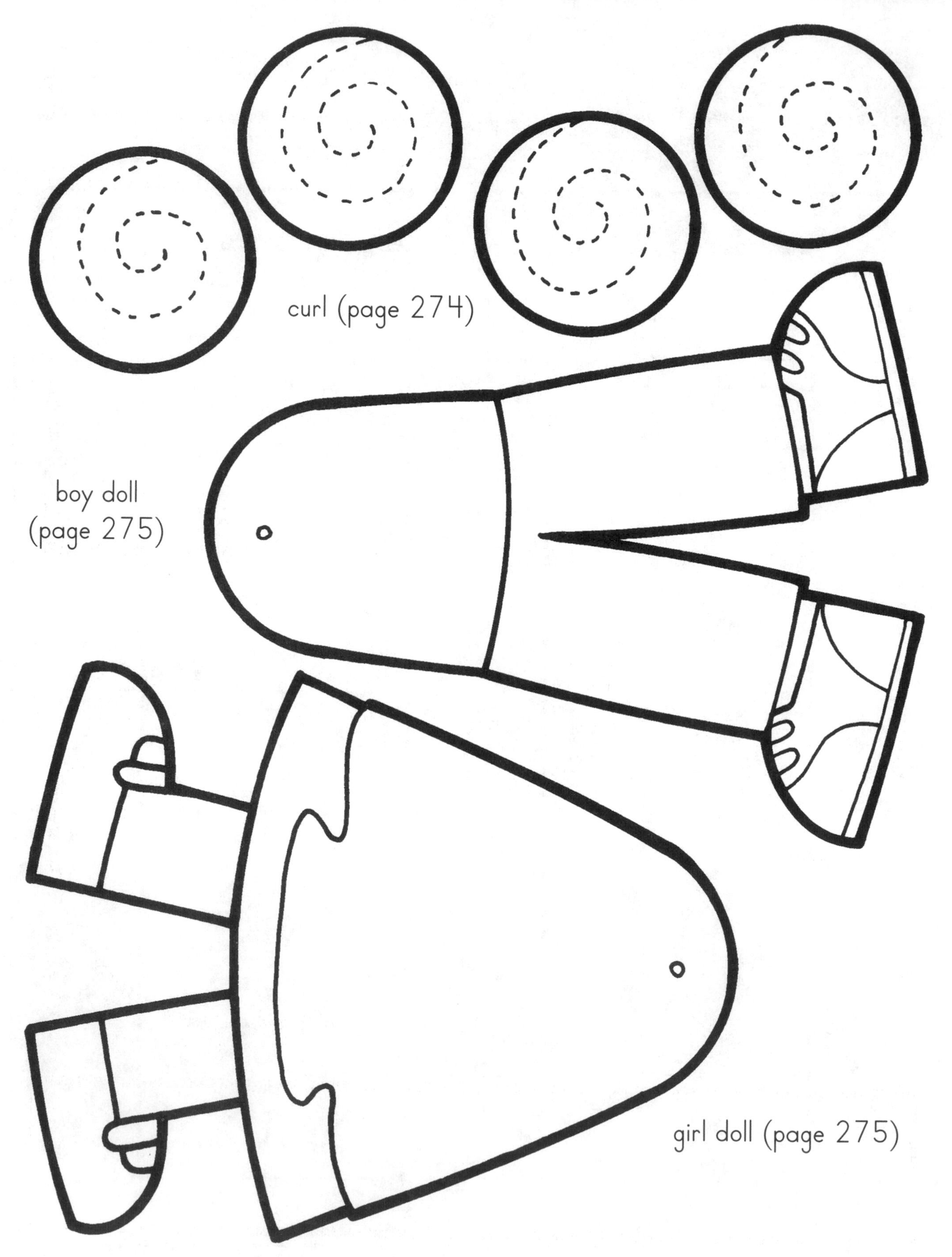

Additional Patterns *(cont.)*

Additional Patterns *(cont.)*

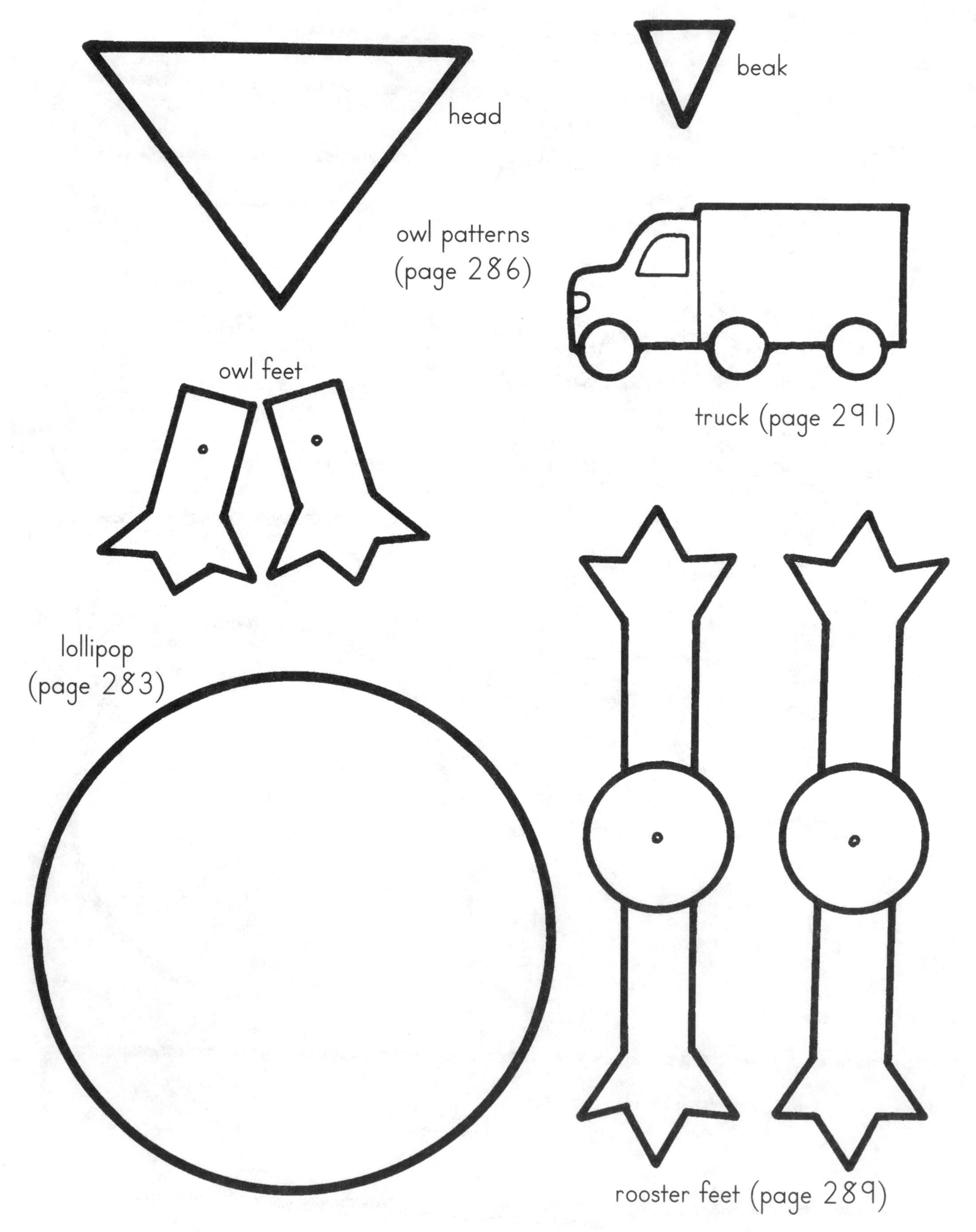

Additional Patterns *(cont.)*

salad patterns
(page 290)

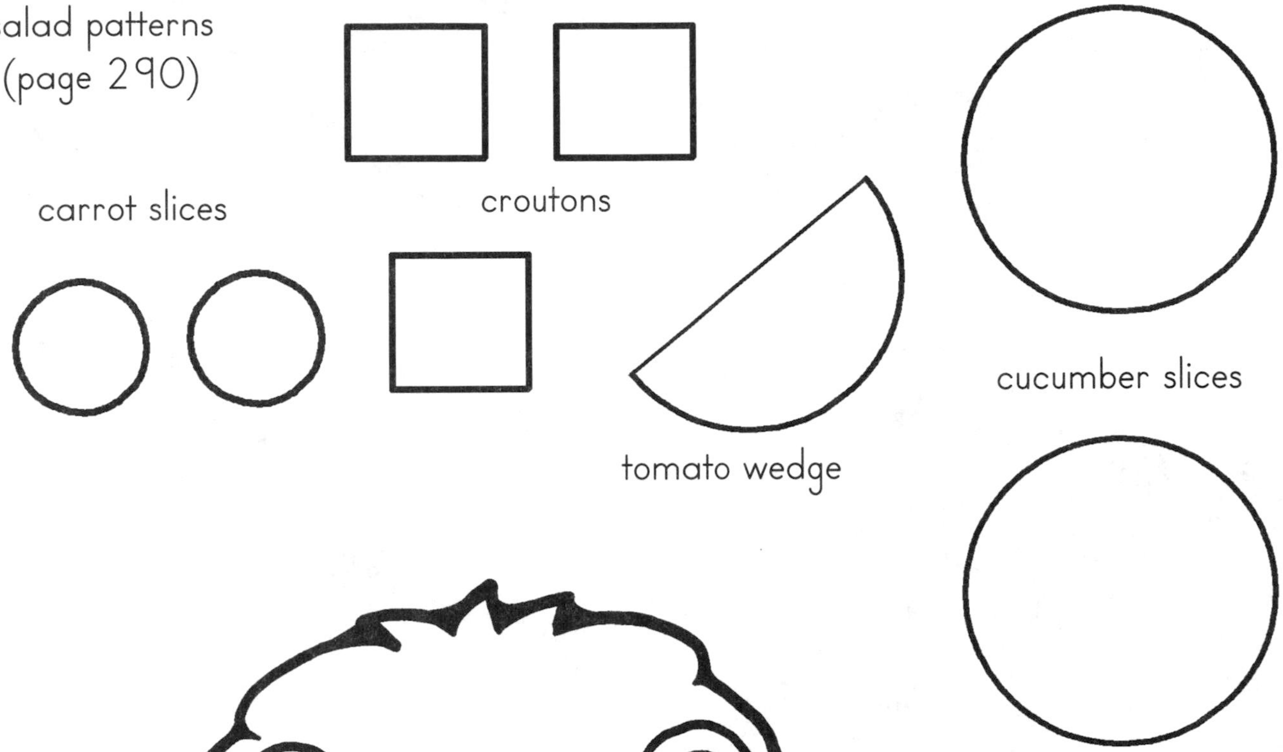

croutons

carrot slices

tomato wedge

cucumber slices

zoo animal
(page 297)

Additional Patterns *(cont.)*

Additional Patterns *(cont.)*

Additional Patterns *(cont.)*

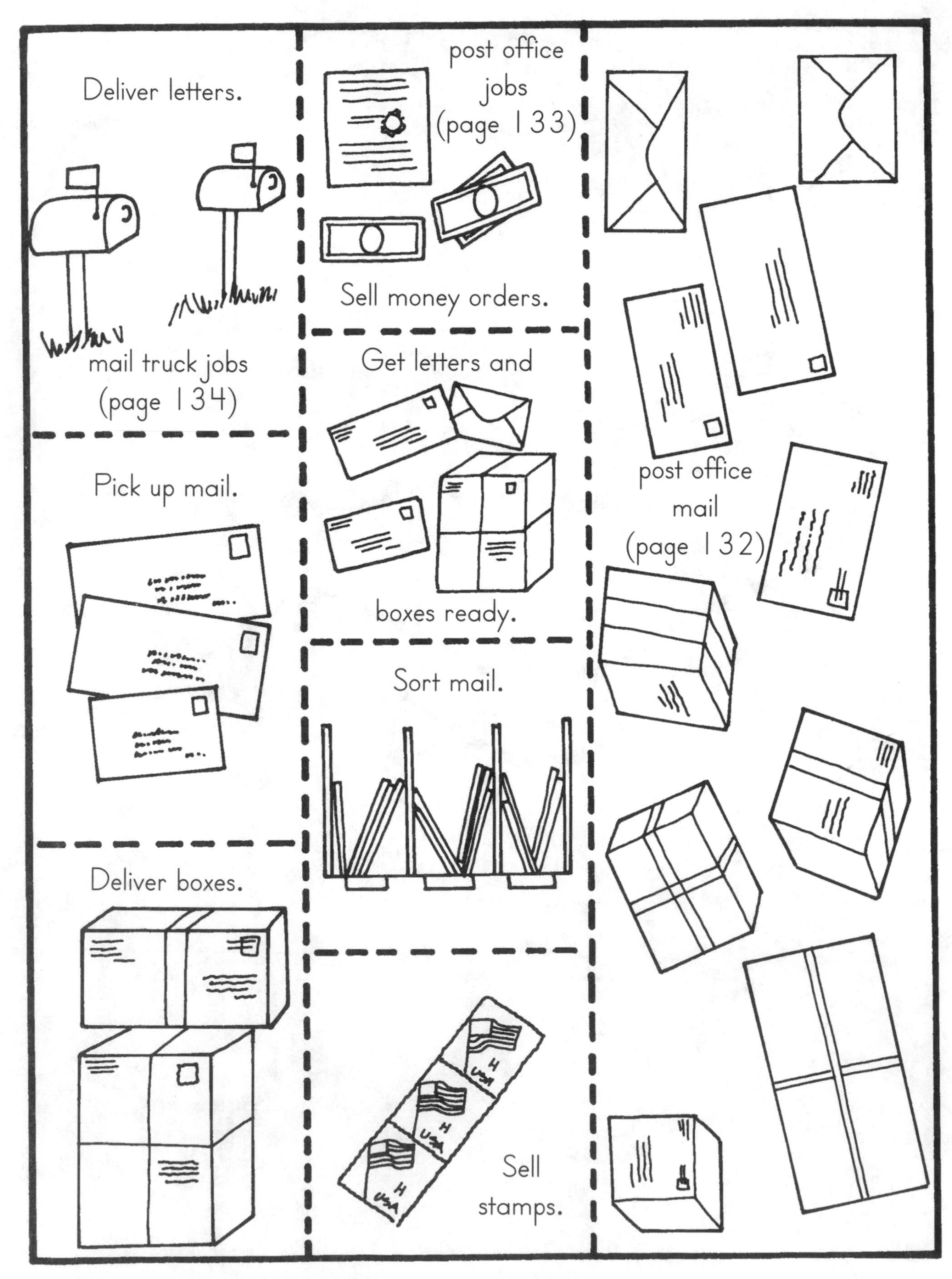

